Tax Management and Tax Evasion

New Horizons in Management Sciences

Edited by Lukasz Sulkowski

Volume 4

PL ACADEMIC RESEARCH

Konrad Raczkowski / Lukasz Sulkowski (eds.)

Tax Management and Tax Evasion

PL ACADEMIC RESEARCH

Bibliographic Information published by the Deutsche Nationalbibliothek
The Deutsche Nationalbibliothek lists this publication in the Deutsche Nationalbibliografie; detailed bibliographic data is available in the internet at http://dnb.d-nb.de.

Library of Congress Cataloging-in-Publication Data
Tax management and tax evasion / Konrad Raczkowski, Lukasz Sulkowski (eds.).
pages cm. — (New horizons in management sciences, ISSN 2194-153X ; volume 4)
ISBN 978-3-631-65190-2
1. Taxation—European Union countries. 2. Tax evasion—European Union countries.
I. Raczkowski, Konrad. II. Sulkowski, Lukasz, 1972-
HJ2599.5.T256 2014
336.20094—dc23

2014032550

This publication was financially supported
by the University of Social Sciences in Warsaw.

ISSN 2194-153X
ISBN 978-3-631-65190-2 (Print)
E-ISBN 978-3-653-04614-4 (E-Book)
DOI 10.3726/978-3-653-04614-4

PL Academic Research is an Imprint of Peter Lang GmbH.

Peter Lang – Frankfurt am Main · Bern · Bruxelles · New York · Oxford · Warszawa · Wien

This publication has been peer reviewed.

www.peterlang.com

Table of Contents

Introduction

Tax management and tax evasion represent an intrinsic element of economic turnover, an area of interest both to the institutional and to the real spheres of national economy. It needs to be said openly that a specific kind of tax engineering flourishes now, in the days of all-pervasive globalisation, when tax burdens impact the overall productivity of production factors, but very often relate to only non-tangible and legal values. Such schemes are devised as a rule by large multinational corporations, which develop international tax strategies adapted to the profile of conducted economic activity; other enterprises follow suit with their strategies. The aim is, of course, such reduction of tax liabilities, using legal means, which will allow for retaining the largest possible profit in the overall profit & loss account, allowing for presentation of the best possible financial result. This way in many countries one meets with major firms, such as trade and service companies, hyperstore chains or all categories of single logo restaurant chains which, irrespective of mass scale presence in multiple locations in the given country, may be paying no taxes in that country, or the sum of such taxes will be disproportionately low in relation to the generated turnover. After all, in international relations it would be difficult to prove that an entity which differentiates costs as part of creative price manipulations in reality transfers profits so as to reduce tax liabilities.

In this context a fundamental question arises, asked above all by the tax authorities seeing such anomalies and webs of international entanglements: to what point is this really optimising of taxes within bounds of the law, and from when can one speak of wilful breaking of laws and tax evasion? How should they suppress the practice of mass scale extortion relating in particular to indirect taxes, and VAT above all else, from budgets of individual states? How to, from the perspective of an entrepreneur, secure oneself against being sucked into a tax carousel, attempts to shift responsibility by a buffer enterprise, and in consequence attempts at punishing in bad faith? How can a state support honest tax competition, as part of securing the economic turnover process with an appropriate, and in particular efficient system of managing taxes? These are fundamental questions, to which it is not only necessary to seek answers, but which in a fundamental way necessitate revisiting and altering given tax policies.

These problems, beyond any doubt, should become the focus of interest for all states having a common market, e.g. the European Union, or the countries which have not introduced the universally binding and highly susceptible to abuses

VAT tax – such as the United States. Such problems certainly fall within the range of interest of every state, since in the present day multinational capital does not ask whether things are well in a given country, but only whether it is possible to reap profits by doing business in that country.

With this in mind we present to you the present monograph, outlining the issues of managing taxes and tax evasion, mainly (though not exclusively) through focus on European Union, with Poland in particular. The choice did not come by accident, since the latter was the only EU member state which in the waning years of the still continuing economic crisis never fell into negative economic growth. Yet the growth was not matched by tax collections which, particularly in VAT, experienced a gigantic fall during 2012–2013, widening the tax gap due to unsatisfactory tax collections. This was exacerbated by the fact that in recent years there was an increase in the number of tax-related court litigations, reviewing complaints of taxpayers in dispute with tax authorities.

The monograph consists of twelve chapters, providing a systematic review of the issues signalled by its title. From presentation of the significance of taxes, their competitiveness, optimising and impact in a global environment plus strategic planning in public finance, all the way to issues connected with the unofficial economy, tax gap, tax fraud and legislation addressing indirect tax crimes.

We hope that the book which we present to you will become an incentive to linking in common the knowledge inherent in the worlds of science, business and politics, in the aim of achieving better understanding of the tax issues still not understandable to the majority, which constitute present day tax engineering. For that reason we have the ambition of starting and joining in extensive, international discussions of this issue, which should above all allow for designing constructive solutions and for their practical implementation in the organisational & legal order of individual states and economic turnover entities.

Konrad Raczkowski, Łukasz Sułkowski

Katarzyna Żukrowska[1]

Taxes as challenge in globalized and open economy with intensified competition. Case study of Poland in the context of Transatlantic Trade and Investment Partnership

Introduction

Polish economy is in transition from a phase driven by effective use of production factors towards innovative use of them. This means the importance of sustainable growth being attractive for certain types of investments, and serve as deterrent to other types. This statement provokes some controversies, as some economists declare that in light of 12% unemployment rate the country should encourage all possible flows of investment and not concentrate only on part of them. Others express the opinion that concentration helps to accelerate the rate of growth of the economy and enables quicker build-up of wealth in the society (notion which replaces well known welfare state). Taxes can play an important role in this process, especially in the context of bilateral opening of the EU and US markets for more intensified trade and investment flows within Transatlantic Trade and Investment Partnership – TTIP. Decisions taken ex ante concerning levels and structure of taxes can have an important impact on the ability to compete and develop by Polish companies in the coming future.

The article will examine the theoretical impact of level and structure of taxes in the context of TTIP, showing the direction of possible changes which can either undermine the rate of growth of the economy or stimulate it. The hypothesis of this article is that improper level and structure of taxes can be considered as an element jeopardizing the area of economic security of the state.

Main assumptions

In this article it is assumed that taxes are considered by investors and management of companies as one of the costs and as such are taken into consideration

1 Professor in economics and political sciences, Warsaw School of Economics, email: zukrowsk@wa.home.pl.

in decisions to either stay in a particular market or move to another location. This context takes into account one of the features of current economic relations, which is the international movement of production factors on top of transfer of goods and services.

Policymakers, including those who decide about taxes, look at them mainly from the position of narrowly considered interest, defined within the context of national economy framework, limiting their role to source of national budget revenues. The observed trend in this area was strengthen by the 2008+ crisis, when growing budget deficits stimulated policy makers to raise the taxes, hoping for increases in the state's budgetary revenues. Such revenues can increase, but only temporary and the increase is short lived. This was proven by, *inter alia,* the experience of countries which were preparing for EMU in the 1990's and applied different policies in area of fiscal policy, where mainly 3 methods of budgetary consolidation were applied [Żukrowska, Orsi, Lavrac, 2004, p. 24–31]. First consolidation method was based on restructuring and at the same time lowering expenditures, and this was called expenditures-based consolidation. The second method used a different approach, focused on increase of revenues by higher taxes, something that is called revenue-based consolidation. Third method was a mix of the two, changing both the revenues and the expenditures and it is known as mixed consolidation strategies featuring one-off measures. The method applied in the US can be classified also in the last category; it was leading the American economy to a balanced budget and with time even to a budget surplus.

Recently most of the developed economies are facing the problem of budget deficits, rarely looking into the experience from the past, despite the fact that some lessons from that practice can be drawn and applied in the current conditions. The importance of that experience seems to increase in the context of effectiveness of applied methods and relative social burdens that they bring. Moreover, TTIP, brings us to the point in which some comparisons between methods applied in the EU states and US market have to be made. At this point both markets strive under budget deficits. EU has enforced its control over the state of budget deficits by providing additional tools to the Stabilization and Growth Pact (S&GP), which are following:

a) European Semester;
b) European Stability Mechanism (ESM)
c) European Financial Stabilization Mechanism (EFSM)
d) European Financial Stability Facility (EFSF)
e) Six new legal arrangements were approved, which are aimed to help in managing of the economy, known as the six-pack;

f) Euro Plus Pack was also established, which is striving to spur efforts enabling convergence of the EU member states national policies, something that is considered to be a measure helping to enhance competitiveness of the Union as a whole[2].

Moreover, indebted economies are supported by financial and expertise aid from both the IMF and the European Commission. This was experienced by Greece, Ireland and Spain after the 2008+ crisis. Also the new regulations increase the external control over the policies applied in particular states in their consolidation policies.

The European Financial Stability Facility (EFSM) is furnished with €60 bln. This amount is a guarantee set up together by all EU states, which can be considered as a ceiling up to which the European Commission can collect capital on the money market, prior to such activity securing the approval for it from ECOFIN. Such a mechanism is backed by guarantees coming from the EU general budget. And as the EU general budget should not end up with a deficit (indicating that expenditures are higher than revenues) when a loan is drawn, than the there are at least consequences of such move. Firstly, it has a defined set ceiling, which cannot be surpassed, something that constrains the state's appetites for money. Secondly, the EU member states take over financial responsibility to cover such a gap. The size of shares of each individual state in financing the gap is defined by its share in the Union's GNP. Financial means available from the financial gap, defined in such way, are additionally supported by means coming from the EFSF and the ESM.

The European Financial Stability Facility, forms a consecutive element of the solutions recently created in the EU serving the purpose of stabilizing the European finances. Often all the mentioned solutions are presented as funds, which is not a proper approach, as the instruments are not created with use of financial means, which would be in disposal of the mentioned solutions, in the sense of money that are ready to be paid. Those instruments are constructed in such a way that they are able to offer defined amounts of money using the guarantees of the EMU member states. The ceiling for such guarantees is the amount of €780 bln. In practice this implies a crediting potential of €440 bln. The stabilization setup, as it was mentioned earlier, includes also the IMF. At the start the share of IMF was set at level of €250 bln. In December 2011, at the EU summit, a proposal was made to raise the share of the IMF by an additional €200 bln.

2 The initiative was born from the common proposal of France and Germany, known also as Pact for Competitiveness, 3.02.2011.

The European Stability Mechanism (ESM) was provided with an active credit potential of €500 bln[3]. The value of ESM accumulated capital is €80 bln and €620 bln. made available to Member States, guaranteed by their allocations. The ESM is designed to supply short and medium-term credits as well as interventions on sovereign debt markets. The ESM loans have to be offered to states interested in drawing them on financially better conditions than those offered by EFSF. Credits drawn in ESM require carrying out budgetary reforms and corrections in economic policies applied on macro scale. The loan can be granted after positive evaluation concerning economic liquidity prepared by ECB, IMF and the European Commission.

Available financial sources listed above are additionally enforced by specific legal arrangements introduced by so called six-pack. Trying to comment on the practical impact which the six-pack exerts on state finances, one can say, that the aim is to introduce a specific automatic mechanism in both application of penalties as well as awards for fulfillment of the convergence criteria. The powers of the European Commission were increased, meaning that it can demand information more frequently and more specific than it has done in the past. Procedures were introduced which enforce the control of state's indebtedness. Those controls are not limited to share of debt in the GNP or indicators of trend in employment. An additional requirement was imposed in regulation of the rate of public debt reduction. In practice this means that those states who's debts surpass the threshold of 60% of GNP, will be required to reduce by 1/20 between the 60% threshold and the level of debt from last 3 years. It also seems to be important that a state is required to deposit an amount equal to 0,2% GNP, when its deficit was ruled excessive under the process of excessive budget procedure. A state punished in such manner loses its deposit unless it introduces solutions effectively limiting the deficit and in result also the debt [Żukrowska 2014 p. 235–252].

It also seems to be interesting to note that in effect of the 2008+ crisis some changes were introduced in the European Central Bank policies. ECB's aims its policies at upholding financial stability in the EMU. This implies a close relation between monetary policy and the inflation goal. This means also close control of prices, which should be close to the market level, allowing for a small difference of about 2.00%. During the years of the 2008+ crisis, the ECB relatively frequently contravened the fixed rules of monetary policy, which were precisely defined within the framework of launching EMU.

---

3 For AAA rating the capital base should be upgraded to €700 bln.

The tensions in achieving this particular goal to a large extent resulted from decoupling of the monetary and fiscal policies one from another. This is so, because monetary policy is applied on the international level, while fiscal policies are conducted on national levels by each of the member state individually. Fulfillment of the requirements concerning fiscal policy have a strong impact on monetary policy. In other words, when the budget deficit shrinks, all remaining criteria improve. Generally all the criteria are mutually dependent when one goes up, the other follow, when one goes down. the other follow down as well. Fiscal policy, namely the way that convergence criteria are fulfilled, has a strong impact on what is done in monetary policy conducted by the ECB. In such circumstances the financial crisis in Greece, economy of which does not surpass 2% of the cumulated EU GDP of all EU member states, can easily turn into systemic changes of the whole EMU. Nevertheless, knowing the past ability of the EU to overcome systemic tensions of the organisation, we can assume that also this crisis will be overcome and will lead to health of the integrating organisation. Such solutions can have a strong influence on the balance of power between the reformers and those member states who support unchanged expenditures of the EU –[Meletcky, 2013][4].

The main problem in EU is that EMU was established by a group of states where part of the participants did not finish the former stage of creating economic union, which was a precondition for the next move, namely monetary union with common currency. The unfinished process of creating economic union embraces full liberalization of the movement of people and services. Labour market should be opened more and be flexible. Services market should be more open and characterized by full competition rather than protection, as it is now. This seems crucial to the GDP creation and employment, and second is lack of flexibility of the labour market, which should replace the role that previously was played by flexibility of national exchange rates.

In such relatively new and complex circumstances we have witnessed two important things. First was positive, as far as integration is concerned, deepening integration by introducing common European currency in circulation, was a solution which has counteracted growing tensions between the members states

4 This divide was clearly seen in the process of preparation of the current Multiyear Financial Framework 2014–2020. This was mainly seen in 2011. Germany, Netherlands, France, Britain and Italy were in favor of cutting spending, while most of the new MS and Portugal, Spain were in opposition to that idea. The divide was labeled as lovers of cohesion transfers and those who finance them.

during the 2008+ crisis. This can be assumed as with national currencies: states would have had devalued their currency, using low exchange rates as a protection tools. On the other hand, applied policies, which led to increase of budget revenues, mainly by increasing taxes, where bringing results in short run but in medium term they were leading towards decrease of revenues, followed by decrease of budget deficit. This shows the vicious circle of the applied policies, when policy makers behave like they did in the past when the economy was national and protected, while today the economy is not only international but also interdependent.

All general characteristics of the specific features displayed by the economy in its current stage indicate that there is need to deepen the integration process, at least covering the liberalisation of service market and increasing flexibility of the labour market. Second, policies applied at the national level should take into account that those policies are applied in an open environment, something that requires changing their contents as well as the instruments applied. If economic policies needed to be applied, they require closer coordination on the EU level or even better on the G-20 scale. Third, increase in taxes in an open environment leads to fall in revenues for the budget. Finally, policy decreasing taxes should be coordinated within the internal market and open coordination does not do the job. Moreover changes in the tax policy area should be introduced in parallel with structural changes of the expenditures, which should be more oriented towards the goals defined in the strategy Europe 2020. This makes the changes even more difficult economically and politically.

Characteristic of the Polish Economy and its tax system

The current Polish tax system has its roots going back to the 1990's, when most of the currently used taxes were introduced. The construction of the system was aimed at encouraging foreign investors. The system consists of direct and indirect taxes. The direct taxes are following:

a) Personal Income Tax – PIT;
b) Corporate Income Tax – CIT;
c) Tonnage tax;
d) Inheritance tax and donation tax;
e) Tax on civil law transactions;
f) Agriculture tax;
g) Forest tax;
h) Real property tax;

i) Transport vehicle tax;
j) Tax on extraction of certain minerals.

The indirect taxes embrace the following:

a) Value added tax - VAT:
b) Excise tax;
c) Gambling tax.

The CIT tax was lowered from 40% to 19%. PIT has two tax rates 18%, and 32% with threshold annual amount of 85528 PLN. The tax system in Poland includes some tax exemptions (deductions), which are gradually being simplified and reduced. Direct taxes are the source of 65% of the revenues. The revenue from PIT (24%), CIT (11%) and VAT (42%) make up nearly 80% of the all revenues to the state budget (Ministry of Finance Data Base 2014). The remaining revenues come from excise duty (22%), games tax (1%), and customs (1%) (Ministry of Finance Data Base, 2014). Proportions between direct and indirect taxes seem to be similar also for current 2014 year. Although one can see gradual fall of the share of VAT as a source of revenues. This is explained with use of three different arguments: increase of VAT by 1%; slow-down of the consumption and purchasing power of the Polish society; difficulties in collecting the tax. There is a strong temptation to compensate fall of revenues from one tax by increases of the remaining categories. This can be seen in area of reducing the 50% costs-deduction by such profession groups as writers, artists, scientists, etc (State Budget Revenue, Ministry of Finance 2014). This move is seen as an additional source of revenues from PIT in 2014, as it has happened in 2013. Revenues from mining are supposed to yield 9,4% of revenues. This resulted in introduction of one of the most complicated tax systems in area of mining gas and oil [Ekonomia i Rynek, 2014].

Expenditures of the Polish Government Sector are shown bellow in Chart 1, prepared by the World Bank [Government Expenditure, 2013].

The government hierarchy consists in Poland of 5 levels, which are:

a) Government level;
b) Region level (województwo);
c) County level (powiat)
d) Municipality/commune level (gmina)
e) Local government.

Time spread analysis shows the evolution of revenues and expenditures (indebtedness) of the state on each of the mentioned levels. World Bank, IMF

Chart 1: Structure of Poland's National Public Budget

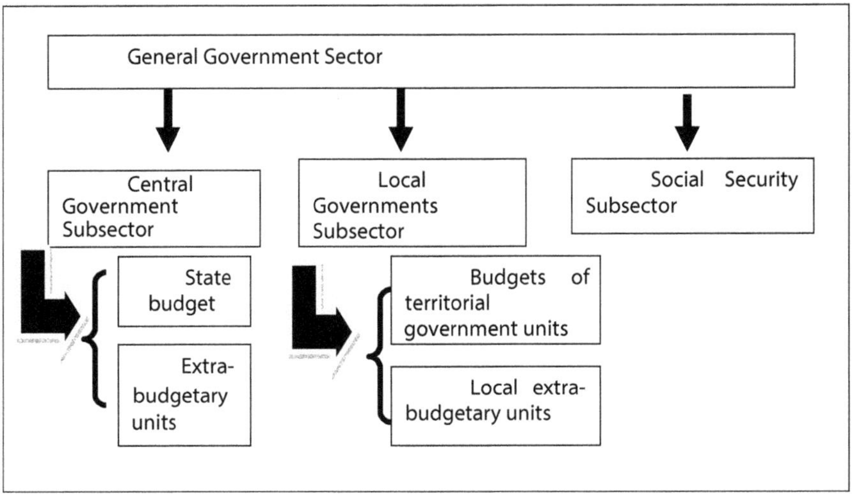

Source: Government Expenditure Database. POLAND. The World Ban December 2013. p. 4.

and OECD prepare detailed analysis of the public debt management in Poland [Melecky, 2013]. Within the procedure which was introduced in 2011 to enforce the Stability and Growth Pact all countries have to report on their macroeconomic policies to the European Commission. This is done with the European Semester Procedure. Poland, same as a number of other EU Member States, is subject to Excessive Budget Deficit Procedure. In June 2013 Poland was given a longer period to finally reduce the budget deficit to the required 3% level. Similar decision was made also towards five other states: France, Netherlands, Portugal, Slovenia and Spain. The Procedure in 2013 was abrogated for Italy, Latvia, Hungary, Lithuania and Romania. Recommendation to open the procedure was also made for Malta. Recommendation was issued by the Commission towards Belgium, suggesting some moves which can help to reduce the deficit. Generally the Report of the Commission on the EBDP shows 20 states which are included into the procedure. In other words EU Members States except Bulgaria, Germany, Estonia, Luxembourg, Malta, Finland and Sweden are subject to EBDP. Abrogation of the procedure for Italy, Latvia, Hungary, Lithuania and Romania and proposal to open an EBDP for Malta, if the recommendations are followed, means that overall 16 Member States are covered by this procedure [Memo, 2013].

The remedy programme of the Polish economy foresees increased economic growth, stimulation of tax revenues. It is expected that in 2014 the Polish budget will change to a 5,8% surplus what will be obtained by overhauling the pension system, something that further on is expected to lead towards budget deficit of -2,5 in 2015 and -1,8 in 2016 [Sobczak, 2014].

General remarks on American and European tax systems

United States of America is a federation of autonomous states with local governments. Taxes in US are imposed on each of the mentioned levels. This concerns all types of taxes, which are deducted from personal and corporate incomes, salaries, capital transactions and revenues, sales, imports, etc.

Income taxes were counted in 2012 within seven brackets, embracing 10, 15, 25, 28, 33, 35, 39.6%. They are calculated for single, married couples or widows, married filing separately (same as for single) and for heads of households (introducing higher bracket levels). The number of brackets was increased in comparison with 2012 by one additional level. This was done by adding 39.6%. The taxes on capital gains are calculated at 6 levels 10, 15, 25, 28, 33, 35. They are also collected in different categories of gains, embracing: long term capital gains, short term capital gains, recapture of depreciation and long term gains on real estate, long term gains on certain small business stocks. Corporate income taxes are graduated into two levels: 15–35 and 34–35. Local taxes are between 1–16%. State and local taxes are allowed as tax deductions in computing federal taxable income. Deductions include: exemptions, standard deductions, dividends received (partial reductions) and organisational costs in special industries such as insurance, extractive industries, regulated investment corporations, real estate investment trusts, real estate mortgage investment conduits, etc. Generally we can say that CIT for industry is higher in comparison with CIT in services. This stimulates development of service sector.

Some states apply individual taxes, others flat rate taxes, remaining are tax free. In some states the taxes are being raised, while in others they are being reduced. States without individual taxes: Indiana, Alaska, Florida, Nevada, South Dakota and Wyoming. Texas does not apply individual income tax but franchise tax on corporations. Such states as New Hampshire applied individual tax of 5% and 8.5 % on business profits. Tennessee – 6% on income from stock and bonds, Washington (0.138–1.9%). Some other states have introduced flat rate taxes. This solution can be found in Colorado (4.63%), Illinois (5.0%), Indiana (3.4%), Massachusetts (5.25%), Michigan (4.25%), North Carolina (5.6%), Pennsylvania (3.07%) and Utah (5%). In Illinois the current level of local tax is foreseen until 2024 and in 2015 it will be replaced by a lowered tax of 3.25%. In Michigan the tax was lowered in 2013 since 2012 by 0.05%. In North Carolina the flat tax is in rise and in 2015 it will reach the level of 5.75%. [State Individual Income Tax rates, 2000–2014]

Most of the analyses of the American tax system stress that the approach to a new, reformed system should lead towards simplification of system, it should make taxes more transparent, stimulating creation of jobs and enabling innovativeness in R&D sectors.

There is a number of solutions to cure the American tax system which are supposed to lead towards reduction of the budget deficit and public debt. The best know proposals can be divided into proposals of President Obama, Congressional proposals, experts ideas.

In September 2011 President Obama announced a 10-year Plan[5] (2012–2021) in which he proposes tax increases for those with higher incomes, supplemented with some changes in structure of expenditures. Changes in expenditures include reduction of expenditures on defence and Medicare[6]. Following the first proposal of 2011, the American President allowed tax cuts of Bush and Clinton to expire in 2012, something that meant an increase in budget revenues caused by return to higher tax brackets. This will result in, among other effects, return to 39.6% level from 33% and 35%.

The Budget Committee of the House of Representatives, which is chaired by Paul Ryan, a Republican, proposed a tax reform which was focused on lowering income tax rates and reduction of expenditures[7]. The project also tried to eliminate the loopholes. The project was to change the Medicare and Medicaid Programs. Compared with the President Obama's proposal it did not reduce significantly the defence spending. This proposal had the lowest share of expenditures and revenues to the GNP in comparison with all other projects reforming the US budget [News-Pressnow, 2014].

A competitive proposal was submitted by the Congressional Progressive Caucus (CPC) [The People's Budget, 2011]. This proposal outlined the path to balance the budget by 2021, at the same time keeping public debt below 60% level. The idea of the project was to increase revenues by increasing taxes and reducing expenditures. Reductions included cuts in defence spending. The project was built upon increasing taxes, restoring some of the taxes which were

---

5 Living Within Our Means and Investing in the Future: The President's Plan for Economic Growth and Deficit Reduction.

6 Solutions proposed by the President are in most cases similar to those o Domenici-Rivlin and Bowls-Simson but the President's proposal foresees relatively higher spending.

7 The Path to Prosperity: Restoring America's Promise and a 2012 budget.

suspended in the past (like estate tax), and calling into life a programme dedicated to creating jobs. This proposal – in comparison with remaining projects – was evaluated as highest shares of spending and tax revenues in the GNP.

Some proposals were also submitted by individual Congressmen. This can be exemplified by the project submitted in 2012 by Jim Cooper (Democratic Party from Tennessee) and Steven LaTourette (Republican Party from Ohio). The project was not approved by the House. Nevertheless, it obtained support of the two parties, 17 from each of them. The project was built upon lowering both corporate and income taxes and by broadening the base. This plan to reform the US budget was considered to be the most radical one in comparison with all proposals submitted to the Congress.

There were also five additional proposals of budget reforms prepared by House Republicans for the Senate. All were launched in 2012. One of the proposals was the already presented proposal of P. Ryan, second was the one announced by President B. Obama. The remaining three were offered by Senators Mike Lee, Rand Paul, Patrick Toomey. All three focused on cutting expenditures. The similar approach was taken by six organizations, such as American Enterprise Institute, the Bipartisan Center, the Economic Policy Institute, the Heritage Foundation, the Roosevelt Institute Campus Network, the Center for American Progress.

Analyses of the proposals were strongly concentrated on the level of shares of revenues and expenditures in GNP. The first of the stated indicators measures the size of state burdens in an economy, while the second indicates the presence of the state in the economy (size of the state sector) [Report, 2013].

Table 1: Ratio of taxes to GDP in years 1995–2012 in Poland, USA and OECD average

Contents	1995	2000	2007	2009	2010	2011	2012
Poland	36.2	32.8	34.8	31.7	31.7	32.3	na
USA	26.7	28.4	26.9	23.3	23.8	24.0	24.3
OECD average	34.4	35.2	35.0	33.6	33.8	34.1	34.6

Source: OECD.

The ratio of taxes to GDP in the US is much lower than the OECD average. Moreover, it indicates a declining trend in the period 1995–2012. In case of Poland a declining trend in the similar indicator is shown, nevertheless the all-in-all ratio of taxes to GDP is higher than the OECD average. The drop in years 2008–2011 in most of OECD states was due to the financial crisis 2008+. In some OECD states the fall of revenues and increase in budget deficit stimulated rises in revenues. Such rises are proved to be temporary. This fact was proved by states which were preparing for EMU entry and trying to meet the convergence criteria of which budget deficit seemed to be the most problematic challenge. There were practically four methods to reduce the budget deficit [Żukrowska, Orsi, Lavrac 2004]:

a) First was based on increase of revenues achieved by increase of taxes. This method was applied by Austria, Finland, Ireland, Netherlands and Spain.
b) Second was based on cuts of expenditures and changing their structure. This method was applied by Belgium, Greece and Portugal.
c) Third method was a mixed one, embracing increase of incomes and cuts of some expenditures. This was applied in France, Germany and Italy.
d) Final method, which can be counted as a mixed one, was applied in the US. It allowed an increase of expenditures but to a lower degree than the increase of revenues. In the past (before the US engagement in the Iraqi and Afghan wars) application of this method led to reduction of the American budget deficit and after some time it led towards a surplus 1998–2001[8].

The current proposals of budget deficit reductions both in the EU states as well as in the US seem to be relatively far from the assumptions that were made in the period when the American Budget Reconciliation Act was launched. Moreover, some of the comments show that in most cases policies addressing the reduction of budget deficit were leading towards recession (www.econdataus.com/thayer1.html). Such assumptions are not backed by practical evidence nor by recommendations made by international organisations to states in area of their fiscal policies. This concerns OECD, G-20, EU, IMF, etc [Supporting, 2011].

Majority of the recommendations point to lowering taxes, restructuring expenditures and reducing the budget deficit as well as public debt. The policies recommended are guided in principle by the ideas which have been used to prepare the Washington Consensus [Serra, Stiglitz, 2008] in macroeconomics or the current strategy Europe 2020 [European, 2010] in applied economic policies.

8 Before the surplus was achieved in 1947, 1948, 1949, 1956, 1957, 1960 and 1969. The reduction in 1998 resulted from The Omnibus Budget Reconciliation Act of 1993 called in abbreviation OBRA-93 or Revenue Reconciliation Act of 1993. This was a federal law which was enacted by the 103rd United States Congress. It was launched into life by President Bill Clinton.

TTIP: what it can bring to the tax systems?

TAFTA is a proposal of Transatlantic Area of Free Trade between North America and the market of the EU Member - States. This idea was born relatively early, it was mentioned several times during the EU-US meetings, G-7 and after G-7/8 summits. Negotiations of such solution in Transatlantic trade were never commenced before the 2013. In 1995 the former EU Trade Commissioner, Leon Brittan declared necessity of creating a Transatlantic free trade area. Nevertheless, his idea was not coined into action due to discrepant interests of the two Partners. A consecutive step towards liberalisation of the mutual trade was undertaken in Spring 2007. On 30th April 2007 during a EU- a common declaration was launched: Framework for Advancing Transatlantic Economic Integration between the European Union and the United States of America (Framework for advancing... 2007). In this declaration it was announced that for a while the partners worked together preparing some specific solutions in their laws, making an effort, where possible, to bring closer the two so different systems. Such activities were undertaken on both sides of the Atlantic and were made transparent on both sides. Often this activity was used as an argument that there is no doubt that legal solutions shape mutual relations between the markets and states as well as their companies. At the same time it was considered that it is high time to introduce liberal solutions in mutual economic relations. From the beginning, when such a decision was taken, there was doubt that it will have a wider impact on international economic relations. In such circumstances attention is turned towards introduction of such solutions which have to promote not only opening of markets but also protection of consumers, their interests as well as protection of the environment. The announcement makes it clear that expectations concerning the agreement between the EU and the US are very big and the plans concerning the applied solutions in the framework of the TTIP agreement are ambitious. In general, the TTIP is seen as an open agreement, meaning that others could join in the future. Moreover, the agreement will affect a number of markets with whom the EU and US have concluded free trade agreements or preferential trade agreements. On a broader scale it will also have impact on those who are excluded from such agreements, as their sensitivity to institutional competitiveness will increase their interest in deciding on more freer trade.

Not only the results of the negotiations themselves, but mainly the solutions which they would introduce are eagerly awaited. It is expected that TTIP will eliminate the customs tariffs but on top of that it is expected to deeply liberalise the transfer of services as well as create more advantageous conditions for business by providing freer access to public tenders. Finally, attention is turned to the necessity of introducing innovative solutions into a number of markets such as: energy, raw materials as well as to sustainable growth and protection of interests of investors and investments. Achievement of all those goals will be possible after reaching consensus on and approving the regulatory pillar of the agreement which will create new conditions for mutual cooperation and will have a direct impact on bilateral conditions of cooperation yielding positive impact on the economic effects for all sectors on both of the markets [Framework for advancing, 2007].

The deadlock in mutual relations over the Atlantic was broken in 2013, when transatlantic negotiations started on TTIP.

At this moment economic relations between the EU and the USA are conducted under the standardised agreement, in which no specific preference conditions are applied in bilateral terms [Woolcock, 2011]. Bilateral terms take into account the MFNC (Most Favored Nation Clause). In US such regulations of the relations are labelled as: Permanent Normal Trade Relations with the third countries. In general they are regulated by conditions which are provided by the membership in such organizations as OECD or GATT/WTO.

There is limited knowledge what the TTIP and TAFTA can bring when they are ready, signed and launched. This remark concerns a number of areas, not only the tax systems. We are aware that TTIP will eliminate the already relatively low – at this moment – tariff barriers, which can reduce the costs of mutual trading. What is more important for the small and medium companies (S&M) which dominate in both of the producing markets in UE and US, are the non-tariff barriers. They create a bigger problem in mutual transatlantic trade and are seen as costly obstacles especially for S&M [Parker, Alemanno, 2014; Roy, Dominique, 2014; Shapiro, 2013].

Nevertheless, analysing the list of experts engaged in the TTIP negotiations and looking at their professional profile specialisation, one can guess that taxes will be part of the deal. The problems linked with taxes, their level, reforms and application form the conditions of competition, are part of the financial services, play some role in government procurement, are also part of the legal and institutional solutions. TTIP is also supposed to regulate some of the sector solutions, where both markets apply specific and differentiated taxes aimed at stimulating specific sectors. Some such solutions were mentioned in reviewing the US case. Another issue is the sector of state owned enterprises. The negotiations seem to be well prepared in advance as tasks groups on law harmonisation work on some approximation of EU and American laws practically since 1972 (year when transatlantic inter-parliamentary relations started). followed by launch of the Transatlantic Legislation Dialogue in 1990. Mutual cooperation also includes the work of Transatlantic Economic Council, which was called into life during the EU-US summit in 2007, while the first meeting of the Council took place in Washington on 9th November 2007. On top of the two mentioned bodies, there is the EU US High level Working Group on Jobs and Growth. This body also supported the vision of eliminating trade barriers.

Conclusions for Poland

Poland, in the light of internal economic problems as well taking into account the future changing conditions of trade and competition, should apply policies anticipating all mentioned changes. This opens a number of areas in which some strategic adjustments should be implemented. Excluded from this will be competition policy and macro-stabilisation which are traditional requirements in current conditions. This will not change. What seems to be important in the light of TTIP for Poland?

First of all, Poland should make a strong effort to decrease the share of tax revenues and budget expenditures in GDP. Those indicators show advancement of the economy as well as natural competitiveness of the economy. In US both of the indicators are below the OECD average, while in Poland the same indicator is above the OECD average. This goal can be achieved by policies pointed at quick increase of the GDP, to be followed by decrease in tax burdens and restructuring of expenditures. All mentioned general lines of change should be designed as future-oriented solutions, which anticipate what will follow conclusion of the TTIP. It was mentioned that once concluded, TTIP will address not only the internal issues of the EU and US but also the problems of growth, development and employment addressed on global scale. This means that the current Polish national interest is to define what has to be done in order to accelerate the increase in GDP, as well as how to restructure expenditures without having to increase the share of state spending in GDP. The former requirement is approvable politically, although methods to come up with the results in this specific area can vary. The latter is more difficult, at least politically, as traditionally with a growing economy there are strong pressures to increase expenditures on certain tasks or at least keep them at unchanged levels. Creation of an institutional and law regime in this area would be helpful. A number of solutions included in such a regime could have been taken from the laws introduced in the EU general budget, such as linking the rate of growth of certain expenditures with the rate of increase in revenues, but at the same time introducing certain limits in form of ceilings.

Now let us move towards some solutions which can effectively stimulate growth. It should be mentioned that no methods will be discussed here in details. In most cases they will be enumerated. As mentioned earlier, Poland is a developed economy in post-industrial phase of development, but it is somewhere in the middle of its way between the stage driven by effectiveness of the available production factors and the stage driven by innovative use of those factors. This means that acceleration of advancement to the highest stage of development is required here. This can be done when Poland will look into the opportunities which are offered by the fact that Poland is a member of the EU, EEA (European Economic Area), OECD, as well as consider the prospects inherent in conclusion of the TTIP.

All mentioned requirements demand higher focus of the applied policies in attracting foreign investors and investments. This in turn throws some light on the tax system, where the taxes are not competitive with other economies in the region. Skilled and productive labour force should no longer be considered as compensation for higher taxes. Such approach reduces the chances to attract FDI into the Polish market, especially as regards S&M companies in innovative areas of the economy.

A major focus in strategy to change the economic conditions for business require reduction of tax burdens, something that can be achieved gradually in order not to destabilise the current system of financing the budget. Such changes can be done when the economy grows. They are less acceptable when the economy slows down. Tax reform can foresee a flat tax as a final goal of the reform. Nevertheless, lowering the level of tax burdens can be spread over a longer time, giving the perspective for business that in the future their fiscal obligations will be lowered. Also personal fiscal obligations should be lowered. The gap between expenses of the state and the revenues can be temporarily filled by selling state-held properties. Such a solution is being proposed in developed economies. The cuts in taxes should include not only direct taxes but indirect taxes as well. Lower energy taxes or VAT both impact on costs of production. Lower costs increase competitiveness of production and of products.

Poland should prepare a wise and thoughtful strategy to promote her economy and all the opportunities that make the market attractive for FDI and foreign managers to stay here with their families. Such a promotion strategy should be complex, well thought out and easily accessible by business. It should be also confirmative. All state institutions should be engaged in that promotion proportionally to their terms of reference and beyond (in sense of directing interested customers to specific institutions able to supply them with detailed information).

Stress should be put on education including practical elements of it, and showing relations between theory and practice. Explaining what in the theories has changed and why (in what circumstances). Changes should involve all generations (those coming into the labour market, those who work already and those who are in the phase of preparing themselves to exit from active workforce), but not forcing anyone.

Such solutions indicate that Poland requires deep revolutionary changes in schooling on all levels, starting from nurseries, through preschool, primary, secondary and high schools and ending at university and third level of education. All of the them should be focused on preparing young generations for their future professional lives, where future requirements of professions are hard to imagine today. Nevertheless, some features of future professions are clear. Just as now, they embrace entrepreneurship, imagination, anticipation and innovation. At the same time they should be strongly relying on ITC, self-sufficiency but not excluding work in teams (often international teams, formed into flexible networks).

In sum Poland awaits its new promotion strategy, it needs deep reforms in the tax system, finally it requires specific changes in the educational system.

Bibliography

An end to Austerity? (2014), 09 March 2014, Ludwig von Mises Institute.

Area Lawmakers Vote in Favor of Ryan Budget. News-Pressnow.com. 10 April 2014.

European Commission Communicaton: Europe 2020. (2010), – A Strategy for Smart, sustainable and inclusive growth (3 March). COM (2010) 2020 final.

Framework for Advancing Transatlantic Economic Integration between the European Union and the United States of America. Washington 30 April 2007.

Government Expenditure Database. (2013), POLAND. The World Bank December.

httOne Economicsp://www.econdataus.com/thayer1.html (2.06.2014).

Living Within Our Means and Investing in the Future: The President's Plan for Economic Growth and Deficit Reduction.

Melecky, M., A. (2013), *Cross-Country Analysis of Public Debt Management Strategies*, The World Bank. Banking and Debt Management Department July 2007. Policy Research Working Paper 4287. Europe Facing More Pressure to Reconsider Cuts as a Cure, The New York Times, 20 April.

Memo 13/463 29.05.2013. Commission takes steps under the Excessive Deficit Procedure. Brussels, European Commission.

Nowe Podatki Utrudnią Poszukiwania w łupkach. (2014), Rzeczpospolita. Ekonomia i Rynek 29.05.

Pact for Competitiveness, 3.02.2011.

Parker R., Alemanno A. (2014), *Towards Effective Regulatory Cooperation under TTIP: A Comparative Overview of the EU and the US Legislative and Regulatory Systems*, CEPS. Series: Thinking Ahead of Europe.

Revenue Reconciliation Act of 1993.

Rodrik, D. (2008), *One Economics, Many Recipes: Globalization, Institutions and the Economic Growth*, Princeton University Press, Princeton.

Roy, J., Dominique R., (ed.). (2014), *The Transatlantic Trade and Investment Partnership between the European Union and the United States*, Thomas-Shore, Inc., Miami-Florida.

Serra, N. Stiglitz J., E., (ed.). (2008), *The Washington Consensus Reconsidered. Towards a New Global Governance. The Initiative for Policy Dialogue Series*, Oxford University Press, Oxford.

Shapiro, G. (2013), *The Global Economy is Counting on A US/Europe Trade Deal*, The Forbes, 8.13.

Small Business Exporting Survey. (2013), NSBA/SBEA (National Small Business Association/ Small Business Exporters Association.

Sobczak P. (2014), *Aims for Narrower Fiscal Deficit In 2015* – Government Document. Reuters. 14.04.

State Budget Revenue. (2014), Ministry of Finance. State Budget department, Warsaw.

State Individual Income Tax Rates, 2000–2014, http://taxfoundation.org/article/state-individual-income-tax-rates. State individual Tax Rates, http://www.usa-federal-state-individual-tax.com.

Supporting the development of More Effective Tax System. (2011), A Report to the G-20. Developed by Working Group by the IMF, OECD, UN and World Bank.

The Path to Prosperity: Restoring America's Promise and a 2012 budget. (2011), House Budget Committee, April 5.

The People's Budget. April 2011.

Transatlantic Economic Council – Annexes to the TEC Joint Statement. 29 November 2011.

TTIP: szanse i wyzwania dla biznesu. Raport Amerykańskiej Izby Handlowej w Polsce TTIP: Chances and Challenges for the Business, The Report of Am Cham in Poland, September 2013) Wrzesień 2013.

Woolcock, S. (2011), *European Union Trade Policy*, London School of Economics, London.

Żukrowska, K., Orsi, R., Lavrac V., (Ed.). (2004), *Fiscal, monetary and exchange rate issues of the Eurozone enlargemenrt*, A Report, Ezone Plus, Instytut Wiedzy, Warsaw, Berlin.

Żukrowska, K. (2011), *Strefa euro w kryzysie – zastosowane rozwiązania naprawcze*, [in:] T. Gruszecki (ed.) *Kryzys a dług publiczny w krajach rozwiniętych*, KUL, Lublin 2014. Pact for Competitiveness, 3.02.2011.

Tadeusz Waściński[1] and Dorota Bienias[2]

Strategic planning of services in performance budgeting of the public finance sector's units

Introduction

The article provides a review of Polish experience to date with strategic planning in the public subsector. A critical analysis of the strategies and plans for the development of entities making up this sector points to shortcomings in transfer from diagnosis to strategic implementation, a habit of avoiding projects of financial implementation, excessive lenient monitoring indicators and blurring the responsibility for achieving goals.

Authors of the article formulate the thesis, that performance budgeting is the link connecting strategic planning with on-going financial planning. It enables direct translation of the financial situation into development policy and operational objectives. It allows to precisely estimating the effects and allows ex-post performance analysis and assessment. Introducing strategic planning to performance budgeting is a chance not only for improving the quality and effectiveness of development policy, but also for implementing an *Evidence Based Policy*. What is more, performance budgeting may very well eliminate the need for drafting local development strategies.

In the article a description was provided of the process of performance budget strategic planning in 7 steps in practical terms, taking into account a new, service approach to the objectives executed by local self-governments.

Development strategies and strategic programmes in the public sector

The public sector is very important for the functioning of the state, because it affects every sphere - in particular in economic security [Raczkowski, 2014, p. 47–49]. Modern strategic planning as a basic function of strategic management has

---

1 Professor, Warsaw Technical University, Management Faculty, email: T.Wascinski@wz.pw.edu.pl.
2 Ph.D. student in Warsaw Technical University, Management Faculty.

become more common in practice of the Polish public sector since the 1990s. This development is not only a reflection of statutory requirements, which relate to the government and local, self-government entities in regions. It stems also from the necessity of enhancing competitiveness with limited resources, the pressure on increasing the social-economic, regional and geographic cohesion of the country, as well as the ambitions of politicians of various levels. In distribution of European Union funds, strategic planning is required as well – compatible with political ambitions in given communities. In Poland, strategic planning on national scale is the responsibility of the Council of Ministers, while on the self-government level it belongs to the legislature of the local community, district or region governments within their terms of reference.

According to J. Stoner and C. Wankel, strategic planning signifies long-term planning, set for defining and executing certain objectives of the organisation [Stoner and Wankel, 1992, 99–100]. The main tool in strategic planning, both in the private and public sectors, is the development strategy. It is a kind of a system plan describing the given government actions over a period of time taking place on the given territory and following set priorities. As put by A. D. Chandler, a strategy covers the arrangements for reaching the long-term goals subjected to the general directions of action, as well as the instructions for allocating the resources crucial to executing the declared objectives [Chandler, 1962]. A properly designed development strategy should rely on a thorough diagnosis of the situation, an assessment of the resources on hand and the entity's needs, analysis of the operating environment and development trends. The strategy document most often contains the following parts: diagnostic, strategic and implementation, financing and monitoring.

There had been so many strategies and long-term government programmes in Poland, that on the 27th November, 2009 the Council of Ministers has implemented a document entitled "*Plan for organising the development strategy*". Its actions resulted in decreasing the number of strategic documents existing and required for presentation to the CoM from 42 in 2009 to 9 new, integrated development strategies, realising the medium- and long-distance strategy of the country's development. The new strategies constitute the so-called "other development strategies" in Article 9 of the Rules of Development Policy Act of 6th December, 2006. [National Physical.., 2012; National Developed.., 2012; Raport końcowy.., 2011].

In 2011, the PSDB consulting firm has carried out an adaptive expert review concerning the results of a crosscheck of 9 integrated development strategies, performed on the level of detailed objectives and the directions of interventions/actions in 11 identified key arenas [PSDB]. In the document, the degree of accommodating the challenges – key arenas – has been assessed. In summary of the research exercise a high level of internal correlation between the set objectives has been noticed; however, the lacking or poorly integrated elements have been listed as well – especially the weak points in correlating the diagnostic and strategic parts. The cure for this weakness for Poland could be the introduction of the *Evidence Based Policy*, first introduced in the United Kingdom by the Government headed by T. Blair. It would allow attaining development goals on the basis of a thorough diagnosis of the situation and needs of a entity, an analysis of requirements, environment and development trends, as well as an analysis and assessment of the results attained instead of a blurry, political vision.

The analysis of the country's strategies performed by the article's author on her own shows also a weakness in the documents' implementation part. Although in strategies the necessity of applying monitoring indicators for the assessment of progress in reaching the set objectives has been accepted, the reference to the financial framework for the execution of indicators was, in fact, all but absent. Monitoring indicators are in many cases set on a low level, basically attainable with no public intervention (we may observe the independent event effect – the *deadweight*).

Monitoring procedures, as well as procedures for performing potential remedial actions in the event of unsatisfactory results of given indicators are also of low quality. The weakness of those elements hinders or even prevents evaluation and execution of the effects. Achieving a concrete effect in a set time with concrete resources, while being the greatest benefit of enterprise development strategies, is the weakness of development strategy in the public sector.

The cause of such a state of events can be ascribed mainly to the insufficient cooperation between the experts drafting strategies and the officials responsible for their execution, the discrepancies between target groups and, last but not least, the alterations of once formulated political aims. For an accurate definition of a strategy's aim it is crucial to make a gigantic analytical graft – an assessment of social-economic phenomena and defining the cause-and-effect correlations. In most cases, the process of defining the precise goals of strategies on the basis of a thorough diagnosis and analysis is purposely avoided, since, as J. M. Keynes stated, "*There is nothing a government hates more than to be well-informed: for it makes the process of arriving at decisions much more complicated and difficult*" [Hunter, 2003, p. 194–196].

In the self-government subsector, the statutory requirement for formulating development strategies applies only on the region self-governments level [Public Finances Act, 2009, Journal of Laws 2013 items 885, 938, 1646]. Despite attempts to extend this duty to the self-government commune and district levels, the Sejm (Parliament) of the Republic of Poland, while introducing the change of the Act stating the rules of development strategies and some other acts on

24th February 2014, has introduced a possibility, but not a fixed requirement, to prepare strategies [59th saession Act, Article 4]. In reference to local communities supported from the European Agricultural Fund for Rural Development, the necessity for defining and stating the range of a local development strategy has been set out in Chapter 2, Article 33 of the European Parliament and Council's Regulation 1303/2013 of 17th December, 2013.

The most important strategic planning document that is currently required in commune-level administrations is the Long-Term Financial Forecast, introduced by the new Public Finances Act [PFA, 2009, Articles 226–232]. Under terms of Article 227 of the Act, starting from 2011, self-government entities draft a long-term financial forecast covering the given and at least three following fiscal years, while the minimum period of the forecast is subject to obligatory prolongation for a period of any forecast long-term expenses (for instance, the first Warsaw forecast created in 2011 was set for the 2011–2013 period, the current is set for the years 2014–2042). The forecast includes the incomes and current expenses of the budget, property incomes and expenses, budgetary result (along with the way of using the surplus or funding a debt), incomes and expenses of the budget (including the current and planned future debt), indicating sources of debt repayment, plus interpretation of the forecast. Introducing the Long-term Forecast was meant to replace the earlier functioning planning documents for communes: the Long-term Investment Plan, limits of programmes and projects expenses financed out of UE funds, non-refundable grants from the EFTA and the debt amount projection.

Aside from the obligatory forecast under other statutes commune administrations are required to come up with a number of other strategic documents, e.g. a study of conditioning and directives for land management, local Land Use Planning, housing stock management programme. Most Polish communes have development strategies as well as specific target strategies, e.g. strategies for solving social problems, interaction with non-governmental organisations programme, environment protection scheme. Furthermore, many specific target documents are or were required for the purpose of filing a request for external aid funds – e.g. revitalisation programmes – which the author finds undue, since in her opinion, it is an unnecessary abuse on the part of the fund-distributing institutions and an excessive multiplying of planning documents that obstruct access to the funds.

There are many reasons for arranging the number and range of strategies and development programmes on the communes level. Communes do not have the proper staffing for creating, monitoring and controlling programmes and they lack funds for external evaluations conducted by experts. Multiplying development plans and strategies is unnecessary, as it often leads to lack of coordination between particular documents and creates contradictions between the aims and objectives contained in them. In a critical analysis of development strategies of communes conducted in 2011 by M. Pytlak, low quality of the development strategies in selected communes has been pointed out [Pytlak M., 2011, p. 373–375]. Pytlak accuses the experts of routine, badly conducted situation diagnosis, directing strategies towards trying to get allocations of UE funds, lack of reference to or cohesion with neighbouring communes, excessive number of strategic objectives, wishful thinking not connected in any way with the social-economic communes' reality.

In addition, many local governments, especially newly elected, find strategies to be a bother in executing their political goals (especially those created by their predecessors). As shown by practice: execution of the self-government politics is, in most of cases, divergent with strategic goals and concentrated on on-going operational management. The officials who assigned with monitoring objectives have problems monitoring and assessing strategies as a result of the rules of monitoring and handing in the reports' faultiness. In most strategies, the reports only consist of one page at the end of the document, along with the list of potential monitoring indicators (without pointing out their base and target values). Moreover, very often the descriptions of implementation fail to specify the range of those responsible, leading to a situation, in which the execution and reporting a strategy's effects resides in no one particular, making the responsibility blurry and unclear. Gaining the monitoring information and its processing are also very difficult, and in the case of financial data – often impossible. Evaluation of a development strategy becomes problematic as well, both because of the errors of implementation and funding systems and the indicators' values and their translation into aims and objectives. Meanwhile, evaluation of a strategy should provide information and managerial recommendations useful in the next stage of strategic programming.

Performance budgeting

Performance budgeting is the chance for introducing strategic planning in correlation with financial planning in the public sector. In the author's opinion, in the public sector the performance budget combined with WPF can replace the local development strategy. There are, however, a few conditions described later in the article, fulfilling which will be necessary to ensure taking full advantage of performance budgeting's potential.

Performance budgeting is, according to OECD, a form of budgeting oriented towards measurable results, in which the gathered results information is used for the allocation of resources, increasing their efficiency and the responsibility

[Performance Budgeting in OECD Countries, 2007, p. 20]. It was first introduced in 1949 the US, when Congress passed the Security Act for the newly created Department of Defence. Performance budget was implemented for the purpose of improving the public resources management and ensuring they would be spent accordingly to the set aims and priorities. An additional effect was the improved transparency of expenses and legibility for decision makers. Performance budgeting is the main tool of the *New Public Management (NPM)* introduced in many of OECD's countries. Moreover, performance budgeting is a part of the *Evidence Based Policy*.

In Polish law the concept of a performance budget was introduced in Articles 2 and 32 of the Public Finance Act [Public Finances Act, 2009, Journal of Laws № 157 item 1240] in reference to the country's budget. According to the Act, it is "*a comparison of a country's budget expenses or a public finance sector's entity's expenses prepared accordingly to the country's function, denoting particular areas of the country's actions, and budgetary objectives grouping the expenses by the aims, budgetary sub-tasks grouping the objectives enabling execution of the objectives' aims, in which those sub-tasks were set out*" along with a description of objectives' purpose and the sub-tasks, base and target indicators of the degree to which the aims have been executed in result of the incurred costs. An obligation to prepare a budgetary performance system covering the given fiscal year and two following years was defined for the following: ministries, executive agencies, budgetary economic institutions, administrators of country's special purpose funds and corporate entities classed into the financial public sector.

Performance budgeting should lead to better allocation of financial, property and staff resources in an entity, for efficient meeting of recipients' needs. Moreover, it answers the postulates in the range of purposefulness of spending financial resources, because it ties a particular expense with the aim that is executed for a recipient through this act, also makes it possible to choose the optimum way of executing the objective.

There are 22 functions in a country. A critical analysis of Function 17: *Forming the local development of a country* in the country's budget for 2013 in a performance system [Bienias, Waściński, 2013, p. 43–56] has brought up many shortcomings in budget planning:

a) lack of integrity between budgetary aims and strategic policy in the local development area,
b) examples of aims and indicators chosen inadequately to the modified budgetary aims,
c) concentrating only on using the European funds,
d) obstructions in evaluating the criteria of effectiveness, efficiency and usefulness.

The obligation to prepare the budget in the performance system does not currently concern the self-government subsector, but 23% of the studies in 2012 cities with district rights have introduced performance budgeting in addition to the traditional one [Korolewska, Marchewka-Bartkowiak, 2013, p. 161]. Among the performance budgeting's advantages were listed: improved effectiveness of spending, generating savings, monitoring the achieved results, evaluation of all executed objectives, clear lines of responsibility for, transparency for the recipients, a tool for managerial control. The research included also the methodology difficulties of preparing the budget – mainly linked to defining objectives, aims and indicators. Problems with reporting were also mentioned.

Introducing an obligation to budgeting in the performance format (instead of the traditional) in communes would require preparing a unified planning and reporting scheme. It would lead to tremendous qualitative changes and make it possible to compare the entities' results. Changes of present arrangements are becoming more and more urgent due to the current state of public finances, cutting expenses, growing indebtedness of the entities, social pressures regarding effectiveness and efficiency, and the need to increase the quality of public services. Performance budgeting is becoming a necessity in contemporary public management. The new form of budgeting, based on planning, monitoring, controlling the expenses and assessing the achieved results requires, however, constant improving of the budgeting process in a cycle similar to that of project management and project approach to objectives (Chart 1).

Chart 1: The cycle of performance budgeting in the public finance sector's entities

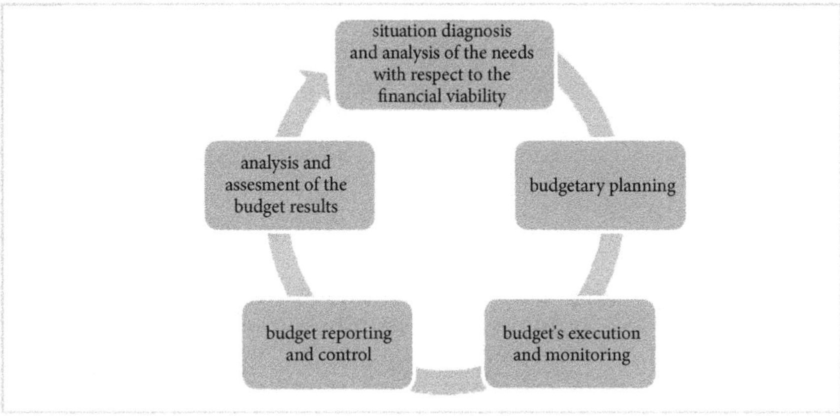

Source: own elaboration.

Currently, research of performance budgets of the self-government entities is hindered because of the lack of sources available. The information available on websites of the entities usually is limited to only the descriptive part of the planned budget. There are practically no results of the performance budget assessment, as either there are none, or their publication would expose the government to the criticism from political opponents.

Strategic approach to public services in performance budgeting of communes

In performance budgeting, a popular belief ascribing the act of preparing the budget to the financial services is proven wrong. The performance budget is the link connecting strategic planning and financial planning, and tying the budget with politics aims, as well as diagnosing the effects and their later analysis and assessment give the full spectrum to the strategic policy of a entity.

The results achieved to date in making use of of the performance budget, especially in the government subsector, are far from satisfactory [Misiąg, 2009; Płoskonka, 2012]. In the self-government subsector the results are slightly better, but self-government administrations, also did not avoid making mistakes in the process of shaping and functioning of performance budgets. It should also be noted, that in performance budgeting the approach "for the office department worker's sake" is used. The main grounds for such a state of events are in the first place:

a) lack of interest in the matters of strategic planning in performance budget on the part of managers in entities,
b) lack of skill to identify the cause-and-effect connection in the process of constructing the budget and translating the diagnosis for the strategic purposes,
c) appointed officials avoiding the responsibility for the achieved budgeting effects,
d) little social engagement observed in inspecting budget' due to poor availability and blurriness of the budget,
e) lack of consistent approach to assessing the achieved results,
f) lack of interest in creating evaluations, which could become the tool of control in the hands of government's opposition.

The approach presented in this article is a pragmatic one; its usage allows to limit the failures when connecting performance budgeting with strategic development, as well as the inconveniences of introducing remedial actions in the event of unsatisfactory results.

In the author's opinion, success of performance budgeting in self-government entities can be achieved with the service approach – from the office client's point of view and properly conducted budget strategic planning process in 7 steps (Chart 2). What is more, this approach is congruent with one of the four models of *New Public Management* – the so-called NPM 4 [Modzelewski, 2009]. The NMP4 model concentrates on the service's recipient: increasing the quality of public service, managing the quality, listening to the recipients' voice and complying with their expectations. In this model the role of certain local societies' representatives is increased, any focus on the market's role in public services is curtasiled, whereas the pressure is put on learning from the citizens, their needs and expectations. The model is oriented towards efficiency and utility (chart 2).

Chart 2: Strategic approach – 7 steps to performance budget planning in a self-government entity

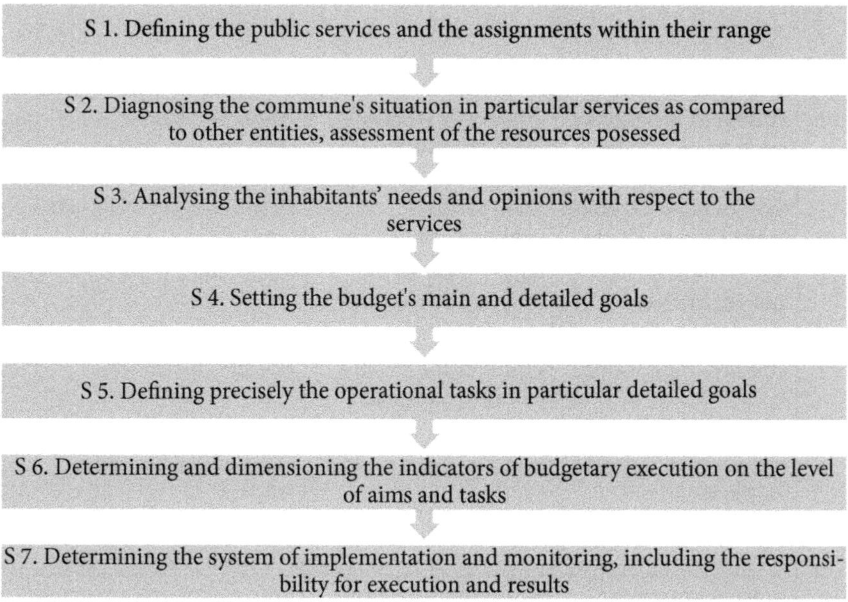

Source: own elaboration.

Following is a brief description of the components of the process of the strategic planning of performance budgeting.

Defining public services and the assignments within their range

The approach from the service recipient's (client's) point of view determines working on the performance budget by the rule: the office department is meant for the inhabitant's sake and not the other way around.

Commune, as the basic entity of a self-government, has the obligation to satisfy the needs of a self-government community consisting of the inhabitants on the local level and accordingly to the Commune Self-government Act [Commune Self-government Act, 1990, Journal of Laws 2013, positions 594, 1318] conducts those public affairs which have not been reserved for other subjects under other statutes. Polish communes execute their own objectives, as well as commissioned objectives. Own objectives were defined in the Commune Self-government Act. The commissioned objectives [Map of Competencies] (e.g. issuing ID cards) are public objectives justified by country's needs, executed statutory or being negotiated. The own and commissioned objectives for the purpose of performance budgeting were called spheres and functions. In the service approach I suggest grouping them in 9 public services (table 1).

Table 1: Functions in cities' performance budget compared to the service approach

Lp.	Functions in Szczecin's performance budget	Spheres in Warsaw's performance budget	Public services in performance budget in the service approach
1	Safety and public order in the city	Transport and communication	Healthcare and social care services
2	Promotional activity and international cooperation	Land zoning and property management	Communication services
3	Education and science	Communal economy and environmental protection	Educational services
4	Finances and various payments	Safety and public order	Safety and public order services
5	Communal economy	Education	Environmental protection, fire and flood protection
6	Housing economy	Healthcare and social services	Land zoning and communal property management services
7	Physical culture, tourism and recreation	Culture and protection of national heritage	Cultural and sport services

Lp.	Functions in Szczecin's performance budget	Spheres in Warsaw's performance budget	Public services in performance budget in the service approach
8	Culture and protection of cultural heritage	Recreation, sport and tourism	Communal services
9	Land and property management	Promotional activity and supporting economic growth	Administrative services
10	Social services and healthcare	Self-government structures management	–
11	Development of civic society	Finances and various settlements	–
12	Transport and communication	–	–
13	Supporting the economic development	–	–
14	Managing self-government structures	–	–

Source: Own elaboration based on: bip.um.szczecin.pl and bip.warszawa.pl.

What is the difference between the approaches? In the structure applied so far, performance budget is constructed from the point of view of the manager, his organisational entity and the entity's officials. For a citizen, however, such a structure is illegible and the word "sphere" or function are incomprehensible. The service approach is constructed from a client's point of view, with focus on the logic of services performed by communes. There is no place, then, for the service "finances and various payments" – because for a citizen this consists in administering the Commune's resources service (table 2).

Table 2: The range of public services in performance budget with a service approach

№	Public service	Range of objectives (own and comissioned)
1	Healthcare and social care services	Healthcare, social care, including guardianship centres, pro-family policy, including providing pregnant women with social, health and legal care
2	Communication services	Local public transport and traffic management
3	Educational services	Public education (elementary, grammar-school and preschool level)
4	Safety and public order services	Public order and safety of the community

№	Public service	Range of objectives (own and comissioned)
5	Environmental protection, public order, safety, fire and flood protection services	Environmental and water economy protection, fire and flood protection, including equipping and maintaining the Commune's flood-fighting facilities
6	Land zoning and communal property management services	Land zoning management, management of the Commune's housing properties, markets and market halls, maintaining the Commune's institutional facilities and installations and administering facilities
7	Cultural and sport services	Maintaining culture facilities, including municipal libraries and other culture institutions, conservation of relics, physical culture and tourism, including recreational areas and sport devices
8	Communal services	Water grids and water supply, sewerage, removing the wastes and water treatment, maintenance of order, cleaning and sanitation, landfills and communal waste treatment, electricity, heating and gas supply, supporting the telecommunication networks (contracted), municipal roads, streets, bridges, squares, municipal greenery and forestation, municipal cemeteries
9	Administrative services	Supporting and spreading the self-government idea, Commune's promotion, cooperation with local communities and regional communities of other countries, executing the administrative commissioned objectives, covering the Commune's personnel's salary costs

Source: own elaboration.

Arranging the services in the Tables 1 and 2 was done in the "most to least important" sequence on a basis of the results of CDS's 2013 research [Bieńkowska, Ulasiński, Szymańska, 2013] for 6 public services conducted with a group of 3717 inhabitants of 12 communes of the Wołomin District and 16 focus group interviews. The communes' inhabitants recognized the health-related services as the most important, followed by communication and educational services. They named the administrative services as the least important. In the study, the inhabitants defined not only the relative importance of given service, but also the factors in public services of greatest importance to them:

a) effectiveness, efficiency and quality of the rendered services connected with high level of skill and kindness of officials and personnel,
b) on-time handling of matters,

c) in respect to communication and communal services – degree of technical infrastructure availability.

Research shows that a public service recipient does not perceive the expenses which need to be incurred on execution of an objective (which is often the main element of the performance budgets' descriptions) as important. The client is more interested in the expenses, e.g. how much does a particular service cost per capita (and why are our taxes such a big part of it?) and the quality. A client of educational service is not interested in the number of school's workers and of which exactly scholarly degree is held by the teachers, but whether the educational service is carried out in proper financial condition, the school operates in one turn, the children are safe at school, the learning conditions are good and if the results compared to other schools in the Commune, district or region are satisfactory. Such analogies may serve in other public services as well. Approaching the subject from the client's point of view determines the choice of monitoring indicators of the budget.

Diagnosing the Commune's status in particular services, compared to other entities, assessment of the possessed resources

In Chart 3 the most important elements of a Commune's situation diagnosis, which should be conducted for the purpose of properly setting the development aims, have been presented.

Chart 3: Actions undertaken while creating a diagnosis of public services

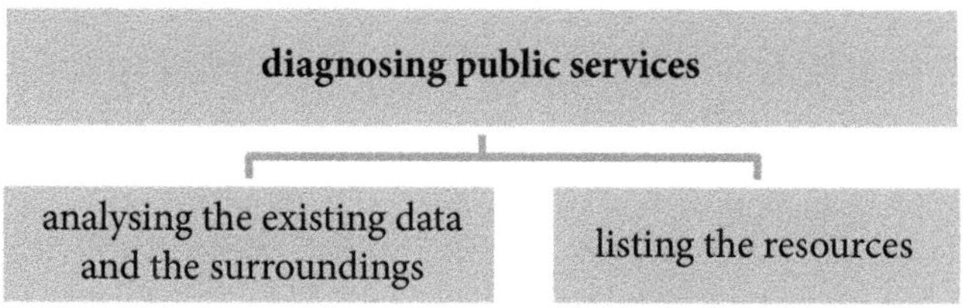

Source: own elaboration.

A diagnosis should rely first and foremost on up-to-date and objectively verifiable secondary source data – e.g. readily available CSOP (Central Statistical Office of Poland) statistics (Local Data Bank, Strateg system), the Regional Examination Board data, obligatory comparison prepared by communes (e.g. fulfilling the budget data, databases). It is necessary to conduct a short comparative analysis with other entities and defining the Commune's score among the neighbouring communes, the other communes in the county, the region and

Poland as a whole. An analysis of the location environment could be performed with the PEST method. The PEST analysis allows creating an overall image of a Commune's macro-environment (phenomena, actions and subjects) and the services rendered. PEST concerns 4 aspects of the surrounding environment: political-legal, economic, social and technological. Defining the factors and their impact (weight) on the Commune's functioning and the relations between them allows for indicating the expected development benefits – prognoses and missions.

Listing the resources currently possessed for the rendered public services is inevitable for the purpose of estimating the organisational, institutional and technical shortcomings as compared to the needs. A list is a specification of all subjects functioning in a given service, e.g. a list of elementary schools, a list of subjects conducting healthcare services. By presenting a list (a so-called map) of resources for public services, one should also take into consideration the non-public subjects, the services of which may influence the quantity, quality and range of public services, and also, in justified cases – to which it may be possible to entrust execution of public objectives under agreement or competition rules.

Analysis of inhabitants' needs and opinions with respect to services

An analysis of inhibitors need's is performed mainly as a result of conducting quantitative and qualitative surveys among the inhabitants - chart 4. Main types of quantitative surveys are PAPI (Paper and Pencil Interview), CATI (Computer Aided Telephone Interviews), or CAPI (Computer Aided Personal Interview) – chart 4.

Chart 4: The analysis of inhabitants' needs in public services

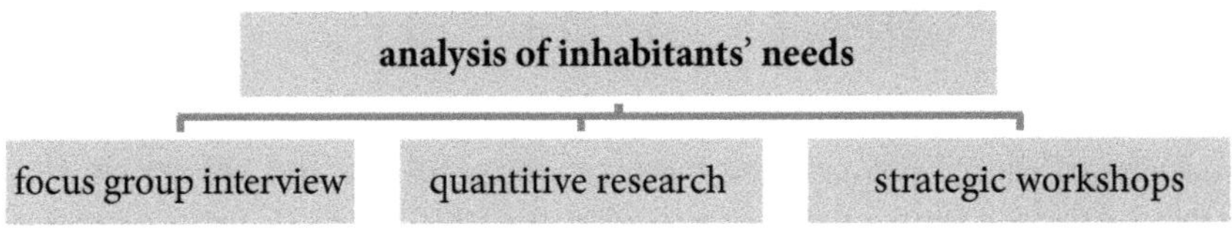

Source: own elaboration.

The selection of the target group is especially important for the research. Besides the random group, for an accurate assessment of needs the purposive sampling must be applied, one including an overrepresentation of additional groups e.g.

large families, people of the age above 65, disabled persons. The focus group interviews, also being a part of the analysis, allow to study the analysed service's context and gather inhabitants' comments, opinions and experiences concerning reception of the public service. In justified cases one of the indicated analyses may be conducted.

Summarizing a diagnostic study and the inhabitants' needs' analysis requires conducting diagnostic worshops and an expert's opinion, since adjusting the resources to the needs is the hardest element of strategic planning in performance budget. Strategic schooling, on the other hand, gathers the self-government entity's representatives capable of assessing the services' execution, representatives of the subjects and organisations involved and the services' recipients. They allow an exchange of opinions by the parties involved on the range of services, conditions of rendering, development priorities and execution possibilities. Within the worshops a number of group work methods can be used: the nominal group technique, discussion in teams and in plenary, facilitated discussion. Thanks to the indicated methods it is possible to work out a common post-worshops exercise position and confronting the agreements with an in-depth analysis of the inhabitants' needs.

Setting the main aim and detailed aims of the budget

Defining the main objective and detailed objectives in a strategic planning of a performance budget requires preparing a SWOT/TOWS analysis on the basis of previously conducted diagnosis and analysis of needs. Without a thorough SWOT/TOWS analysis it is not possible to correctly build the problems and objectives tree.

The SWOT/TOWS (Strengths, Weaknesses, Opportunities, Threats) analysis is a tool for identification and measurement of internal (weak and strong sides of a Commune) and external tendencies (opportunities and threats), here in the context of public services. Generally the strong sides should be strengthened, weak – eliminated, opportunities – used, threats – avoided. Defining the particular indicators' weight in the impact on a Commune's criterion allows for arranging them starting from the most to the least important. One should avoid the, all too often seen in development strategies of communes, lists of wishes and threats which do not come from a diagnosis and, what is more, are not indicated in the objectives. The SWOT/TOWS analysis' results often coincide with a part of the PEST analysis (the internal chances and threats for a Commune). It is then a confirmation of a correctly concluded diagnosis.

The last element before setting the strategic objectives for a performance budget is an analysis of problems and objectives. The first part of the analysis consists of identifying the Commune's problems and arranging them by defining the cause-and-effect correlations among the factors. The basic hardship in the process of constructing the problems and objectives tree and setting their hierarchy concerns identifying – distinguishing between the consequences of problems and the actual problems themselves along with their causes, pointing out the actual problems and not their symptoms. A problem tree gives an overall view of a bad situation on hand and is a tool for defining the factual "bottlenecks", which the concerned persons perceive as the most critical and are trying to adress. The purpose for creating a problem tree is defining the "key problem", to which a performance budget should relate. A complete problem tree includes a focused key problem, which has to be accepted by the recipients of the services and the Commune's governing body. The objectives tree, on the other hand, shows the overall desired future situation, which is created on the basis of the problem tree and is a positive mirror image of it – the negative state is transformed into positive results (effects), the correlation between the means and objectives reflected, the hierarchy pictured. The tree of problems and objectives should be prepared for each of the 9 public services in a Commune (chart 5).

Chart 5: Problem tree and objective tree

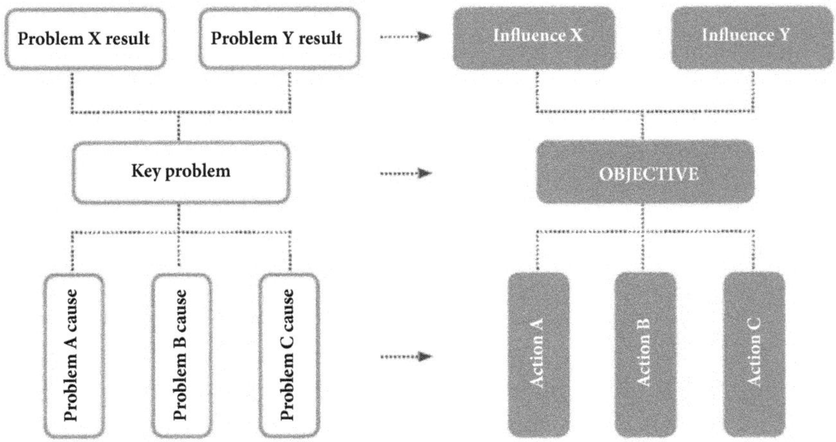

Source: Dziemianowicz W., Szmigiel-Rawska K., Nowicka P., Dąbrowska A. (2011), Planowanie strategiczne. Poradnik dla pracowników administracji publicznej, Ministerstwo Rozwoju Regionalnego, Warszawa.

After building the problem tree and defining aims for the public services we gain the detailed aims of a performance budget and we set one strategic goal of performance budgeting. While pointing the strategic and detailed aims, one should remember the SMART rule, according to which the aims should be: Simple, Measurable, Achievable, Relevant and Timely Defined. The mission and vision often seen in development strategies need not to be defined, since it is, intuitively speaking, the best possible management of available resources for the growth of a local society.

Defining operational objectives in particular detailed aims

For each of the detailed aims an operational objectives list should be prepared. Identifying the objectives may take place in the middle of strategic worshops. Below, example detailed aims and operational objectives for communal services have been depicted (Table 3).

Table 3: An example of strategic and detailed aims and operational objectives in a communal service

Strategic aim	Detailed aim	Operational objectives
Strategic goal 1 Optimising access to the water and sewage service and to water treatment	Aim 1.1. Achieving physical integrity in a Commune by planning the technical infrastructure's growth	WPI's verification in respect to covering the whole Commune with the water supply and sanitary and drain sewer networks
	Aim 1.2. Providing the inhabitants with access to the water supply and sanitary sewer networks	Building and modernising the water supply and sanitary sewer networks
	Aim 1.3. Providing access to efficient and cheap industrial water treatment	Modernising the existing industrial water treatment
	Aim 1.4. Providing access to the storm drain system	Building a storm drain system
	Aim 1.5. Improving the inhabitants' interest in connecting to the water supply and sanitary sewer grids	1. Creating a system to help fund the grid lines wires (including starting loans for 50% of the lines' cost) 2. Lowering the charges for connecting to the grid.

Strategic aim	Detailed aim	Operational objectives
	Aim 1.6. Improving the inhabitants' ecological awareness	Execution of ecological actions
	Aim 1.7. Improvement of the efficiency of executing the law in respect to water and sewerage economy	Controlling the grid lines and the contracts for water supply and sewerage

Source: own elaboration based on „Strategia rozwoju usług komunalnych. Planu proponowanych działań partnerskich na lata 2014–2020 na obszarze Powiatu Wołomińskiego, CDS.

Defining and measuring the execution of the budget indicators on the level of aims and objectives

An analysis of the available performance budgets points to the problem of choosing the indicators (measurements), both in government and self-government subsectors. The indicators most often appear on the objective level and are chosen in a way so that they would be easiest to monitor for the officials. In many cases they do not show the core of the objective. Generally, quantitative indicators are used for objectives (for instance the entity cost, average cost per capita, the number of pedagogic workers in translation to job posts). Qualitative indicators, due to being hard to achieve, are used sporadically. The indicators should also rely on readily available data (e.g. Local Data Bank), so that the level of their fulfilment in a particular period of time could be easily, and objectively, verified. The choice of indicators is not the only one crucial task, as there still is the matter of proper measuring of their (measurements') base and target value. The strategy's worth is dependent on them, as well as the performance budget. Should the aims be of long-distance and ambitious nature, and the indicators be of very low value which did not allow reaching the target objectives, this always indicates mistakes made during planning or that the creation of development's vision has replaced setting the detailed or strategic aim. A proper measuring of the indicators is, in turn, dependent on the correct diagnosis of the Commune's situation and the availability of resources,

In the service approach to performance budgeting, just as in strategic management in the public sector, three levels of indicators can be used: strategic aim, detailed aims and objectives indicators (chart 6). Using the indicators only for objectives does not, however, reflect the level of a Commune's development, so it seems more advantageous to use one or two more additional indicator levels – e.g. of synthetic nature. Synthetic indicators are collective indicators, created from a set of variables processed according to a formula, which gives a more complete view on a Commune's development in comparison to other communes. Common usage of synthetic indicators would make it possible to compare the development level of Polish communes. The levels of indicators have been presented in Chart 6, and the example indicators in Table 4.

Chart 6: Aims, objectives and indicators in strategic planning of a performance budget

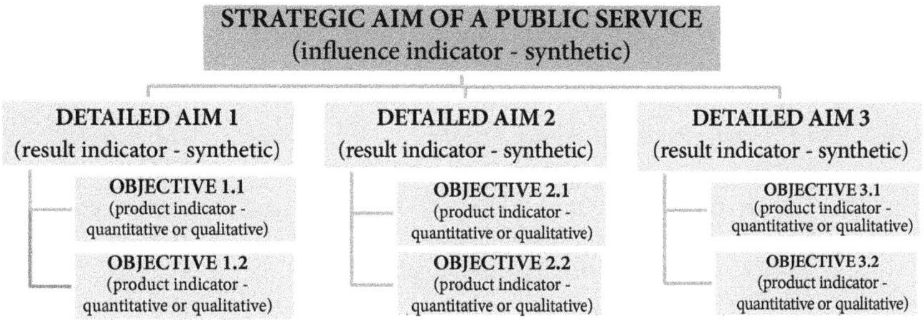

Source: own elaboration.

Table 4: Example indicators of aims and objectives in reference to Table 3

Aim №	Indicator	Entity	Source
Strategic aim 1	Synthetic – the arithmetic mean of the following indicators: • change in the number of inhabitants using the water supply grid by the county's communes, • change in the number of inhabitants using the sanitary sewer grid by the county's communes, • change in the number of inhabitants served by water treatment stations.	individuals	Local Data Bank, Central Statistical Office of Poland
Aim 1.1.	Quantity of formulated plans of covering the Commune with water supply and sanitary sewage grids ensuring the Commune's physical integrity	pieces	Municipality Office
Aim 1.2.	The percentage of a Commune's inhabitants using the water supply grid The percentage of a Commune's inhabitants using the sanitary sewer grid	individuals	Local Data Bank, Central Statistical Office of Poland

Aim №	Indicator	Entity	Source
Aim 1.3.	The percentage of inhabitants served by the industrial water treatment	%	Local Data Bank, Central Statistical Office of Poland
Aim 1.4.	Changes in the length of the storm drain in the Commune	km	Local Data Bank, Central Statistical Office of Poland
Aim 1.5.	The quantity of inhabitants connected to the grid as a result of the conducted initiatives of encouragement and support	individuals	Municipality Office
Aim 1.6.	The quantity of educational actions conveyed	pieces	Municipality Office
Aim 1.7.	The quantity of monitoring campaigns conducted in communes / Quantity of grid connections started as a result of the conducted campaigns	pieces	Municipality Office

Source: own elaboration.

Defining the implementation and monitoring system, including the responsibility for the execution and results

Performance budget is implemented and monitored by the appointed entities of an office or by organisational and executing entities performing public objectives on behalf of a Commune while using the agreed tools and internal procedures. Setting the assessment of the set aims' realisation and completion mechanisms, along with creating a verification system, is crucial for the strategic approach to performance budgeting's success. The monitoring system should provide information on the degree of execution of strategic aims and objectives. In case the value of an indicator differs from the planned value, an explanation of causes and an introduction of managerial remedial actions will be needed. The forwarding medium and dates of handing in the reports should be the same as in the system used to date – quarterly and annual reports.

Summary

There are many reasons to arrange the quantities and range of development strategies programmes on the commune level. Communes do not possess enough staff to create such programmes, to monitor, control and evaluate them. Multiplying the numbers of development plans and strategies is counterproductive,

Table 5: Examples of monitoring report on execution of performance budget

№ and name of aim	Name of objective	Indicator and entity	Base value 2013	Value 2014	Value 2015	Target value 2017	Value reached in 2017	Comment on value of the achieved indicator in the particular monitoring year (corrections)
Aim 1.4 Ensuring access to the sanitary sewer system	Building the sanitary sewer grid	Changing of the sanitary sewer grid length in the Commune (change of x km)	24,00 (length of the sanitary sewer grid in the Commune)	+4,00 km	+5,00 km	32,00	33,00	Indicator reached in 103,13%

Source: own elaboration.

often causing lack of coordination between particular documents and creating contradictions between aims and objectives contained in them. And, as the practice shows: execution of self-government policy is, in most cases, divergent with strategic aims and concentrated on the current operational management. Combining the contents of a communes' Long-Term Financial Forecast with performance budgeting is enough for conducting a strategic and realistic development policy on the commune level.

Performance budgeting is a chance for introducing strategic planning in correlation with financial planning in the public sector. The currently applied approach does not ensure the basic objective of performance budgeting – raising the effectiveness and efficiency of public funds disbursement in respect to the actual needs and development aims of communes. Introducing the service approach and performance budgeting in 7 steps will allow the qualitative changes of development management in communes.

Bibliography

Bienias, D., Waściński, T. (2013), *Czy budżetowanie zadaniowe w polskich jednostkach sektora finansów publicznych przynosi oczekiwane rezultaty?*, Zeszyty Naukowe UP-H w Siedlcach 97 Series: Administering and managing No. 24.

CDS (2013), *Research on the Wołomin County's communes*. Operational Technical Help Program, Kraków.

CDS. Communal Services Development Strategy. (2013), Plan of the planned partner actions in the years 2014–2020 in the Wołomin County, Wołomin.

Dziemianowicz W., Szmigiel-Rawska K., Nowicka P., Dąbrowska A. (2011), *Planowanie strategiczne. Poradnik dla pracowników administracji publicznej*, Ministerstwo Rozwoju Regionalnego, Warszawa.

Hunter, David J. (2003), *Evidence-based policy and practice: riding for a fall?* Journal of the Royal Society of Medicine 96(4).

Korolewska, M., Marchewka-Bartkowiak K. (2013), *Budżet zadaniowy w samorządach terytorialnych - analiza wyników badania ankietowego oraz studium przypadków na przykładzie miast na prawach powiatu*, Studia Biura Analiz Sejmowych Kancelarii Sejmu, Warszawa 1(33).

Lubińska, T (red.). (2007), *Budżet państwa i budżet zadaniowy w kontekście zasad budżetowych*, Difin, Warszawa.

Map of Competencies, http://www.mapakompetencji.org/index.php?option=com_content&view=article&id=13&Itemid=106.

Modzelewski, P. (2009), *System zarządzania jakością a skuteczność i efektywność administracji samorządowej*, CeDeWu, Warszawa.

National Developed Strategy 2020. (2012), Attachement to Resolution No 157 of the Council of Ministers of 25 September.

National Physical Development Concept 2013. (2012), Ministry of Regional Development, Warsaw.

Performance Budgeting in OECD countries. (2007), Organization for Economic Co-Operation and Development, Paris.

Poland. Public Finances Act. 27th August 2009, Journal of Laws No 157, point 1240 with the latter changes.

Poland. Rules of Development Policy Act. December 6th, 2006, Article 9.

Poland. Sejm of the Republic of Poland. Act enacted on the 59th meeting on 24.01.2014, awaiting the President of Poland's signature.

PSDB. Expertise Report concerning the crosscheck of 9 integrated development strategies. Warszawa: WYG Group, 2011. Source: http://www.mir.gov.pl/rozwoj_regionalny/Polityka_rozwoju/System_zarzadzania_rozwojem/Zintegrowane_strategie_rozwoju/Documents/Kontrola_krzyzowa.pdf, access on 23.03.2014 r.

Pytlak, M. (2011), *Planowanie rozwoju społeczno-gospodarczego communes-krytyczna analiza strategii rozwoju wybranych gmin zachodniego pasma aglomeracji warszawskiej*, Wyższa Szkoła Rozwoju Lokalnego w Żyrardowie, Rocznik Żyrardowski XI, Żyrardów.

Raczkowski K. (2014), *Współczesny model tetrarchii zarządzania a bezpieczeństwo ekonomiczne obrotu gospodarczego*, [in:] K. Raczkowski (ed.), *Bezpieczeństwo ekonomiczne obrotu gospodarczego. Ekonomia. Prawo. Zarządzanie*, Wolters Kluwer business, Warszawa.

Robinson, M., Last, D. A. (2009), *Basic Model of Performance-Based Budgeting*, International Monetary Fund, Washington.

Raport końcowy. (2011), *Ewaluacja ex-ante Strategii Rozwoju Kraju 2020*, Zachodniopomorska Grupa Doradcza, Szczecin, October.

Stoner J. A. F, Wankel C. (1992), *Kierowanie*, PWE, Warszawa.

Zawadzka-Pąk. (2013), U.K. *Budżet zadaniowy w jednostkach sektora finansów publicznych*, ODDK, Gdańsk.

Konrad Raczkowski[1]

Intellectual capital management in tax administration and country's economic growth determined by competitive taxation

Inroduction

Ever more changeable socio-economic environment, in which international factors exert a significant impact on defining the realities of individual economies, forces national states to strive for improving their competitive standing. That may be shaped in diverse ways within the twelve pillars proposed by the World Economic Forum [Schwab, 2014, p. 4–9], yet from the perspective of the present chapter should be considered through (a) fundamental requirements for ensuring effectiveness of the institutions which support macroeconomic equilibrium; (b) factors raising effectiveness, connected with improving the education and skills of tax administration staffs as regards understanding effectiveness of the market held in balance for the common good; and (c) innovation and development factors, directed at promoting enterprising attitudes, supportive for enterprises, and on the other hand taking up effective fight against unfair competition operating outside the bounds of law. This should be supplemented with one more, important and fundamental factor, namely tax competition. Both for the countries associated in integration groupings, and in other national states, important are the opportunities for attracting capital in particular, as a mobile factor of production, contributing to creation of new jobs, investment and development of the given economy. Hence it is not surprising that economic development of a country, even of a region, is decided by tax policy and tax administration which acts as its practical executive arm. Through its actions it exerts a direct impact on the functioning of business entities, their condition, efficacy and competitiveness. Interactions taking place between the tax administration and entities involved in economic turnover are critical to development of businesses, shaping the state of public finances. For that reason management of intellectual potential in tax administration may be of key significance to

1 Prof. Ph.D., Institute of Economics in Warsaw, University of Social Sciences, email: raczkowski.konrad@gmail.com.

structuring proper relations, fostering security of economic turnover and sustainable development of the state.

Notion and Importance of Intellectual Capital in Tax Administration

Intellectual capital is certainly a strategic asset for any organisation. It is defined as the sum of "knowledge held by the people forming an organisation, enabling transformation of its resources into a defined financial value of the enterprise – hence encompassing the entirety of inter-relations between its various component elements and the entirety of knowledge transfer between them in the form of processes to generate, acquire, transform and accumulate knowledge, and as the results of these relations in the form of intellectual property" [Karoń, 2012, p. 36]. Intellectual capital is identified as knowledge in itself, that is the wealth inherent from holding knowledge [Łucki, 2005, p. 126]. At the same time, L. Edvinsson and M. S. Malone rightly note that this term is to be understood as the spread forming between the market value and the book value of an enterprise – the so-called sum of concealed resources which are not reflected in financial accounts. These resources cover general knowledge and specialist expertise, experience and trade skills, technology and organisational culture – everything through which an organisation is capable of developing and meeting the needs of its customers and achieve a competitive edge [Edvinsson, Malone, 2001, p. 39–40].

In the broad sense, intellectual capital is defined as "entirety of non-tangible assets of people, enterprises, communities, regions and institutions which, properly applied, may become the source of present and future wellbeing of a country" [Report, 2010, p. 85]. In a similar sense of intellectual capital can be defined as "all intangible resources that are available to an organization that give a relative advantage and which in combination are able to produce future benefits" [Cegarra-Navarro, Sánchez-Polo, 2010, p. 330].

One cannot, however, speak of intellectual capital and its development when the conditions within an organisation are not conducive to transfer of know-how within an organisation, and stimulation of the learning process is no more than just declarative. Individual employees have to be aware of that, and their own knowledge should develop [Adamkiewicz-Drwiłło, 2010, p. 347; Bojewska, 2013, p. 147] as regards:

a) permanent monitoring of economy functioning and the market mechanisms accompanying economic processes;

b) making use of organisational, technical and technological advances, particularly in active, but also in passive ways;
c) shaping self-organisation networks dedicated to development of know-how and exchange of best practices, through developing and implementing new services and products;
d) drawing up the business case for application of know-how creating processes;
e) advanced marketing and information transfer – both within, but particularly to the macro-environment of the organisation;
f) shaping other desirable attitudes.

This implies that the managers themselves need to know the timing required for learning, delegating leadership, building teams bent on co-operation, committing strongly to the work performed, gaining satisfaction from it, or handling crisis situations [Adamkiewicz-Drwiłło, 2010, p. 347]. Most important in this process is the skill for appropriate and rapid learning, aiming at innovations, accepting creative approach to action (manifested as skill in resolving problems) or adapting to new conditions as part of the risk of implementing new approaches, understood as innovations [Bojewska, 2013, p. 148]. A contemporary manager in an organisation which makes pragmatic use of intellectual capital must show a specific capability for taking the right decisions, frequently reacting *just in time* to surfacing problems, something that is not very common in public administration.

In a way split into categories and broadly circulated delineation of intellectual capital was proposed in the Scandia definition, that intellectual capital is understood as human capital and structural capital, as two main pillars [Karoń, 2012, p. 39]. A third pillar which should be recognised, is the customer capital. Management may apply at the same time to both a single entity of one human being, a team of employees and the organisation as a whole (micro, mezzo, macro, mega levels) and should be focused on supplying high-value products, services and broadly defined improvement of productivity, customer satisfaction, contributing directly to the general increase in value [Skrzypek, 2005, p. 56].

"It should also be remembered that intellectual (human) capital is the property of each employee and cannot be taken over, but only to a certain degree made use of with consent of its owner. Every time that an organisation acquires capable, highly competent employees, it extends the intellectual capital, in other words bolsters the development trend. The same thing happens when an organisation moves by other ways towards a learning organisation, thanks to operating flexibly, acting with dynamism, adapting to new conditions and applying supercompensation in progressive and planned development" [Raczkowski, 2010,

p. 91–92]. By the same token, the notion of intellectual capital is strictly imbedded in the concept of knowledge management, though due to the value approach may be equally well developed from the financial perspective.

From the vantage point of the is publication, the primary consideration is to have human capital, as an element of intellectual capital, related to taxes and economic development. It has been demonstrated that tax evasion declines when productivity and human capital increase. This explains the situation where the more developed countries, marked by more welfare, become ever more developed by increased accumulation of human capital, experiencing a parallel decline in tax evasion ratios [Schneider, Raczkowski, 2013, p. 71].

It is to be noted that intellectual capital of tax administration in many countries carries different connotations. This is linked with the fact of parallel co-existence, at times similar and at times quite diverse functioning models of the public levies administrations themselves (Graph 1).

Graph 1: Comparison of tax administration operating scope in OECD countries

Country	**Character of operations**	**Main tax categories collected by tax authorities**						
		PIT	**Social Security**	**CIT**	**VAT**	**Excise**	**Real Estate**	**Remaining taxes: Real Estate: E; Enrichment: W; Motor Vehicles: M**
OECD countries								
Australia	USB	+	n.app.	+	+	+	x	-
Austria	SDMOF	+	x	+	+	+	x	M
Belgium	MDMOF/1	+	x	+	+	+	x	M/1
Canada	USBB	+/1	+/2	+/1	+/1	+	x	/ 2
Chile	USB/1	+	x/2	+	+	+	+	E -/3
Czech Republic	USB	+	x	+	+	x	+	E, M
Denmark	USB/1	+	x	+	+	+	+	
Estonia	SDMOF	+	+	+	+	+	+	M/2
Finland	USB	+	+	+	+	x/1	+	E
France	SDMOF	+	x	+	+	x	+	E, W, M
Germany	Other/1	+	x	+	+	x	+/2	
Greece	MDMOF	+	x/1	+	+	+	+	E, W, M
Hungary	USB	+	+	+	+	+	x	E, M
Iceland	USB	+	+	+	+	+	x	W, M

Country	Character of operations	Main tax categories collected by tax authorities						
		PIT	Social Security	CIT	VAT	Excise	Real Estate	Remaining taxes: Real Estate: E; Enrichment: W; Motor Vehicles: M
Ireland	USB	+	+	+	+	+	x	E, M
Israel	SDMOF	+	x	+	+	+	+	M
Italy	Other/1	+	x	+	+	x	x	-
Japan	USB	+	x	+	+	+	x	E, M
Korea	USB	+	x	+	+	+	+/1	E
Luxembourg	MDMOF/1	+	x	+	+	+	x	E, W
Mexico	USBB	+	x	+	+	+	x	
Netherlands	SDMOF	+	+	+	+	+	x	E, M
New Zealand	USB	+	n.app.	+	+	x	x	-
Norway	USB	+	+	+	+	x	x	E, W
Poland	MDMOF/1	+	x	+	+	x	x	
Portugal	SDMOF	+	x	+	+	+	+	E, M
Slovakia	USB	+	x/1	+	+	x	x	M
Slovenia	USB	+	+	+	+	x	+	
Spain	USB	+	x	+	+	+	x	
Sweden	USBB/1	+	+	+	+	+	+	
Switzerland	SDMOF/1	+	x	+	+	x	x	-
Turkey	Other/1	+	x	+	+	+	+	
United Kingdom	USBB	+	+	+	+	+	+	E
United States	USBB	+	+	+	n.app.	+	x	E

MDMO - Multiple directorates in Ministry of Finance
SDMO – Single directorate in Ministry of Finance
USB- Unified semi-autonomous body
USBB - Unified semi-autonomous body with formal board or advisory group comprised of external officials
Source: Tax Administration 2013. Comparative Information on OECD and Other Advanced and Emerging Economies, OECD, Paris 2013.

From that perspective it is possible to distinguish centralised models and decentralised models. The models with homogenous competences regarding all the main public levies (e.g.: Estonia, Hungary, Ireland, Sweden, or United Kingdom), and those splitting powers regarding different levies, of which Poland can serve as an example. The model adopted in that country (Poland) provides for operation of three separate organisational entities, that is tax administration, treasury inspection and Customs Service, all within the finance administration set-up under auspices of a single Finance Ministry, which in total within all its different units is served by a total staff of nearly 68 thousand people (Table 1).

Table 1: General organisational frames of finance administration in Poland

FINANCE ADMINISTRATION			
Entities	**Employment**	**Structure**	**Main responsibilities and powers**
Ministry of Finance	2680	Currently in reorganisation phase.	– drafting, executing and controlling execution of State Budget; – responsible also for execution of state budget revenues and expenditures, including tax revenues, and for financial, credit and payment relations with other countries and for implementation of regulations regarding customs and treasury inspections.
Training Division	170	Finance administration professional education centre (head facility plus 5 field facilities)	– execution of training responsibilities of the Ministry of Finance and the entities subordinated to or supervised by the Minister of Finance; – ensuring employees of finance administration permanent professional development opportunities.
Treasury Inspection Division	5690	16 Treasury Inspection Offices (UKS); 8 field offices (UKSOZ).	– safeguarding State Treasury interests and property rights as well as ensuring effective execution of tax levies and other levies constituting revenues of state budget or state defined purpose funds.

FINANCE ADMINISTRATION			
Entities	**Employment**	**Structure**	**Main responsibilities and powers**
Customs Service Division	15330	16 customs chambers (IC); 46 customs offices (UC); 151 customs posts, including 51 at border crossings (OC)	– implementation of customs policy element concerning importation and exportation of goods as well as performance of other tasks under separate regulations, and in particular: 1) performance of operations connected with awarding commodities customs status; 2) assessment and collection of: a) customs and other charges connected with importation and exportation of goods, b) tax on goods and services (VAT) for imported goods, c) excise tax, d) gaming tax and fees and surcharges, e) fuel tax;
Tax Administration Division	44070	16 treasury chambers (IS); 400 treasury offices.	– collecting tax revenues in the most effective, equitable and efficient manner, – ensuring regular and timely inflow of revenues from taxes and other tax levies, the State Budget and self-government budgets of Community ("Gmina") administrative units.

Source: own elaboration based on Report on State of Real Estate, Transportation Vehicles and Office Equipment in Organization Entities of Finance Administration (in Polish), Ministry of Finance, Warsaw – November 2013 and Ministry of Finance Information Brochure (in Polish), Warsaw 2014.

Presentation of the Polish reference model is warranted given the changes which took place in that country over the past twenty five years. The real rate of economic growth in Poland generally matched both growth and decline European trends, with given turning points for Poland set markedly more beneficially than in EU states; over the years 2002–2014 growth never went into such a GDP decline which would result in negative economic growth (Chart 1). Still, it did involve an increase of the national debt.

Chart 1: Real GDP value in Poland 2002–2018 (with projection for 2014–2018).

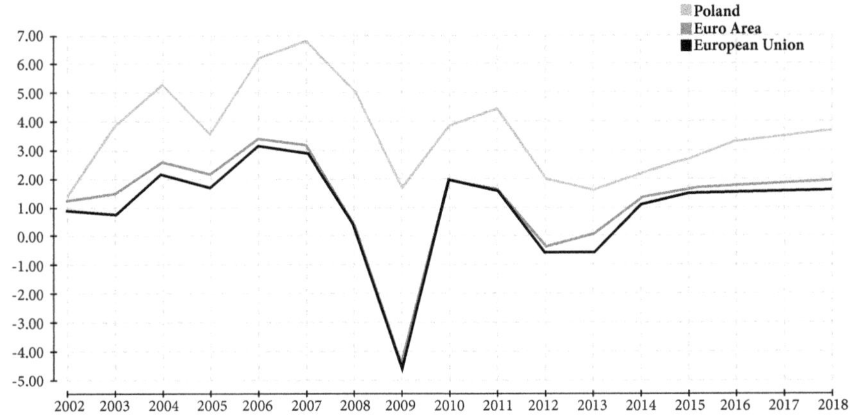

Source: generated from: real GDP growth in Poland, Eurostat 2014.

Polish economy is certainly among the fastest growing in the region, yet insufficient tax revenues in the past two years (from both direct, but particularly from the indirect taxes) resulted in the deficit rising by end 2013 to the level of 4.4% of GDP. It seems also that the tax administration seems unable to keep step with the dynamically shifting business environment, in effect resulting in a considerable so-called tax gap, which according to PwC [PWC, 2013, p. 15] in just the Value Added Tax for 2012 could have amounted to between PLN 36.5 and 58.5 billion (USD 12.1 – 19.4 billion).

Reform of the pension system bolstered public finances, limiting gross public debt in 2014 to 50.3% of GDP [European, 2014, p. 89]. Still, the solutions adopted as part of new national accounts ESA 2010 in principle only slightly change the statistical situation of public finances. European Commission also stated that by 2015 Poland still needs to address the problems of excess deficit. Reaching this goal and restructuring both revenues and expenditures in such a way as to save 2.2% of GDP [Council, 2013] requires reforming public finance along with reform of the entire apparatus of state finance (the finance administration). Notable in this context are the conclusions stemming from the EY 2014 report, treating the twenty five years of shaping and functioning of the tax system, within new organisational structures which claim the need for [System, 2014, p. 3–5]:

a) striking a balance between the taxpayer and the state, manifested by uniform law and its interpretation;
b) treating the tax system as part of the approach shaping competitive terms for the state as a whole (after all, it operates within EU structures and in an

environment of universal globalisation). Shaping a transparent fiscal policy, while motivating business to involvement with research & development, and fostering innovativeness;
c) consulting tax law with the business community – before enactment, rather than only during the time when a statute already becomes binding;
d) creating a new tax law system from the grounds up, immune to changes on the political scene;
e) permanently educating tax collection personnel and enforcing taxes in an efficacious manner, rather than relying on impunity of officials shrouding ill will or substantive uncertainties.

Tax administration, same as most public institutions, shows typical traits of organisations, such as: organisational structure, links and interdependences within and without. In its operation it relies on four categories of resources within classically defined management, that is planning and decision making, organising, leading and controlling, which consist of [Griffin, 2004, p. 5–6]:

a) human resources – officials and support personnel (should be viewed as intellectual capital);
b) financial resources – financial capital at its disposal, allocated by law;
c) tangible resources – in the form of all kind of specialist equipment and office premises;
d) information resources – indispensable and key to performing the assigned statutory responsibilities, directed to taking multi-criteria decisions.

Employees of the tax apparatus can certainly contribute to facilitating economic processes or in contrast, constitute their negation. Most important in this respect are two aspects, considered as part of efficacy: efficiency and effectiveness. This concerns making wise use of resources (efficiency). This is linked with creative approach of the given manager, but also an official not entrusted with a managerial role in the tax administration, directed to making use of own skills and know-how, which will permit utilisation of available resources as part of efficient operation. At that, "according to the theory of organisation, effectiveness is the superior category in relation to such subordinate terms as output, productivity, profitability, success and even rationality. Effectiveness is a major tool in measuring success of management (…), illustrating the speed of response to market challenges, and also expectations of its participants, is a proven tool in building up a competitive edge, and also allows for the right response to signals coming in from outside" [Skrzypek, 2012, p. 313–325]. Many studies have shown that effectiveness of tax administration within its institutional shape depends on trust in government and its institutions [Wintrobe, Gerxhani, 2004] as part of economic freedoms, competitive law, low crime rate [Riahi-Belkaoui, 2004, p. 135–143] or sense of social capital [Ritsatos, 2014, p. 252].

At this juncture it appears imperative to propose a split-down definition of intellectual capital accruing to a given tax administration (Chart 2).

Chart 2: Intellectual capital in tax administration

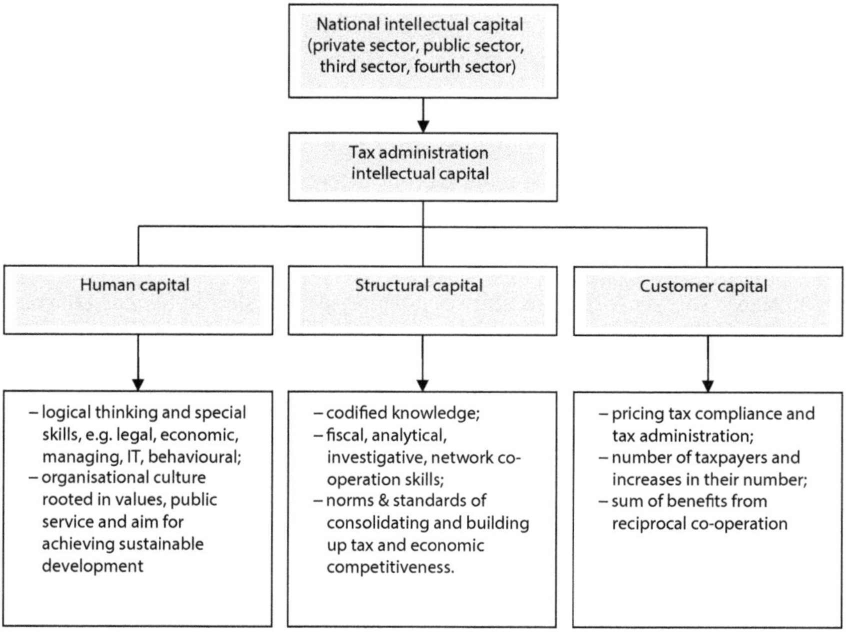

Source: own elaboration.

In this model intellectual capital of tax administration is built up on the basis of domestic intellectual capital represented by enterprises and other entities of economic turnover (first sector), the entire public sector, so called third sector (including civil society) and households. Domestic intellectual capital comes from knowledge of all members of a given society, who hold diverse interests, hold different bodies of data and information and represent divergent perspectives in real and institutional perceptions of the state [Käpylä, Kujansivu, Lönnqvist, 2012, p. 349]. Important also is the very perception of a public administration official by the tax administration as client, stakeholder who may perform his or her mission well and to whom the organisation should ensure conditions for harmonious development. This is the key to building up structural, and particularly customer capital, in which the most difficult feat concerns attaining such an effect where the employee will get to like the administration for which he or she works, not forgetting that in reality this is public service (though within full freedom of thought) and will consider that each taxpayer paying in taxes fosters economic growth and broadly defined development.

Taxes and Their Impact On Economic Development

Public levies are an intrinsic element by which any state functions, the criteria of which concern net increase in property or sources of generated income. Under the first criterion income is defined as basically all sources and conditions in which such income was generated (including inheritances, donations and other increments in property). In the theory of sources, the essence is represented by new property value which for the given individual is a fixed source of regularly obtained revenue [Litwińczuk, 2013, p. 32]. In general terms, public levies consist of "taxes, dues, fees, shares in profits of state-owned enterprises and single shareholder State Treasury companies, as well as other monetary encumbrances, the requirement of paying which to the benefit of the state, regional self-government entities, state-operated defined purpose funds and other entities of the public finance sector stems from other statutes" [Flis, 2010, p. 98–99].

A good tax system does not necessarily have to be responsible for economic growth, but it is certain that a bad tax system may lead to retarding development [Bird, 2010, p. 2]. It has been proven empirically that reducing taxes from corporate entities can reduce the inclination to evade taxes, can increase investment, support new business formation, result in increasing sales, and finally bring about higher GDP [Bruhn, 2011, p. 5]. This was also confirmed by the studies conducted in Canada and elsewhere over the years 1977–2006, which showed that a reduction of CIT by 1% results in a temporary boost of economic growth by precisely 0.1–0.2% [Ferede, Dahlby, 2012, p. 587] (obviously assuming that businesses do not resort on a massive scale to tax optimising arrangements, which have connotations closer to tax evasion). This was also supported by research carried out in the United States, covering 1945–2010, which proved that top tax rates, including top rates of capital gains taxes, have no or only negligible impact on economic development. In turn reductions in these rates correlated with improvements in productivity, investment and savings [Hungerford, 2012, p. 16], while maintaining rates at unchanged levels encouraged the same taxpayers to opt for various forms of unofficial economy [Thornton, 2012, p. 449]. In addition, introduction or maintenance of certain group of taxes at unchanged levels or within a set statutory-organisational infrastructure may be, on the one hand, problematic for the state budget, yet at the same time contribute to economic growth. Already now the European Union is coping with serious problems regarding VAT fraud and notorious attempts to swindle budgets of individual countries on refunds of that tax, where: "missing intra-community trader fraud is one of the most prevalent types of cross-border fraud in the area of VAT" [Combating, 2013, p. 4].

On the other hand, the unending search for hypothetical possibilities, opportunities and threats involved in introducing such a tax is being considered by the United States, which ponder whether introduction of a value added taxes would be warranted economically and would not result in excessive tax evasion. Already at present, 70% of U.S. GDP is generated by consumer spending. Should there be introduction of a 10% VAT, then GDP should hypothetically increase 7%. At the same time revenues from this tax could not be lower, due to reluctance of authorities as regards borrowing needs (in particular with respect to health care) or difficulties with taxation of housing according to its value [Feldstein, 2011, p. 119]. System changes, specifically with regard to taxing medical care seem unavoidable, since the United States already now spends the highest GDP percentage of any country on these needs, which by 2035 may amount to no less than 26% of GDP [Baicker, Skinner, 2011, p. 39].

A different situation with regard to VAT can be observed in Latin America countries (e.g. Argentina, Chile, Brazil, Mexico), where it is an effective instrument increasing tax revenues, enabling their further redistribution. At that it does not have an excessive impact on the functioning and distortion of economic turnover. In contrast, income tax in these same countries is basically unproductive and does not improve effectiveness of revenues. This is in part due to the fact that these countries have a high proportion of tax exemptions and reliefs, high shares of informal economy, and the tax rates themselves are held down to a low level [Canavire-Baccareza, Martinez-Vasquez, Vulovic, 2013, p. 21–22].

After all, economic growth requires using three basic factors of production, namely labour, capital and technological advances. Taxes may be both a development opportunity for the economy and a threat [Zipfel, 2012, p. 2], creating entry and functioning barriers for defined economic entities on the given market. So it is possible to claim that taxes, reflecting on aggregate productivity of production factors, impact economic growth [Myles, 2000, p. 141–169;

Myles, 2009], in as much as they become stimulators of economic processes within an effectively operating state institutional system responsible for contribution of public levies.

Present day tax systems around the world are in many areas systemically maladjusted to the changing global realities. A high proportion of corporations function by basing their operations on trade in non-tangible and legal values, rather than the physical products tangibly accessible at the given location. In the latest PwC report "The global results on Paying Taxes study 2014" a general trend is noted in reducing tax rates [Paying, 2014, p. 23]. The countries with heaviest taxation burdens in 2014 were Gambia (283.2%) Comoro Islands (217.9%), Congo (118.1%), Argentina (107.8%) or Uzbekistan (99.3%). On the other extreme of tax burden scale (lowest tax burden), one notes such countries as Vanuatu (8.4%) or Macedonia (8.2%).

The United States, as the world's largest economy, maintains total tax burdens on the level of 46.3% GDP. This is a level close in percentage terms to that of Japan (49.7% GDP) and much lower than in the case of China (63.7% GDP) – Chart 3.

Chart 3: Tax burdens on world's three largest economies (% GDP)

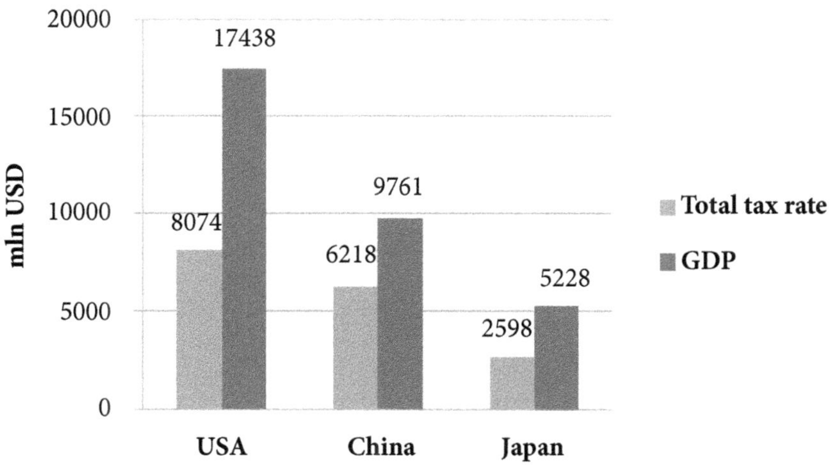

Source: own elaboration based on GDP calculated at current prices – World Economic Outlook 2013 and Paying Taxes 2014, op.cit., s. 173–175.

In turn, European Union countries have highly differentiated total taxation burdens, varying between 19.8% (Croatia) and 65.8% (Italy), with differing rates of capital gains tax [Paying, 2014, p. 173–175] – Chart 4.

Chart 4: Total tax rate vs. capital gains tax total rate in the EU

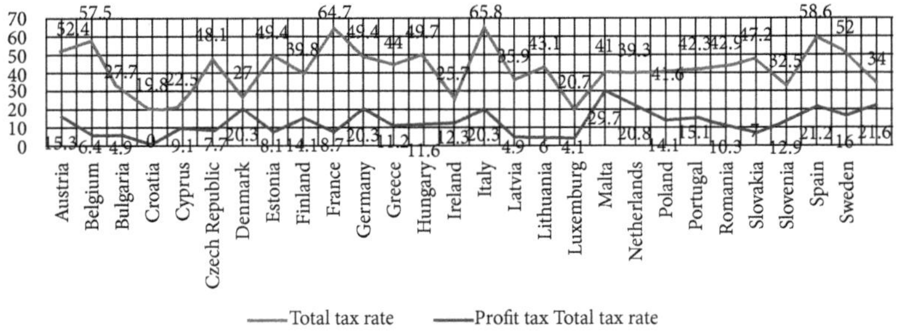

Source: own elaboration based on Paying Taxes 2014, op.cit., s. 173–175.

At the same time tax revenues as percentage of GDP vary between individual EU countries from 21.1% GDP (Spain) to 43.4% GDP (France) – Chart 5. In principle, in each country tax revenues are directly linked to GDP (function of revenues and expenditures). This is connected with the fact that cyclically calculated revenues are calculated in relation to projected GDP falling within the forecast trend [Romer, Romer, 2007, p. 15–16], which in the near future may turn out to be either lower or higher.

Chart 5: Tax revenues in EU countries (percentage of GDP)

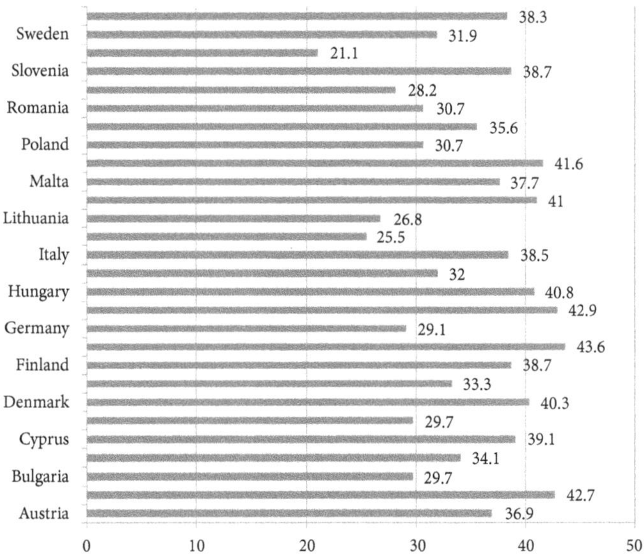

Source: own elaboration based on International Monetary Fund, Government Finance Statistics Yearbook and data files, World Bank, OECD GDP estimates, World Bank 2013.

Among all the EU countries, a reduction of tax revenues as percentage of GDP in 2012 was noted in six countries, that is in Denmark, Hungary, Portugal, Slovakia, Spain and Sweden. The average of these revenues came to 35% (of GDP). The data differ slightly from Eurostat 2012 statistics, which reported that the taxes collected amounted to 40.6% GDP of the entire EU budget.

It may be said, therefore, that taxes can impact economic growth, and their appropriate compliance and redistribution may contribute directly to launching new investments, jobs, or programmes of activating the unemployed on the labour market – which leads to economic growth. Lack of tax revenues in state coffers is undesirable for obvious reasons, and for that reason it is important to have tax morality and a specific form of tax patriotism. Tax optimisation, often adopting the shape of tax evasion as part of, among other things, choice of tax jurisdiction, provide unitary revenues and may drive a given economy (not always the one where the firm has its head office and actual place of conducting business). Unfortunately, it also spurs unfair competition, contributing to elimination of honestly operating economic entities from the market, and by the same token constitutes a more severe threat of systemic character to the entire economic fabric. For that reason, both nation states as an element of modernising their own fiscal systems in adjusting their economies, and particularly business people themselves, seek opportunities presented by given tax jurisdictions, competing with each other in both economic and in taxation terms (Table 2).

Table 2: Ranking of economic-tax competitiveness in EU countries

Country	**GCI 2013–2014**		**Tax compliance and tax administration**	
	Rank	**Score**	**Rank**	**Score**
Austria	16	5.15	9	0.86
Belgium	17	5.13	11	0.83
Bulgaria	57	4.31	25	0.49
Croatia	75	4.13	-	no data
Cyprus	58	4.3	16	0.78
Czech Republic	46	4.43	26	0.42
Denmark	15	5.18	6	0.9
Estonia	32	4.65	1	0.97
Finland	3	5.54	4	0.93

Country	GCI 2013–2014		Tax compliance and tax administration	
	Rank	Score	Rank	Score
France	23	5.05	10	0.86
Germany	4	5.51	14	0.81
Greece	91	3.93	22	0.7
Hungary	63	4.25	18	0.72
Ireland	28	4.92	5	0.93
Italy	49	4.41	19	0.72
Latvia	52	4.4	20	0.71
Lithuania	48	4.41	12	0.83
Luxembourg	22	5.09	2	0.95
Malta	41	4.5	-	no data
Netherlands	8	5.42	8	0.88
Poland	42	4.46	24	0.67
Portugal	51	4.40	21	0.71
Romania	76	4.13	15	0.81
Slovakia	78	4.1	23	0.68
Slovenia	62	4.25	17	0.76
Spain	35	4.57	13	0.83
Sweden	6	5.48	3	0.94
United Kingdom	10	5.37	7	0.9

GCI – Global Competitiveness Index
Source: own elaboration based on The Global Competitiveness Report, op.cit. and Excellence in public administration for competitiveness in EU Member States, European Union 2012 – dataset 1, s. 5.

Economic competition is currently something natural, and such main factors as institutions, infrastructure, macroeconomic equilibrium, health and education, higher learning and life-long learning, efficient goods and labour markets, developed financial market, technical preparedness, size of the market itself, quality of business environment, innovation – determine the foundations for development of a state [Schwab, 2014, p. 4–9].

Tax compliance and tax administration examined two main components: total time for preparing and filing a tax return and the administrative costs of taxation. For instance in Poland these values are more than 42% worse than the

EU average in terms of time required and 30% worse in administrative costs of taxation [Excellence, 2012, p. 5].

Building up competitiveness of an economy basing on tax competitiveness is a pragmatic and reasonable approach. Any tax harmonisation under bilateral or multilateral arrangements may be needed, but always involves a risk for the weaker – mainly less developed countries. This stems from reduced capacity for competing on the global market, something that may be manifested through lessened activity of domestic economic entities, outflow of investment and general economic slowdown.

Already now many consulting firms advise enterprises about the business model scenarios to be applied or on how to decrease tax liabilities while staying on the right side of the law, at that increasing the revenues gained. Large holding corporations have entire structures doing nothing but devising tax optimising schemes. The countries with appropriate institutional systems responsible for the tax sphere outright strive for publishing such open competitiveness reports. After all, what sort of decisions can the entrepreneur take when learning that total tax costs are 46.4% lower in Canada than in the United States or 63.3% higher in France than in the United States [Competitive, 2014, p. 2]. Such information always encourages reflection and search for best ways to optimise.

Conclusions

The sum of knowledge represented by staff of given tax administration in the light of constant tax competition, both the crawling tax competition and the outright unfair tax competition, is a key element of attention devoted to public finance as part of economic development. Already now there is an evident intellectual abyss between the market creators of tax engineering and the tax administration personnel, reflected particularly in declining tax revenues and elimination of fairly operating economic entities from the market by dishonest entities, often impossible to locate – as perpetrators of deeds prohibited by law.

Differing tax rates in many countries, diverse scope of powers within defined structures, disparities in total tax burdens and finally different scopes of tax and also economic competition are, in a global world, an unstable standard which requires regular close scrutiny, regarding which conclusions need to be drawn and own mechanisms adjusted for efficient functioning. Effectiveness of a given country's tax administration itself will not improve when its staffs will be barred, politically or by the powers that be, from disseminating and implementing the conclusions drawn from performed analyses. It will not improve unless employees of given tax administration themselves will raise their capabilities and skills necessary for understanding the mechanisms of international tax strategies, optimising operation of enterprises. It will not improve unless the tax administration of its own accord will not start promoting enterprising spirit and attitudes negating and suppressing tax offences.

The general global trend towards reducing taxes notwithstanding, the share of taxes in the budget of a given state will have to be sufficient to ensure its functioning. That is not to say, obviously, that higher taxes will ensure higher revenues, or lower tax rates will contribute less to generating GDP. Understanding of these phenomena, understanding that tax administration intellectual capital may have a substantial impact on individual sector policies and in consequence on economic growth is vitally important. Today this part of public administration in a given country which, next to the central bank and financial supervision, acts as guardian of financial stability. Managing the tax administration intellectual potential is today the key to understanding the rôle of institutions in the economic process and their influence on economic growth and welfare.

Bibliography

Adamkiewicz-Drwiłło H. G. (2010), *Konkurencyjność przedsiębiorstw w świetle uwarunkowań współczesnej gospodarki* [Competitiveness of Enterprises in Light of Conditions in Contemprary Economy], Dom Organizatora, Toruń.

Baicker K., Skinner J. (2011), *Health Care Spending Growth and the Future of U.S. Tax Rates*, Tax Policy and the Economy, Vol. 25, No. 1, September.

Bird R. (2010), *Taxation and Development*, Economic Premise, The World Bank, Number 34, October.

Bojewska B. (2013), *Kapitał ludzki w gospodarce opartej na wiedzy* [Human Capital in a Knowledge Based Economy], [in] R. Bartkowiak, P. Wachowiak (scholar editors), *Wiedza i bogactwo narodów. Kapitał ludzki, globalizacja i regulacja w skali światowej. Zarządzanie* [Knowledgee and Wealth of Nations. Human Capital, Globalization and Regulation on Global Scale. Management], Oficyna Wydawnicza Szkoła Główna Handlowa, Warszawa.

Bruhn M. (2011), *Reforming Business Taxes*, View Point, Public Policy for the Private Sector, Note Number 330.

Canavire-Baccareza G., Matinez-Vasquez J., Vulovic V. (2013), *Taxation and Economic Growth in Latin America*, IDB Working Paper Series, No. IDB-WP-431, August.

Cegarra-Navarro J. G., Sánchez-Polo M. T. (2010), *Linking National Contexts with Intellectual Capital: A Comparison between Spain and Morocco*, The Spanish Journal of Psychology, Vol. 13, No. 1.

Combating tax fraud and evasion. (2013), Commission contribution to the European Council, Brussels, 22 May.

Competitive Alternatives. (2014), *Special Report: Focus on Tax*, KPMG, Canada.

Council Recommendation with a few to bringing an end to the situation of an excessive government deficit in Poland, COM (2013) 906 final, Brussels, 15.11.2013.

Edvinsson L., Malone M. S. (2001), *Kapitał intelektualny* [Intellectual Capital], Wydawnictwo Naukowe PWN, Warszawa.

European Economic Forecast. (2014), *European Economy*, European Commission, Brussels, No. 2.

Excellence in public administration for competitiveness in EU Member States, (2012), European Union - dataset.

Feldstein M. (2011), *Preventing a National Debt Explosion*, Tax Policy and the Economy, Vol. 25, No. 1, September.

Ferede E., Dahlby B. (2012), *The impact of tax cuts on economic growth: evidence from the Canadian provinces*, National Tax Journal, September 65(3).

Flis P. (2010), *Główne źródła dochodów budżetowych w Polsce* Main Sources of Budget Revenues in Poland], [in:] G. Gołębiowski (editor) *Polityka budżetowa* [Budget Policy], Studia Biura Analiz Sejmowych Kancelarii Sejmu, BAS, Warszawa.

Gillman M. (2014), *Tax Evasion, Human Capital, and Productivity-Induced Tax Rate Reduction*, Journal of Human Capital, Vol. 8, No. 1, Spring.

Griffin R. W. (2004), *Podstawy zarządzania organizacjami* [Basics of Managing Organisations], Wydanie drugie zmienione, Wydawnictwo Naukowe PWN, Warszawa.

Hungerford T. L. (2012), *Taxes and the Economy: An Economic Analysis of the Top Tax Rates Since 1945*, Congresional Research Service, September 14.

Käpylä J., Kujansivu P., Lönnqvist A. (2012), *National intellectual capital performance: a strategic approach*, Journal of Intellectual Capital, Vol. 13, No. 3.

Karoń S. (2012), *Zarządzanie wiedzą i kapitałem intelektualnym w organizacji* [Managing Knowledge and Intellectual Capital in an Organisation], [in:]

D. Jelonek, (red.), *Wybrane problemy zarządzanie wiedzą i kapitałem intelektualnym w organizacji* [Selected Issues in Managing Knowledge and Intellectual Capital in an Organisation], Sekcja Wydawnictw Wydziału Zarządzania Politechniki Częstochowskiej, Częstochowa.

Litwińczuk H. (2013), *Ogólna klasyfikacja podatków dochodowych*, [in:] H. Litwińczuk, *Prawo podatkowe przedsiębiorców*, Wolters Kluwer business, Warszawa.

Łucki Z., Kozarkiewicz-Chlebowska A., Brenk D. (2005), *Nowoczesne metody zarządzania w górnictwie naftowym i gazownictwie. Zarys teorii i przykłady* [Modern Methods of Management in Oil Extraction and Gas Industry], PGNiG, Oddział Zielona Góra, Kraków.

Myles G. D. (2000), *Taxation and Economic Growth*, Fiscal Studies 21 (1).

Myles G. D. (2009), *Economic Growth and the Role of Taxation—Disaggregate Data*, OECD Economics Department Working Paper No. 715. Organisation for Economic Co-operation and Development, Paris.

Paying Taxes 2014. (2014), PwC, World Bank, London.

PwC Raport. (2013), *Straty Skarbu Państwa w VAT – luka podatkowa, oszustwa, wyłudzenia oraz problematyka podatku od towarów i usług w Polsce* [State Treasury Losses from VAT – Tax Gap, Fraud, Swindles and Issues of Tax on Goods and Services in Poland], Fundacja Naukowa – Instytut Badań Strukturalnych, Warszawa.

Raczkowski K. (2010), *Zarządzanie wiedzą w administracji celnej, w systemie bezpieczeństwa ekonomiczno-społecznego* [Knowledge management in Customs Administration, within system of economic-social Security], Difin, Warszawa.

Raport o Kapitale Intelektualnym Polski. (2008) [Report on Poland's Inteellectual Capital (2008)], Kancelaria Prezesa Rady Ministrów, Warszawa.

Riahi-Belkaoui, A. (2004), *Relationship between tax compliance internationally and selected determinants of tax morale*, Journal of International Accounting, Auditing and Taxation, Vol. 13.

Ritsatos T. (2014), *Tax evasion and compliance; from the neo classical paradigm to behavioural economics, a review*, Journal for Accounting and Organizational Change, Vol. 10, No. 2.

Romer C. H., Romer D. H. (2007), *The macroeconomic effects of tax changes: estimated based on a new measure of fiscal shocks*, National Bureau of Economic Research, NBER Working Paper Series 13264, Cambridge, July.

Schneider F., Raczkowski K. (2013), *Size and development of the shadow economy and of tax evasion within Poland and of its neighbouring countries from 2003 to 2013: some new facts*, [in:] K. Raczkowski, F. Schneider (eds.), *The Economic Security of Business Transactions. Management in Business*, Chartridge Books Oxford, Oxford.

Schwab K. (2014), *The Global Competitiveness Report*, World Economic Forum, Geneva.

Skrzypek E. (2005), *Kapitał intelektualny jako szansa na poprawę jakości zarządzania w warunkach globalizacji*, [Intellectual Capital as a Chance for Improving Management Quality Under Conditions of Globalization], E. Skrzypek (editor), t. 1, Wydawnictwo UMCS, Lublin.

Skrzypek E. (2012), *Efektywność ekonomiczna jako ważny czynnik sukcesu organizacji* [Economic Effectveness as an Important Success Factor of an Organisation], Prace Naukowe Uniwersytetu Ekonomicznego we Wrocławiu, Wrocław No. 262.

System stworzony od podstaw, czyli prawdziwa historia 25-lecia polskich podatków [System Shaped From Scratch, Or True Story of 25 Years of Polish Taxes] (2014), EY, Warszawa.

Tax Administration. (2013), *Comparative Information on OECD and Other Advanced and Emerging Economies*, OECD, Paris.

Thornton D. (2012), *The U.S. Deficit/Debt Problem: A Longer Run Perspective*, Fed. Reserve Bank St. Louis Rev. 94 November/December.

Wintrobe, R. and Gerxhani, K. (2004), *Tax evasion and trust: a comparative analysis*, Proceedings of the Annual Meeting of the European Public Choice Society.

Zipfel F. (2012), *The impact on tax system on economic growth in Europe*, EU Monitor, Deutsche Bank, Frankfurt am Main, October 5.

Jolanta Szołno-Koguc[1] and Małgorzata Twarowska[2]

Transfer pricing as an instrument for tax optimisation

Introduction

The aim of the paper is to present the transfer pricing as an instrument for tax optimization, as well as data on the controls of transfer pricing in Poland. The paper also presents a comparison of the situation in scope of transfer pricing in Poland and other OECD countries.

The new, stricter regulations and legislations combined with the need for more public revenues cause an increase number of the transfer pricing controls by tax authorities around the world. This affects the deterioration of the conditions for business activity. Companies are often in the face of necessity for income adjustments, which can result in additional tax payments and deterioration of the financial results.

The OECD in 1979 published report "Transfer Pricing and Multinational Enterprises in 1979" (OECD Guidelines). As a result of discussion this report was replaced in 1995 by the "Transfer Pricing Guidelines for Tax Administrations and Multinational Enterprises". In 2010 the OECD made further revisions to the Guidelines in order to ameliorate double taxation as well as a hierarchy of transfer pricing methodologies [OECD, 2010, p. 5].

Transfer pricing policy

Transfer pricing is related to the shifting income – as a result of different from market pricing in transaction between related parties [Jamroży, Kudert, 2013,

1 Prof. Ph.D., Public Finance Department, Faculty of Economics, Maria Curie-Skłodowska University in Lublin, Poland, jszolno@hektor.umcs.lublin.pl.

2 Ph.D. Student, Public Finance Department, Faculty of Economics, Maria Curie-Skłodowska University in Lublin, Poland, gosia.twarowska@wp.pl.

p. 147]. Transfer pricing applies to the cross-border transactions between related entities, which could involve the transfer of goods, services, intangible property (e.g. technology, brand names) or financing [KPMG, 2011, p. 4]. International corporation could gain huge profits from transfer their income that are not economically justified. It is possible only while applying non-market transaction prices. The benefits from transfer pricing are less available for companies operating in one country scale [Szołno-Koguc, 2009, p. 399].

In the literature there are many definitions of transfer pricing. Transfer price is a price charged by individual entities for goods or services supplied to one another in multi-department, multi-office, or multinational firms. According to S. Sojak, the transfer price is a price fixed by the affiliated enterprises, subsidiary, plant or department of a multinational enterprise for the products or services supplied to the plant, department or subsidiary of the same company [Sojak, 2001, p. 145]. Transfer price is also defined as the price fixed by the multinational corporations for intra-corporate trade i.e. in export-import transactions between subsidiaries and their parent company [Najlepszy, 1993, p. 219].Transfer price is defined by OECD as "a price, adopted for book- keeping purposes, which is used to value transactions between affiliated enterprises integrated under the same management at artificially high or low levels in order to effect an unspecified income payment or capital transfer between those enterprises" [OECD, Glossary of Statistical Terms].

Based on these definitions it can be concluded that the objects of the transfers are mainly finished and semi-finished products, but also services (including financial, administrative and managerial services), intangible assets and participation in the costs (including research and development costs). Many authors claim that transfer prices are a instrument to manipulate used by multinational corporations in order to avoid high taxes, customs barriers, exchange rate risk and restrictions in transfer of dividends [Kamińska-Blichowska, 2003, p. 7].

Transfer price policy is aimed at 1) evaluating financial performance of different business units (profit centres) of a conglomerate, and to 2) shift earnings from a high tax jurisdiction to a low-tax one [RSMI, 2009, p. 3].

A key aspect of transfer pricing is the definition of related parties. Most often these entities are defined by specifying the threshold share of the capital, which exceeding means that we have related parties. In Poland this share of capital is 5% and it is one of the lowest in the world. The Table 1 shows the thresholds of capital relations in selected countries.

Table 1: The thresholds of capital relations in selected countries

Country	The thresholds of capital relations
Poland	5%
Slovenia	25%
Japan	25%
Norway	50%
Portugal	10%
Russia	20%

Source: Own Calculations, OECD 2013.

In 2011 OECD published the report "Multi-country analysis of existing transfer pricing simplification measures", which are described in the simplification measures of tax documentation used by OECD member countries. The report shows that in Poland there is one mechanism of transfer pricing simplification measures. This simplification measure is for small transactions and involves no obligation documentary for the low turnover of related parties. The total amount (or its equivalent) resulting from the contract or the total amount, actually paid in a tax year, of performances enforceable in the tax year is lower than the equivalent of [OECD, 2011, p. 101]:

- 100,000 EUR if the value of the transaction does not exceed 20% of the initial capital,
- 30,000 EUR in the case of performance of services, sale or making available intangible assets and legal values,
- 50,000 EUR in the remaining cases.

According to the OECD report, the exceptions are transactions for which the payment of amounts due as a result of such transactions are made for the benefit of an entity having its place of residence, board of management or seat within a territory of or in a country allowing deleterious tax competition if the total amount from the contract or the total amount, paid in a tax year, of performances enforceable in the tax year is higher than the equivalent of 20,000 EUR [OECD, 2011, p. 101].

These thresholds were introduced to the Corporate Income Tax Act 2001 and and since then have not been indexed for inflation. Consequently, their practical application is negligible, because related entities exceed the thresholds in the first month of fiscal year. In this context it is interesting to know that simplification measures are used by other countries (Table 2).

Table 2: The simplification measures in selected countries

Country	The simplification measures
Czech Republic	Absence of simplification measures. In tax law there is no difference between taxpayers. All are obliged to refer and explain their transactions according to the arm's length principle to the tax authority. Although there is no specific documentation requirement on transfer pricing in the Czech tax law because of possible administrative burden for taxpayers, taxpayers can use the Recommendation in respect of the scope of transfer pricing documentation issued by the Ministry of Finance as guidance in this field. The tax authority takes circumstances into account case by case.
Denmark	Exemption from documentation requirements: Small transactions, Immaterial both in scale and frequency, SMEs: Groups with: - fewer than 250 employees, and either: - annual balance sheet less than 125 million DKK, or - annual turnover less than 250 million DKK
Estonia	Exemption from documentation requirements for SMEs Resident companies and non-resident persons operating in Estonia through a permanent establishment which, considered with related persons: - hire fewer than 250 employees, - had turnover in the financial year preceding the transaction of less than 50 million EUR, and - have consolidated balance sheet total of less than 43 million EUR
Finland	Simplified documentation for small transactions: The total amount of transactions between two parties during a tax year does not exceed 500,000 EUR. Exemption from documentation requirements for SMEs: Small and medium-sized enterprises as EU definition (2003/361/EC).
Germany	Reduced APA charge for small transactions: - less than 5 million EUR turnover in goods - less than 500,000 EUR turnover in services Simplified documentation for small transactions (as above), SMEs and routine company: - low risk distributor, - low risk manufacturer, and - low risk service provider - contract research and development
Ireland	Exemption from transfer pricing Rules for SMEs: Small and medium enterprises as defined in the Annex to European Commission recommendation 2003/361/EC of 6 May 2003

Source: Based on: OECD, 2011, p. 47, 50, 53, 56, 62, 72.

The research carried out by the OECD shows that 27 out of 33 respondent countries have transfer pricing simplification measures in place. Since some countries have several measures in place, the total number of simplification measures reported by these countries is 58. According to research carried out by the OECD, measures benefitting SMEs account for 36% of the available simplification measures, measures benefitting small transactions account for 24% of them, measures for low value added services account for 11% and measures benefitting loans account for 10% of the available simplification measures (Figure 1).

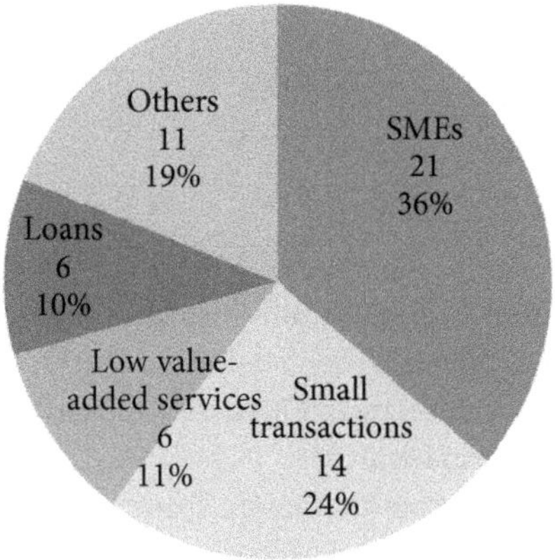

Source: OECD, 2011, p. 10.

In the OECD report simplification measures are classified as follows [OECD, 2011, p. 11]:

- Documentation: "Exemption from documentation requirements", "Simplified documentation" and "Exemption from disclosure requirement",
- Pricing: "Simplified transfer pricing method", "Safe harbour arm's length range" and "Safe harbour interest rate",
- Advance pricing arrangement ("APA"): "Simplified APA procedures" and "Reduced APA charge",
- TP rule: "Exemption from transfer pricing rules" and "Exemption from transfer pricing adjustment",
- Penalty: "Exemption from penalty" and "Alleviated penalties".

Figure 2: Types of simplification measures

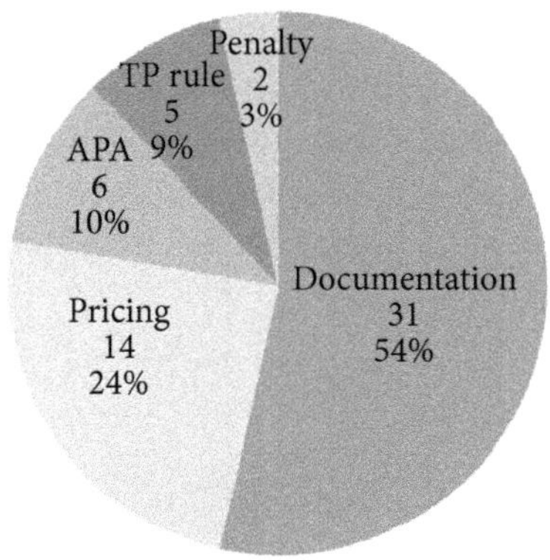

Source: OECD, 2011, p. 11.

The research shows that simplification measures related to documentation account for 54% of the available simplification measures, while measures related to pricing account for 24% of them and measures related to APA account for 10% of the available simplification measures.

Moreover, the research shows that in six countries (Argentina, Chile, Czech Republic, Korea, Luxemburg and Switzerland) there are no transfer pricing simplification measures.

Tax effects of the transfer pricing policy – example (subsidiary in EU)

In order to present the effects of transfer pricing policy, it is assumed that the Polish entrepreneur in a limited liability company (parent company) has for more than two years 100% of the share capital of a company resident in an EU country (subsidiary). Both companies are connected by contract for services. The parent company plans to increase payment for services provided for the subsidiary. How will change the overall tax burden of income if the parent company instead of dividends received increased payment for services in the amount equivalent to increase of the payment? Alternatively assumed that the increased payment for contractual relationship (for service):

a) still is the normal market payment,

b) the tax administration abroad considers the increased payment for income shifting.

In both cases, it is assumed that foreign subsidiary generated a profit (before tax and before taking into account the amount of increase in payment for the service) of 100 monetary units. In assumption, the increased payment will cause the total income of subsidiary equal to 0 monetary unit. The corporate income tax rate abroad is 30%.

In the case of dividends received by the national parent company is applicable the exemption from withholding tax under the relevant national legislation transposing Council Directive 2011/96/EU of 30 November 2011 on the common system of taxation applicable in the case of parent companies and Subsidiaries of different Member States.

Dividends paid by a company resident in the EU (or the European Economic Area) are also exempt from income tax in Poland, provided they have sufficient capital share (10%) for at least two years.[3]

In case of increase the payment, which is still in an acceptable price range considered market prices, there will be no tax burden at the level of the subsidiary (increased tax costs will cause the income will be equal to zero); this payment will be subject to taxation at the level of the parent company. In the situation, where the foreign tax authority contest the increase in payment for services, recognizing that the increased price does not correspond to the market price, there is double taxation in the economic sense: once at the level of the subsidiary, the second time at the level of the parent company.

Table 3 shows a comparison of the amount of income after tax in Poland and abroad in the analyzed three variants:

1) the payment of dividend,
2) the payment of higher wages, regarded as market price and tax costs,
3) the payment of higher wages, unrecognized as tax costs of the subsidiary.

Table 3: The comparison of the amount of income after tax in three variants

	Dividend	Market payment	Non-market payment
Income abroad	100	0	100
Foreign income tax	-30	-	-30
Foreign tax on dividends	-	-	-
Income before tax in Poland	70	100	100

3 Article 20, paragraph 3 of the Corporate Income Tax Act of 15 February 1992.

	Dividend	Market payment	Non-market payment
Corporate income tax – CIT (19%)	-	-19	-19
Income after tax	70	81	51

Source: Jamroży, Kudert, 2013, p. 161.

The analysis of the tax consequences resulting from the presented facts showing that receiving payment from services may be more favorable than the dividends, particularly in situations where the level of tax burden is higher abroad than in Poland. Under the conditions described in the example, subsidiary profit is the subject to a higher tax abroad, which is not compensated with tax liability in Poland (dividend is exempted from Polish CIT). This statement is changed, if the amount of payment for services is not considered as a tax cost of foreign subsidiaries. Then there is double taxation of income. The procedures for eliminate the double taxation are time-consuming and may not be effective [Jamroży, Kudert, 2013, p. 162].

Therefore, in tax planning the decision-making process of transfer pricing should be preceded by analysis of market data (price benchmarking). In the case of transfer price risk the functional analysis, cost analysis or an analysis of the expected benefits should be carried out. The source documents, which confirm the costs, market conditions or provision of services should be also systematically collected. This applies particularly to intangible benefits, including services.

Controls of transfer pricing in Poland – research results

The transfer pricing rules and regulations are rapidly evolving in recent years as a result of the development of the international corporation, long term growth in international trade and the growing fiscal deficits. The above mentioned conditions have resulted in an increase government control of transfer pricing issues, including financing transactions, intellectual property migration, attribution of losses, business restructuring and others.

The Tables 4 presents data on controls of transfer pricing in Poland. The conclusions of the analysis of data contained in this table are as follows:

- the number of controls of transfer pricing carried out by tax offices is increasing and the number of controls carried out by treasury control offices is decreasing each year;

- the total amount of additional income estimated by tax offices and treasury control offices is increasing each year;
- the controls carried out by tax offices result in a much lower average amount of estimated additional income compared to the estimation carried out by treasury control offices.

Table 4: Data relating to controls of transfer pricing carried out by tax offices and treasury control offices in Poland in 2010–2012

The controls of transfer pricing	**2010**	**2011**	**2012**
The total number of controls carried out by tax offices and treasury control offices	2 925	3 286	3 293
The number of controls carried out by tax offices	2 662	3 086	3 108
The number of controls carried out by treasury control offices	263	197	185
The total number of controls carried out by tax offices and treasury control offices resulting in estimation of income	1 396	1 835	1 717
The number of controls carried out by tax offices resulting in estimation of income	1 372	1 835	1 689
The number of controls carried out by treasury control offices resulting in estimation of income	24	16	28
The total amount of additional income estimated by tax offices and treasury control offices (in thousand PLN)	196 906	218 439	219 469
The amount of additional income estimated by tax offices (in thousand PLN)	38 687	27 968	48 469
The amount of additional income estimated by treasury control offices (in thousand PLN)	158 219	190 471	171 000
The average amount of additional income estimated by tax offices (in thousand PLN)	28	15	29
The average amount of additional income estimated by treasury control offices (in thousand PLN)	6 592	11 904	6 107

Source: Own Calculations, Treasury Control Department, Ministry of Finance, http://www.mf.gov.pl/pl/kontrola-skarbowa.

Summary and concluding remarks

The current market condition makes that more and more important is suitable risk management of transfer pricing, among other things, using such instruments as tax documentation, advance pricing agreements, tax statement or the elimination of double taxation. The role of tax risk management is to optimize the tax burden in a way that at the same time does not cause an increased or economically unjustified tax risk.

The analysis shows that the following changes in the transfer pricing rules are needed:

1) changing the thresholds requiring to prepare the tax documentation - thresholds of 30 000 EUR and 50 000 EUR were introduced in 2001 and as a result of inflation are currently too low;
2) changing the threshold of the capital share - the threshold of 5% is the lowest in Europe;
3) simplification of documentation for small and medium-sized enterprises;
4) clarification of the rules for the calculation of thresholds documentation;
5) changing the conditions and procedures for obtaining advance pricing agreements - the current system is inefficient.

Bibliography

Corporate Income Tax Act of 15 February 1992.

Council of the European Union (2011), *Council Directive 2011/96/EU of 30 November 2011 on the common system of taxation applicable in the case of parent companies and subsidiaries of different Member States.*

Kamińska-Blichowska, T. (2003), Ceny transferowe oraz spółki offshore jako narzędzia unikania opodatkowania w korporacjach transnarodowych, „Zeszyty Naukowe nr 1 Wyższej Szkoły Ekonomicznej w Bochni.

KPMG. (2011), *Global Transfer Pricing Review,* Swiss.

Kuchciak, I. (2008), *Wykorzystanie rajów podatkowych w celu zwiększenia wartości przedsiębiorstwa,* Studia i Prace Wydziału Nauk Ekonomicznych i Zarządzania nr 6.

Jamroży, M. and Kudert S. (2013), *Optymalizacja opodatkowania dochodów przedsiębiorców,* LEX a Wolters Kluwer Business, Warsaw.

Jamroży, M. (2011), *Optymalizacja poprzez ceny transferowe,* Komentarz Vademecum Doradcy Podatkowego, Wolters Kluwer, Warsaw.

Majdański, M. (2011), *Transfer pricing as an instrument for planning and optimizing Special Economic Zones tax exemptions,* BT&A, Polish Market Review, No. 10 (170).

Najlepszy, E. (1993), Międzynarodowe finanse przedsiębiorstw, Bafina, Poznań.

OECD (2010), *Transfer Pricing Guidelines for Multinational Enterprises and Tax Administrations 2010,* OECD Publishing.

OECD. (2011), *Multi-country analysis of existing transfer pricing simplification measures*, OECD Publishing, June 2011.

OECD. (2013), *Action Plan on Base Erosion and Profit Shifting*, OECD Publishing.

OECD. (2013), *Addressing Base Erosion and Profit Shifting*, OECD Publishing.

OECD. (2013), *Public Consultation: Draft Handbook on Transfer Pricing Risk Assessment*, OECD Publishing.

OECD. (2014), *Transfer Pricing Comparability Data and Developing Countries*, OECD Publishing.

PWC. (2014), *Spory w zakresie cen transferowych w Polsce. Następstwa polskich i międzynarodowych zmian legislacyjnych, jak i praktyczne wnioski z kontroli podatkowych oraz postępowań sądowych*, Warszawa.

RSMI. (2009), Tax View and Compliance, Volume 3, Series 16.

Sojak, S. (2001), *Ceny transferowe. Teoria i praktyka*, Wydawnictwo Naukowe PWN, Warszawa.

Szołno-Koguc, J. (2009), *Problem cen transakcyjnych w polskim systemie podatkowym*, Zeszyty Naukowe Uniwersytetu Szczecińskiego. Ekonomiczne Problemy Usług, No. 36.

Dominik Gajewski[1]

Is the concept of the Common Consolidated Corporate Tax Base an innovative measure in the context of economic and tax-related consequences?

Introduction

At the time of economic globalisation, holding companies are gaining more and more significance. They are the ones setting trends in the operations of economic entities. Cross-border holding companies are of special importance. They have become the most widely used legal form of operation. However, their activity is hindered by a multiplicity of tax jurisdictions which differ considerably from one another. This problem is also observable within the European Union.

The fundamental basis of Community law is total elimination of all obstacles to operations of the internal market. Lack of regulations relevant to holding companies conducting cross-border activity constitutes one such obstacle. The tax base for companies being part of such a group is calculated according to the rules prevailing in the countries where these companies have their registered offices. Determining what part of the group's total income should be attributed to a given company in the country of its residence poses serious problems, especially in the light of complicated rules and procedures concerning transfer pricing. As a consequence, cross-border activity generates higher administrative costs connected with taxation. There is also a risk that groups of companies will use any available instrument in order to avoid or evade taxation.

In order to satisfy the expectations of groups of companies, the European Commission has attempted to solve this problem by creating the concept of the Common Consolidated Corporate Tax Base (CCCTB). The CCCTB constitutes an advanced proposal for a draft directive which is first and foremost aimed at creating a legal basis for removing obstacles to the operations of the internal market of the EU. The purpose of this concept is to create a tax base for companies conducting cross-border activity in a joint market.

---

1 Prof. Ph.D., Warsaw School of Economics, Poland, emil: d.gajewski@op.pl.

The CCCTB is currently the most advanced concept aimed at harmonisation of taxation of companies within the EU. Therefore, it seems justified and at the same time necessary to carry out an analysis of the measures offered by the CCCTB and its structures, which will form the basis for further discussion. The above-mentioned analysis will also serve to indicate the economic and tax-related consequences that will follow from the CCCTB concept for international holding companies operating within the EU and for the budgets of particular EU member states as well.

The creation of the CCCTB is a result of proceedings by the Common Consolidated Corporate Tax Base Working Group appointed by the European Commission, which has been operating since November, 2004 and whose members were experts from both the member states and the EC. Later, the composition of the Working Group was expanded with inclusion of representatives of business and academic centres. The first propositions within the concept of the CCCTB were put forward in 2001 in the Communication of the European Commission entitled: *Towards an internal market without tax obstacles*. The initial propositions within the concept of the CCCTB were further developed by the EC in an informal document issued on 7 July, 2004, entitled: *Common Consolidated EU Corporate Tax Base* published in *A Common Consolidated EU Corporate Tax Base, Commission Non-Paper to informal Ecofin Council,* 10–11 September, 2004.

The proposition of the CCCTB is a response to requests submitted out of the need to harmonize corporate taxation within the EU by way of elimination or reduction of the number of abundant problems concerning, among others: complying with many restrictions connected with the use of transfer prices, impossibility or limitation of the possibilities to settle cross-border losses and, last but not least, the issues regarding the phenomenon of international double (or even multiple) taxation.

The concept of the CCCTB is based on several fundamental assumptions. The main one is the presentation of common rules for calculating a tax base (i.e. the CCCTB as a common base). Such a base would be used by entities regardless of the place where they conduct economic activity. This is applicable especially in the case of entities that conduct their activity within the territories of several countries, which causes them to be subject to several tax jurisdictions [Supera, 2011, p. 26].

The second pillar of the concept of the CCCTB is the consolidated tax base of related companies which are granted the status of a CCCTB Group (with the CCCTB as the consolidated base). The common tax base would be the total income subject to taxation generated by the CCCTB Group, i.e. by all the member companies of the Group. Intra group transactions would not be included in the consolidated tax base and would be neutral to taxation. Consequently, the entities being members of a Group would not be forced to comply with the regulations concerning transfer pricing with respect to financial operations taking place between the Group members. Another benefit would be the possibility to settle losses within the whole Group without delay. Finally, the processes of dividend distribution among the members of a Group would be tax neutral [Supera, 2011, p. 26].

After consolidation has been performed, it is necessary to determine the share of each Group member company in the consolidated tax base. The tax will be calculated with regard to the determined share on the basis of a tax rate relevant for the country of residence of a given company. One should note that the CCCTB concept is aimed at creating a common system for calculating a tax base whereas setting the tax rates remains the sovereign right of each member state [Supera, 2011, p. 27].

Entities entitled to use the CCCTB system

Whether an entity will be subject to the CCCTB or not is determined by way of reference to the domestic legal regulations of the member states. This means that as far as the CCCTB is concerned, becoming a taxpayer is possible for the entity (company) which has the status of a legal person in line with the internal regulations of its state of tax residence. At the same time, legal persons must be subject to taxation under one of the taxes on legal persons enumerated in the annex to the directive. Thus, taking into account the above-mentioned conditions and the legislation in most member states of the European Union, it is possible to enumerate the entities that may use the CCCTB: joint-stock companies, limited liability companies, companies in the process of formation, organisational units without legal personality except for partnerships, cooperatives and public sector companies or tax capital groups.

The CCCTB concept could also be applied to companies with registered offices in third countries which have a legal form similar to those of companies operating in the EU (as regards the above-mentioned conditions). At the same time, these companies must be subject to taxation in their countries of residence with taxes of comparable nature to the taxes enumerated in the annex to the directive. However, an essential prerequisite for the use of the CCCTB for companies of third countries is the existence of a permanent establishment owned by these companies situated within the territory of a member state providing them with income. This is covered in the following document: CCCTB WP/057/2007, *CCCTB possible elements of a technical outline*. Thus, the system is usable not only for a third country company itself but for its permanent establishment (in a member state) which has income (profit) generated in the member state (as a source state) attributed to it [Staringer, 2008, p. 122; Supera, 2011, p. 28].

It is also worth mentioning that the CCCTB is applicable to both entities conducting cross-border activity and to entities limiting their operations to the territory of one country as a group or individually. Nevertheless, it seems that in terms of taxation, the CCCTB will be most beneficial for groups of companies operating in various EU states.

One important aspect of the CCCTB is that its application is voluntary. This would allow entitled entities to choose whether they prefer to be taxed according to the rules based on the CCCTB [Kołowski, 2011, p. 155; Staringer, 2008, p. 124] or on the basis of domestic tax regulations. Companies which are entitled to use the CCCTB may apply for being taxed in accordance with the rules included in the CCCTB concept. This tax regime is valid for five years and is automatically renewed for successive three year periods unless a motion for cessation of the practice of applying the CCCTB rules is filed.

Undeniably, it is a topic for discussion whether or not the voluntary form is more beneficial than an obligatory one. There are certainly many arguments for and against each particular option. An issue advocating voluntariness of the CCCTB is often raised since it would avoid an accusation of discrimination and infringement of basic freedoms should domestic regulations turn out to be more advantageous than those of the CCCTB concept [Hey, 2008, p. 100; Keen, 2001, p. 759; Spengel, 2008, p. 124]. Additionally, voluntariness of these tax options will make implementation of this concept in the member states "easier" since there will be no need to introduce changes in the existing tax systems [Litwińczuk, 2006, p. 13; Sinn, 1997, p. 258].

On the other hand, the biggest drawback of a voluntary form is that it will be associated with quite a heavy cost needed to cover the tax administration because, apart from the existing domestic fiscal bodies, new tax administration bodies will have to be created for the purpose of the CCCTB which will be financed from the budgets of the member states [Fuest, 2008, p. 731; Schreiber, 2008, p. 125; Staringer 2008, p. 128].

As a consequence of choosing the CCCTB option, if an entity is eligible for the CCCTB system and chooses to use it and has not specified differently, it ceases to be subject to the domestic system of corporate taxation with respect to all matters regulated in the directive.

Tax-related consequences of the CCCTB concept

In line with the CCCTB, income will constitute the difference between the tax revenue and tax deductible expenses. Therefore, in order to calculate income, it will be necessary to define the notion of revenue and expense. The CCCTB Working Group has stated that both revenue and expenses would be defined:

a) on the basis of monetary consideration equal to the price of purchase or vending or established in a different way;
b) on the basis of market value in the case of transactions partially or completely non-monetary;
c) on the basis of the arm's length price in the case of transactions between related parties not undergoing consolidation - Document: WP/057/2007.

The value of revenue and expenses will be calculated in a monetary form. Both the revenue and expenses as well as the tax base will be measured in EUR or translated in EUR from the domestic currency if a country is not a member of the Eurozone. Any difference resulting from conversion would be included in the tax base in the year when it has been made up [Supera, 2011, p. 55].

The revenue would be calculated as net revenue (i.e. not including the output tax on added value – VAT). The same is relevant for deductible expenses which would be included in the net value as long as the input VAT would be partly or wholly irrecoverable. The settlement period would be a tax year, specifically 12 successive months of an accounting period [Fuest, 2008, p. 731; Schreiber, 2008, p. 125].

The tax base should be calculated on accruals basis, both in the case of revenue and expenses (*Various detailed aspects of the CCCTB*, CCCTB/WP066/doc/en, Brussels, 27.3.2008) whereby expenses and revenue should be included in the reporting period in which they were incurred regardless of whether they were settled between the receiver and the supplier in a form of payment [Supera, 2011, p. 56].

In accordance with the CCCTB, the tax base is harmonized which means that its value is calculated in line with common rules applicable to all companies in EU member states included those within the CCCTB area. In the light of the CCCTB, the tax base will constitute the difference between: revenue subject to taxation reduced by the revenue exempt from taxation; and tax deductible expenses and other deductibles. It may be devised in the form of the following formula:

CCCTB = (revenue – deductible expenses) – other deductibles

Notably, considering this formula, one may notice that the difference between revenue and deductible expenses is the same as the notion of income expressed in the Polish legal regulations - Article 7 of the Corporate Income Tax Act

[Orłowski, 2008, p. 76]. Moreover, normative rules for calculating a tax base are indicated in the CCCTB concept:

a) the rule of accruals basis;
b) the rule of incurring (gains and losses are recognised only at the time when they are incurred);
c) the rule of individual evaluation (transactions and tax events are evaluated individually);
d) the rule of coherence (calculation of income is carried out in line with uniform guidelines).

It seems that inclusion of the above-mentioned rules directly into the draft directive will lead to harmonization of the rules for interpretation and allow for avoidance of competing interpretations originating in particular EU member states [Kołomański, 2008, p. 66]. Moreover, implementation of these rules is a beneficial alternative to the measures available in the provisions of the Polish tax law (Article 12 section 3 of the Corporate Income Tax Act), which bind companies only as to the rule of the accruals basis and not the remaining three rules - Document: WP/066/2008.

In line with the CCCTB, the amount of tax will be calculated as the value of income multiplied by the domestic nominal tax rate which will be set individually by each state. One should note that the nominal value of the rate is directly dependent on the legal acts regulating national corporate taxes. Considering the tax rates straightforwardly may lead to misleading conclusions about the tax burdens born by enterprises and, in consequence, about the investment attractiveness of a given country, or lack of it. However, it is noteworthy that the nominal nature of a tax rate may be confusing since it constitutes only one of a number of elements influencing the actual amount of tax imposed on a company [Spengel, 2008, p. 32; Orłowski, 2008, p. 78]. It should be noted that the tax rate is only one of the instruments that may be used in order to shape the effective amount of tax and thus, for instance, instead of increasing the rate of corporate tax, it is enough to limit the number of deductible expenses. Consequently, the interdependence of the nominal rate and the effective tax rate is insignificant.

The issues connected with calculation of the tax base for an individual taxpayer compose a much wider array within the CCCTB. The concept touches upon issues concerning: tax-exempt revenue, the definition of costs and their negative list, settlement of revenue and expenses during a period of time, evaluation for the purpose of taxation, ways of settling long-term agreements, the notion of uncollectible receivables or even amortization itself. The volume of this paper does not allow for thorough discussion of these issues [Kołomański, 2008, p. 68; Orłowski, 2008, p. 78].

It is also necessary to distinguish – still within the CCCTB – between the issues of calculating the tax base for an individual taxpayer and that regarding the consolidated tax base calculated for groups of companies [Staringer, 2008, p. 124; Fuest, 2008, p. 729].

International holding companies versus the concept of the CCCTB

A group of companies is one of the key measures within the CCCTB concept. The CCCTB was created especially for entities conducting business activity within a territory of more than one country. Currently, the tax base for companies being members of such a group is calculated according to the rules applicable in a country in which each company has its registered office. Determining what part of the group's global income must be attributed to a given company in a country of its residence is often quite problematic, especially taking into account the issues connected with transfer pricing. Hence, creation of a group of companies on the basis of the CCCTB is supposed to satisfy the needs of contemporary reality. A CCCTB group comprises a parent entity and related entities which are related by sharing the voting rights at shareholders meetings. The relation may be direct or indirect and should amount to no less than 75% of ownership of the voting rights. In order to ensure continuity of the chain of indirect relationships within a group, a special system for calculating the share of the holding company in the subsidiaries is introduced. It is accepted that in the case of indirect share in votes, the direct holding of over 75% is counted as 100% and the holding below 50% as 0% [Spengel, 2008, p. 32; Baretti, Huber, Lichtblau, 2002, p. 639].

In order to calculate share, the concept of the CCCTB offers the "75% test". It is connected with the condition inevitable for the creation of a CCCTB Group requiring the parent company to have 75% ownership of the voting rights in a subsidiary. Meeting this requirement would be compulsory at the beginning and at the end of a tax year. The holding may not go below the level of 50% at any time of the year. If a new company is willing to enter a Group, it is necessary for it to meet the 75% requirement within a period of 6 months before the day of becoming a member of the Group. However, a group loses its status of the CCCTB Group if two situations are brought about: if the holding falls below 50% (at any time); or if the holding is below 75% at the moment when the tax year ends [Kołowski, 2011, p. 152; Staringer, 2008, p. 124].

Entities which should be entitled to be members of a CCCTB Group are: the holding company and subsidiaries, all of which are companies with share capital having legal personality, and permanent establishments. In order to specify which companies may become members of a Group, an exhaustive list of such companies for all states will be provided in the directive. Such a way of defining the list of eligible entities reflects the way used in other directives up to the present (Directive 90/434/EEC and Directive 90/435/EEC).

The entities entitled to use the CCCTB are – as a matter of principle – companies having a registered office within the territory of the EU. Nonetheless, as far as companies whose states of residence are third countries (from outside the EU), a proposition has been put forward to prepare a non-exhaustive list of entities which would be able to indirectly make use of the provisions of the CCCTB. It is, however, necessary to note that this is relevant for a party being a resident of a third country that earns income (profit) by means of an establishment situated in a member state [Staringer, 2008, p. 124]. The CCCTB concept requires that the type of third country entities should be similar to the type of member states companies which are eligible to calculate a tax base in line with the CCCTB.

Membership to the CCCTB Group of the holding company will constitute its right and not obligation. Yet, if the holding company makes a decision to apply the rules of the CCCTB, it should result in all the directly or indirectly related companies accepting the rules of the CCCTB. Thus, consequences from the decision of the holding company will follow for both the company itself and for the subsidiaries as well [Staringer, 2008, p. 128; Gordon, Wilson, 1986, p. 1362].

As far as relations between the members of the CCCTB Group and subsidiaries outside the group are concerned, it will probably be necessary to apply the provisions of the member states concerning taxation of related entities in such a case - Document: RD/001/2010. In consequence, the effects of enforcing the arm's length rule will be difficult to neutralise by way of consolidation of incomes with the use of the consolidated tax base. It appears that for the purpose of avoiding artificial transfer of income outside the entities under the CCCTB, it will be necessary to apply rules preventing avoidance of taxation within the tax systems of member states. The use of complicated and costly instruments and procedures regarding transfer pricing in the case of subsidiaries which are not consolidated as part of the CCCTB may lead the proposed CCCTB project not to produce the expected benefit of simplification of tax settlement and decrease in costs incurred from it [Bourgeois, von Frenckell, 2008, p. 202; Fuest, 2008, p. 736; Staringer, 2008, p. 132].

As part of the CCCTB, it is planned to abolish the collection of withholding tax and other forms of taxation in the states of source (i.e. countries of residence) of income generated by companies within one CCCTB Group. However, dividends, interest payments, and licence fees paid by a Group member company to an external entity will be subject to taxation under withholding tax within the country of residence. In the case of withholding tax collected on account of interest payments and licence fees, the revenue from this tax will be distributed among the Group members and attributed in line with the sharing mechanism. On the other hand, in the case of dividends, the revenue from the withholding tax will remain in the state collecting tax and will not be distributed among Group members.

Consolidation is to play a major role as far as the CCCTB is concerned. For the purposes of consolidation it will be possible to apply the all-in or all-out rule stating that consolidation will be mandatory for all companies making the decision to accept the CCCTB system if they have subsidiaries entitled to be subject to the CCCTB or a permanent establishment in an EU member state.

The consolidation threshold which should be required will concern the following criteria:

a) an appropriate ownership share – the threshold for which is 75% share in a subsidiary;
b) exercising control – ownership of over 50% of the voting rights is required;
c) the right to participate in profit – over 75% of the right to participate in profit is needed.

These criteria are relevant to the three main aspects of holding a company in terms of economy. These criteria have to be met altogether or separately over a period of 9 months before entering a group and while already being a member – during a tax year as well [Staringer, 2008, p. 132].

Predominantly, a holding company establishes a CCCTB Group if it has a subsidiary in another member state. Various compositions of entities within a group are possible. Hence a company being an EU member state resident might create a group with:

1/ its permanent establishment situated in another member state, and (or)
2/ a permanent establishment in EU owned by its subsidiary which is a resident of a member state, and (or)
3/ its directly or indirectly related companies which are residents of one or more member states, and (or)
4/ one or more companies being residents of the same member state if all these companies are subsidiaries of a company of third country [Spengel, 2008, p. 34; Tenore, 2008, p. 480].

One must keep in mind that there are still many more combinations of possible relationships built up in order to form a CCCTB Group.

The crucial advantage of starting a CCCTB Group is the possibility of intra group settlement of losses. Such settlement will be made by way of consolidation. While combining the tax bases of all group members, the loss incurred by one entity will be automatically compensated for by the income of other entities within a group. If the value of the consolidated base is negative, the loss should be carried forward – in order to compensate it from income generated in future periods, or back – in order to compensate it from income generated in previous periods. This is necessary for purposes of ensuring taxation of net income.

The concept of the CCCTB stipulates two mechanisms of carrying losses over time. The first comprises allocating a loss to each group member company in line with the sharing mechanism. The attributed share in the losses of a group may be carried in time on the level of each entity belonging to the group and compensated for with the share in the positive tax base in the previous or forthcoming years. The second mechanism comprises carrying losses on the level of the group. It seems that the first mechanism assumes some kind of symmetry in terms of treatment of both losses and tax revenues since both the share in income and in losses within the consolidated tax base are attributed to each group member [Bourgeois, von Frenckell, 2008, p. 202; Staringer, 2008, p. 135].

In accordance with the CCCTB concept, losses incurred by a company before entering a group will not be taken into account in the consolidation of the tax base. Such losses should be offset against the share in the consolidated tax base attributed to a given company. The domestic provisions concerning settlement of tax losses in time ought to be applicable in this case. As a consequence, tax losses incurred before consolidation remain subject to the domestic tax system in which they were made.

If a given company leaves the CCCTB Group, the tax losses will remain within the group and will not be attributed to a company which leaves the group. Such losses will be settled with future income of a group [Spengel, 2008, p. 39; Tenore, 2008, p. 480].

Another key instrument of consolidation within the CCCTB is deferred recognition for the purpose of taxation of profits and losses incurred from intra group transactions. The final settlement of these transactions is dependent on the kind of asset being the object of a transaction. Assets subject to amortisation are considered separately. Recognition of such profits or losses for the purpose of taxation, which are incurred on account of transfer of such assets as a result of intra group transactions, should, as a matter of principle, be deferred until a given asset leaves the group (e.g. when it is sold). The CCCTB concept assumes that the income subject to taxation of each group member is calculated in the same way as among unrelated entities. The results of such individual settlements are combined on the level of a group where intra group profits and losses are neutralised in a separate joint statement of the group.

Conclusions

The concept of the CCCTB is undeniably an innovative and modern measure taking into account the specific characteristics of the cross-border operation of entities in the EU. It will unquestionably be attractive to the taxpayers themselves who will not be limited to economic activity within the EU. Implementation of all the above-mentioned mechanisms might constitute a challenge for the administration of the EU member states since it would require adaptation of internal regulations of 27 countries. However, the profit from the implementation of the CCCTB concept will surely compensate for this effort. It is worth mentioning that these measures are of voluntary nature hence the entities interested in the CCCTB will be able to choose between domestic measures and the CCCTB concept. On the other hand, it will lead to a high cost of the CCCTB. The optional nature of this concept will have to result in the development of tax administration on the central level, which will serve the functions appointed to it by the provisions of the CCCTB. Unmistakeably, it will allow for centralisation of administration with regard to groups of companies conducting cross-border activity and at the same time will assign new functions and tasks to these administrative bodies, i.e. verification of the consolidated tax declarations, issuing binding interpretations in terms of the provisions of the directive. Nonetheless, appointing new administration will surely lead to accusations that the cost of maintenance of this directive is high and will constitute a burden for the member states.

The issue of whether the CCCTB concept will be attractive enough to groups of companies conducting cross-border activity (international holdings) should also be considered as currently such groups may evade taxation by means of abundant measures used contrary to their aim and purpose, which is of course against the law.

The scope of the directive will be very wide. The directive will be touching upon a number of issues, often new and complicated. Furthermore, the list of entities entitled to use the CCCTB system is vast since apart from groups of companies (which seem to be the main addressees of this directive), it also encompasses all kinds of companies and entities serving the function of economic entities (e.g. enterprises) as well. It might result in evincing strong interest in the directive among a wide range of taxpayers from all over the EU.

Undeniably, introduction of the rules concerning the calculation of income and the tax base directly into a directive will lead to harmonization of interpretative rules and will allow for preventing competing interpretations given by particular EU member states. Additionally, implementation of these rules will be a beneficial alternative to the measures applicable in the particular EU member states.

An important advantage of the formation of a CCCTB Group will be the possibility to settle intra group losses. Such settlement will be made by way of consolidation. While combining the tax bases of all group members, the loss incurred by one entity will be automatically compensated for by the income of other entities within a group which will certainly be the benefit of the concept of the CCCTB.

Another key instrument of consolidation within the CCCTB will be deferred recognition for the purpose of taxation of profits and losses incurred from intra group transactions. It will constitute a significant economic and tax-related consequence for international holding companies.

Unmistakeably, the CCCTB concept might introduce new European standards based on the model of bringing accounting and taxes together. It seems that the concept is well thought out and constitutes some kind of a compromise between the taxpayers' expectations and the representatives of the tax services in the EU member states.

Bibliography

Baretti C., Huber B., Lichtblau K. (2002), *A tax on tax revenue. The incentive effects of equalizing transfers. Evidence from Germany*, International Tax and Public Finance, Vol. 9, No. 6.

Bourgeois M., von Frenckell E. (2008), *Relation to taxpayers outside the group* [in:] Common Consolidated Corporate Tax Base, Linde Verlag, Wien.

Fuest C. (2008), *The European Commission's proposal for a common consolidated corporate tax base*, Oxford Review of Economic Policy, Vol.24, No. 4.

Gordon R., Wilson J. (1986), *An Examination of Multijurisdictional Corporate-Income Taxation under Formula Apportionment*, Econometrica, Vol. 54, No. 6.

Hey J. (2008), *CCCTB – optionality* [in:] Common Consolidated Corporate Tax Base, Linde Verlag, Wien.

Keen M. (2001), *Preferential regimes can make tax competition less harmful*, National Tax Journal, Vol. 54, No. 4.

Kołomański Ł. (2011), *Ustalenie dochodu podatkowego w koncepcji CCCTB* [w:] *Wspólna korporacyjna podstawa opodatkowania w UE a opodatkowanie dochodu spółek w Polsce* [Calculation of tax revenue within the CCCTB concept [in:] Common Consolidated Corporate Tax Base in the EU versus taxation of the income of companies in Poland], Oficyna Prawa Polskiego, Warszawa.

Kołowski K. (2011), *Grupa spółek w koncepcji CCCTB a PGK* [w:] *Wspólna korporacyjna podstawa opodatkowania w UE a opodatkowanie dochodu spółek w Polsce* [Group of companies within the CCCTB concept versus a tax capital group[in:] Common Consolidated Corporate Tax Base in the EU versus taxation of the income of companies in Poland], Oficyna Prawa Polskiego, Warszawa.

Litwińczuk H. (2006), *Wspólna skonsolidowana podstawa opodatkowania dla osób prawnych - koncepcja i szanse opodatkowania*, [Common Consolidated Tax Base for legal persons – the concept and opportunities in taxation], Prawo i Podatki [Law and Taxes], No. 9, 2013.

Orłowski W. (2008), *Propozycja Wspólnej Skonsolidowanej Bazy CIT - wpływ na polską gospodarkę*, [Proposition of the Common Consolidated CIT Base – the influence on the Polish economy], Warszawa.

Schreiber U. (2008), *Evaluating the Common Consolidated Corporate Tax Base* [in:] A Common Consolidated Corporate Tax Base for Europe. Eine einheitliche Korperschaftsteuerbemessungsgrundlage fur Europa, Springer-Verlag and Heidelberg GmbH and Co., Berlin.

Sinn H. (1997), *The selection principle and market failure in systems competition*, Journal of Public Economics Vol. 66, No. 2.

Spengel Ch. (2008), *Concept and Necessity of a Common Tax Base - an acad-edemic introduction* [in:] A Common Consolidated Corporate Tax Base for Europe. Eine einheitliche Korperschaftsteuerbemessungsgrundlage fur Europa, Springer-Verlag and Heidelberg GmbH and Co., Berlin.

Staringer C. (2008), *Requirements for Forming a Group* [in:] Common Consoldated Corporate Tax Base, Linde Verlag, Wien.

Supera-Markowska M. (2011), *Wspólna korporacyjna podstawa opodatkowania w UE a opodatkowanie dochodu spółek w Polsce* [Common Consolidated Corporate Tax Base in the EU versus taxation of the income of companies in Poland], Oficyna Prawa Polskiego, Warszawa.

Tenore M. (2008), *Requirements to consolidate and changes in the level of ownership*, Common Consolidated Corporate Tax Base, Linde Verlag, Wien.

Ewa Lotko[1] and Urszula K. Zawadzka-Pąk[2]

Fiscal sustainability as a condition of economic security

Introduction

Fiscal sustainability "relates to the ability of a government to assume the financial burden of its debt in the future. Fiscal policy is not sustainable if it implies an excessive accumulation of government debt over time and ever increasing debt service. Sustainability means avoiding an excessive increase in government liabilities – a burden on future generations – while ensuring that the government is able to deliver necessary public services, including necessary safety net in difficult times, and to adjust policy in response to new challenges. There is no defined upper limit of sustainable debt levels. Sustainability limits differ across countries and over time" [Fiscal, 2012, p. VII].

In order to achieve satisfactory results in maintaining fiscal sustainability two kinds of instruments should be implemented simultaneously: firstly, instruments rationalising and limiting expenditures and secondly, instruments mobilising and securing revenues. In many countries for a long time the main emphasis was put on the first group of instruments. Relatively recently, when it turned out that the actions almost exclusively on spending are insufficient as well as under the influence of activities of international organizations (such as the International Monetary Funds or the European Union) the national policy makers started to pay more attention to the budget revenues as an instrument of ensuring financial and economic security.

The objective of this chapter is to determine general conditions of fiscal sustainability obtained with the instruments concerning both the state budget expenditures and the state budget revenues based on French and Polish experiences. The selection of France and Poland results from the fact that both countries struggle with excessive deficit and are incited (or even obliged) by the European Union institutions to introduce instruments ensuring sustainability of public finances. However, the level of French public debt is much

1 Ph.D. student, University of Białystok, Faculty of Law, Department of Public Finances and Financial Law, Poland, email: ewa.lotko@wp.pl.

2 Ph.D., University of Białystok, Faculty of Law, Department of Public Finances and Financial Law, Poland, email: zawadzka.urszula@yahoo.com.

more higher than the Polish one (details below) and as a consequence the urgent needs strongly force French authorities to seek effective solutions ensuring fiscal sustainability and to take much more diverse actions than in the case of Poland. Consequently, choosing these two countries enables gathering information about different instruments aiming at reduction of public debt and public deficit.

Instruments ensuring fiscal sustainability in France - Current situation of French public finances

Since the beginning of the current century, France has been struggling with growing deficit. The excessive deficit procedure was initiated in 2003 [Council Decision No 2003/487/EC, 2003] and abrogated in 2007 [Council Decision No 2007/154/EC, 2007]. Afterwards, due to the global, economic and financial crisis, the situation of the French public finances became significantly worse. Since 2009 the country again has been covered by the EU excessive deficit procedure [Council Decision 2009/414/EC]. Initially, the Council recommended France to eliminate excessive deficit by the end of 2013, however despite considerable efforts, which resulted in deficit decline from 7.5% of GDP in 2009 to 4.8% GDP in 2012, France was not able to do it within that time limit and the Council recommended to correct French excessive deficit by 2015. Persisting for several years, excessive deficit caused an increase in general government debt. Starting from 64.2% in 2007, the ratio of debt to GDP reached 90.2% in 2012. The EU authorities expect the debt ratio to peak at 94.3% of GDP in 2014 and then to drop to 88.2% in 2017 [Fiscal, 2013, p. 56–57].

Instruments concerning budgetary expenditures in France

In France in 2001 the organic Act on finance laws [Loi organique n° 2001–692, 2001], called "New Financial Constitution, LOLF" that fully came into force in 2006, introduced the first crucial changes concerning the expenditures of the state budget replacing the traditional budget by a performance one. This change enabled to take more effective and more efficient decisions regarding the allocation of budgetary resources. In the traditional budgeting the main emphasis (in the phases of budget planning, execution and control) is put on the expenditures limits, whereas in the performance budgeting, apart from the legality criterion, the effectiveness (quality) and the efficiency (relation between delivered public goods or services and their cost) of public spending are also taken into consideration in every phase of budgetary procedure. To measure these results, new expenditures classification was introduced, consisting of functions, programs and tasks, as well as containing the "performance part" (composed of objectives and indicators).

Although in France the transition from the traditional budgeting to the performance one improved the efficiency and effectiveness of spending public money, the role of this new method of budgeting should not be overestimated. In fact, it is only a tool (an instrument) which may (or may not) be used to rationalise public expenditures. To fully take advantage of its possibilities it is necessary to identify the areas where the specific changes should be made to facilitate making right decisions regarding amendments of certain legal provisions or conducting broader reforms. Such actions are called public policies evaluation defined as a search for legal, administrative and financial means whose implementation would enable to achieve results expected from this policy and aims determined for this policy [Décret nº 90–82, 1990].

France has a relatively long tradition of evaluation practices which started in the 1960s. Among the activities undertaken at the beginning of the current century, special attention should be devoted to the comprehensive review of public policies (fr. *Revision Générale des Politiques Publiques*, RGPP) realised in 2008–2010 as an extension of the public finances reform started by the LOLF. This review consisted of a thorough analysis of legal solutions and tasks financed from public funds and carried out by teams of auditors representing both the public and the private sector. On the basis of these results, a specially appointed institution – the Council for the Modernisation of Public Policies (fr. *Conseil de modernisation des politiques publiques*) took hundreds of decisions on the directions of reforms. Its aim was to improve the functioning of the state. The reforms concentrated on six strategic objectives: adapting the state's tasks to the challenges of 21st century, improving the quality of services provided to the citizens and enterprises, modernising the state and enhancing binding procedures, improving the quality of working conditions and increasing promotion possibilities in public administration, broadening the concepts of effectiveness and efficiency, rebalancing public finances and using every Euro effectively [Zawadzka-Pąk, 2014a, p. 62–64].

After the presidential elections in May 2012, when François Hollande replaced Nicolas Sarkozy, the next stage of public administration modernisation started (fr. *modernisation de l'action publique*, MAP). The main difference in the implementation of these two reviews concerns the fact that the RGPP was a one-time evaluation, while the MAP is a continuous action.

The multiannual programming of public finances constitutes another important instrument of ensuring fiscal sustainability. The first important step of its reinforcing in France consisted of modification of the Constitution by the constitutional Act of July 23, 2008 [Loi constitutionnelle n° 2008–724, 2008] that introduced a new category of law, i.e. acts on the multiannual planning of public finances (in short acts on multiannual planning). Their content was detailed by the organic law on the programming and management of public finances [Loi organique n° 2012–1403, 2012]. Currently binding Act on the multiannual planning of December 17, 2012 covering the period of 2012–2017 introduced three rules aiming at reinforcing fiscal sustainability [Loi n° 2012–1558, 2012], i.e.

a) The public finances balance rule – the Act on the multiannual planning of 2012 contains forecast of cyclical and structural balance (deficit/surplus) of the public finance sector, as well as of particular sub-sectors (government, local government and social security). The separation of the cyclical and structural balance is related to the introduction of a corrective mechanism (described below).
b) The expenditure rule – in accordance with this rule, the expenditures of the state budget (with the exception of tax returns and deductions) in each year of programming cannot exceed a certain limit (370,5 billion EUR in 2012, in the next years of programming this amount is updated annually taking into account only the inflation rate). Additionally, the expenditure rule determines the proportion of public expenditures in relation to the planned GDP for each year of programming.
c) The debt rule – the Act on the multiannual planning of 2012 indicated the path of gradual restoration of the safe level of debt for each year of the programming period (it is assumed that in 2017 the French public debt will reach the level of 82.9% GDP).

All these rules do not have strictly binding character and therefore balance, expenditures and debt forecasts can be exceeded. As a consequence, to enhance their enforceability (especially the planned balance) a special body was created, i.e., the High Council of Public Finance (fr. *Haut Conseil des finances publiques*) belonging to fiscal councils created in many countries around the world. The French High Council is an institution independent from the government and the parliament and connected to the Court of Auditors (fr. *Cour des comptes*). The High Council assesses whether there are significant deviation between the balance planned for the previous year in the Act on the multiannual programming and its actual realisation. The deviation is significant, when the structural balance planned in the Act on the multiannual exceeds at least 0.5% of GDP for the year or at least 0.25% of GDP on average per year in two following years [Loi organique n° 2012–1403, 2012]. In such a case, the Council of Ministers, within a corrective mechanism, is obliged to present the justification for the reasons of this situation and to implement corrective actions no later than in the next annual finance act[3] or eventually in the act on financing social insurance.

Instruments concerning budgetary revenues in France

Although the above-mentioned "New Financial Constitution" introduced important changes concerning budgetary expenditures it has not made any changes concerning the budgetary revenues, whereas to ensure financial and economic stability not only efficient and effective public spending is necessary but also "the protection of tax revenues". The French expression – *sécurisation des recettes fiscales* – was used for the first time by the President of the French Court of Auditors in May 2000.

The phenomena of tax fraud and tax evasion constitute serious problems affecting the decrease of public funds and threatening economic security of the state [Zawadzka-Pąk, 2013, p. 90–99]. In France two main approaches aiming at combating these problems are applied: the punitive approach and the preventive approach. The first one is realised by strengthening legal provisions concerning the fight against fiscal frauds and fiscal evasion. Therefore, recently two laws have been promulgated: the Organic Act on the Financial Prosecutor of the Republic [Loi organique n° 2013–1115, 2013] and the Act on the fight against tax evasion and the great economic and financial delinquency [Loi n° 2013–1117, 2013]. The preventive approach, which is still elaborated, consists of resigning, at least partially, from unilateral determination of rules by public authorities and of establishing rights and obligations of tax administration and taxpayers together in the form of so-called preventive fiscal agreements that are, e.g. in the form of advance pricing agreements [Bouvier, 2010, p. 1–2].

Additionally, to secure budgetary revenues was made an important reform of public administration and was created the General Directorate of Public Finances (fr. *Direction générale des Finances publiques, DGFiP*), from the fusion of two units: Directorate General for Taxes (fr. *Direction générale des Impôts*, DGI) and the General Directorate for Public Accounts (fr. *Direction générale de la Comptabilité publique, DGCP*). The separation of authorities responsible for tax assessment and tax collection was specific to France due to a historic

---

3 In France the budget which is included in the financial acts (fr. *loi de finances*) is modified by a special sub-category of the financial acts (fr. *loi de finances rectificatif*) at least once a year, before the approval of budget execution by the parliament in the so-called *loi de règlement* that constitutes the third type of financial acts.

but archaic principle (coming from the 14th century) for the separation of tax assessment and tax collection that prohibited the same person from executing these two functions [Arthuis, 2010, p. 161]. The aim of this "emblematic reform" was to provide a single tax contact for individuals, as it had already been done in the case of tax services for enterprises by *les Services des impôts des entreprises.* It enabled to create "the single tax interlocutors" for individuals - the change important for the effectiveness and efficiency of tax assessment and collection from the point of view of public administration but also an individual taxpayer, as it had taken place earlier in other European countries, i.e. in Great Britain in 2004 [Parini, 2010, p. 153–154].

The fusion of two directorates and the creation of the DGFiP aimed at simplified tax administration and cost reduction but it was particularly difficult to implement due to the strong resistance of the French trade unions defending the existing workplaces (social pressure was the reason why three previous attempts of such a fusion had failed). This successful fusion was announced in 2007 by the new President of the French Republic, Nicolas Sarkozy and was realised in 2010 (however to facilitate the transition, each department of DGFiP had an assistant director till 2012. Both vacant positions were removed in 2013 by a decree). The reform was implemented gradually by: shifting functions from two previous directorates to the one newly created, modifying legal provisions as well as by making organisational changes and dismissal of employees.

It is also important to emphasise an instrument ensuring fiscal sustainability and, as a consequence, economic security which is related to the control of tax and social expenditures levels (fr. *dépenses (niches) fiscales and sociales*). There is no unequivocal definition of tax (social) expenditures because there are no international standards to which they derogate. In general, this notion is related to the legislative or regulatory provisions whose implementation leads to a loss of state revenues and thus to taxpayers relief from their tax burden compared to the situation in which they should pay on the general principles of the French tax law. There is no harmonised definition across the OECD countries and some countries have introduced additional criteria, i.e. Belgium elaborated a number of features characteristic of these expenditures, Germany defines them as the equivalent of budget subsidies, in the United Kingdom their qualification is based on the theoretic possibility of replacing them by a direct expenditure [Perrotin, 2010, p. 3].

The first step of ensuring fiscal sustainability within tax and fiscal expenditures should consist of making their list and evaluate their cost in order to get to know how much the state loses by different deductions and allowances accorded to natural and legal persons. While in the case of the French state taxes, the authorities already have general information on this issue, in the case of local taxes there are no even basic data. The second step should consist of gathering precise information on derogatory mechanisms, definition of governance principles enabling to control and evaluate these tax expenditures as well as optimisation practices they cause and focusing on their real objectives.

In France a special department in the Ministry of Finance was created to evaluate current situation concerning tax and social expenditures and to elaborate the complex vision of controlling them (fr. *Comité d'évaluation des dépenses fiscales et des niches sociales*). Additionally, a number of reports describing current situation and containing general and detailed suggestions about the rationalisation of tax expenditures system was prepared by different public institutions, including the National Assembly [Migaud, 2008], the Senate (Marini 2011), the Council of Mandatory Payments (fr. *Conseil des Prélèvement Obligatoires)* connected to the Court of Auditors (fr. *Cour des Comptes*) [Migaud, 2010]. However, the issue of a better control of tax and social expenditures in France is still open.

Instruments ensuring fiscal sustainability in Poland - Current situation of the Polish public finances

Poland from the moment of accession to the European Union has been struggling with the problem of too high level of public finances deficit. Therefore, Poland with the deficit of 5.7% in 2004 was covered by the excessive deficit procedure [Council Decision n°2005/183/EC, 2005] which ended in 2008 [Council Decision n°2008/622/EC, 2008] and then since 2009 Poland was again covered by the excessive deficit procedure [Council Decision n°2009/589/EC, 2009]. Despite the initial recommendations to reduce the deficit by 2012, and despite Poland's efforts which brought a decline in the deficit from 7.4% of GDP in 2009 to 3.9% of GDP in 2012, the procedure has been extended till 2015. It is worth noting that in 2013 economic growth lower than expected and overly optimistic budget revenues prognosis obliged Polish authorities to modify the Budget Act and to increase the planned deficit of about 16 billion PLN. The excessive deficit that has persisted from several years results in public finances sector debt increase (even if, the situation of the Polish public finances compared to the level of the French public debt remains much more favourable). In 2007 the debt of the Polish public finances sector amounted to 45.5% of GDP, while in 2012 – 55.6% of GDP. The European Commission predicts that in 2014 it will reach 59.0% of GDP [Report, 2013, p. 63–64], while predictions of the Polish government are much more optimistic. According to the Polish authorities the general government debt will reach the level 49.9% of GDP in 2014 and during the next 4 years will fluctuate within the limits of 50.1% of GDP [Ministerstwo Finansów, 2013, p. 4].

Instruments concerning budgetary expenditures in Poland

In order to rationalise public spendings in Poland, similarly as in France (and in more than 50 countries all over the world), the method of a performance budgeting started to be implemented at the beginning of the 21st century. However, contrary to France, in Poland the traditional budget was not replaced by a performance one. Still, the traditional budget based on the administrative expenditures classification constitutes the basis for financial management, whereas the financial plan in the structure of functions, tasks and actions (the performance plan) constitutes an appendix to the justification of the Budgetary Act prepared by the Polish Ministry of Finance. Having executed the traditional budget, the information about the realisation of the performance plan is elaborated by the Ministry of Finance. Such a solution has mainly informative function, whereas it has limited possibilities of influencing the effectiveness and efficiency of public spending. Moreover, in Poland, contrary to France – where the performance budgeting has become an instrument of wider reforms consisting of different forms of public policies evaluation – till this moment it is not related to similar actions so necessary to increase the efficiency and effectiveness of public spending. Instead, the performance planning in Poland (similarly as in France) is linked with the multiannual programming of public finances, even if pursuant to the latest changes in the content of the multiannual plans (details below), these relations are much less visible.

The multiannual planning of public finances in Poland constitutes the second important instrument of maintaining fiscal sustainability. It is mainly realised by the governmental resolution, the State's Multiannual Financial Plan (pl. *Wieloletni Plan Finansowy Państwa,* WPFP), which is elaborated for the budgetary year and three consecutive years. Regarding the content of WPFP plan, it has evaluated since its introduction to the Polish legal system in 2010. The first four plans (i.e. for the following periods: 2010–2013, 2011–2014, 2012–2015, 2013–2016) specified the objectives of the socio-economic and fiscal policy, the forecasts of public debt as well as the basic data on the state budget. Additionally, these plans also contained the attachment where every function (the highest level of functional expenditures classification) of annual performance budget was described in multiannual perspective (i.e. description of function, its objectives and indicators, the values of indicators planned separately for every of the four years of programming, as well as planned expenditures for the next year and together for the last three years of programming). Currently binding WPFP plan for the period of 2014–2017 consists of the Convergence Programme (presented annually to the European Commission) and an artificial description of the objectives of the main state functions together with indicators of their realisation (generally only the value achieved at the beginning of 2014 and the value planned for 2017 are presented) [Zawadzka-Pąk, 2014b].

Another extremely important instrument of maintaining fiscal sustainability and protecting against over-indebtedness has been incorporated into the provisions of the Polish Constitution. According to the Article 216 (5), it shall be neither permissible to contract loans nor provide guarantees and financial sureties which would engender a national public debt exceeding 3/5 of the value of the annual GDP [Konstytucja, 1997]. It is an absolute prohibition and its violation entails political, constitutional and criminal responsibility of persons responsible for ensuring the appropriate level of public debt, its monitoring and taking prudential actions sufficiently early. It should be emphasised that Poland is one of several countries in the world which included it its Constitution the limit of the public debt.

To ensure the compliance with the Constitution, the provisions of subsequent Public Finances Acts (PFA) of 1998, 2005 and the currently binding PFA of Aug. 27, 2010 have provided the existence of one prudential procedure and two remedial ones [Tyniewicki, 2013, p. 367–368]. The first procedure (the prudential one) determined by the PFA restrictions should be applicable to the preparation of the Budget Act (compare below) in the event when the value of the ratio of public debt to GDP is above 50% but below 55%. The second (first remedial) procedure includes restrictions applicable to the preparation of Budget Act and other consequences provided by the PFA when the ratio of public debt to GDP is above 55% but below 60% and finally the third (the second remedial) procedure should be applied when the ratio of public debt to GDP is equivalent to or higher than 60% [Ustawa z dnia 27 sierpnia 2009 r., 2009].

The consequences of applying these procedures were slightly modified with time, however the most important changes were made in 2013. Firstly, the Polish legislator temporarily suspended the prudential procedure (started when the debt achieved the level of 50%–55% of GDP), so the restrictions resulting thereof were not applied during the preparation of the budget for the 2014 [Ustawa z dnia 26 lipca 2013 r., 2013], and then he definitely removed it from the Polish legal system with the beginning of 2014 [Ustawa z dnia 8 listopada 2013 r., 2013]. Analogously, the first amendment suspended the application of the Article 112a of PFA establishing "the temporary expenditures rule" in force between 2011–2013 [Ustawa z dnia 26 lipca 2013 r., 2013] and the second amendment totally abrogated it [Ustawa z dnia 8 listopada 2013 r., 2013]. This rule assumed that public expenditures level can be higher in the next year maximally by the level of inflation forecasted for the next year increased by 1%. This rule did not concern: the expenditures on public debt, the expenditures on social security, own resources of the EU and obligatory contributions paid to international organizations, the expenditures on programs involving funds from the EU budget and the aid provided by the EFTA countries.

Running of the prudential procedure meant that for the following year the Council of Ministers was obliged to pass a Budget Act where the ratio of the state budget deficit to state budget revenues could not be higher than the ratio of the state budget deficit to state budget revenues from the current year resulting from the Budget Act. The obligation of maintaining this ratio existed in 2012, because the public debt in 2011 reached the level of 53.5% of GDB.

Thus, the ratio of state budget deficit to state budget revenues defined in the state budget for 2012 could not be higher than this proportion from the previous year and effectively in the Budget Act for 2013 the ratio was on the same level, i.e. 11.9%. This prudential procedure would have also be applied to the Budgetary Act for 2014, if the legislator had not suspended and then abrogated the prudential procedure [Lotko, 2014, p. 91].

Polish legislator explained the reasons for the prudential procedure abrogation by its replacement with a new instrument, i.e. stabilising expenditures rule (compare below). However, it is difficult to understand the behaviour of the Polish parliament when having exceeded the prudential threshold, it abrogates the application of prudential procedure in order to be able to adopt a budget for the next year with a higher deficit. Especially that the prudential and remedial procedures aim at guaranteeing the compliance with the constitutional public debt limitations. Currently, the government is obliged to take determined actions resulting from the remedial procedures only when the ratio of debt to GDP exceeds 55%. Such action should be assessed negatively, even if we can only presume that the government at all costs wanted to avoid starting once again prudential procedure (limiting the deficit level and consequently the expenditures one), perhaps in fear of the consequences of political and social assessment expressed during next parliamentary elections.

As we have mentioned, instead of the prudential procedure and temporary expenditures rule repealed from the 1 of January 2014, the stabilising expenditures rule (expressed by two mathematical formulas) was introduced and should enable taking countercyclical actions. This rule covers about 90% of the expenditures of the general government sector (outside the scope of the rule are: firstly, the costs of units which do not have the ability to generate high deficits, and secondly, budget expenditures of EU funds and that part of the expenditures which is financed by means of non-refundable grants from the EU and EFTA countries). The limit is aggregated, what means that the expenditures of some units may grow faster at the expense of a slower growth or a decrease in expenditures of other entities subjected to the limit. In order to avoid pro-cyclical adjustments, the rule assumes that it will be suspended in case of a projected decrease of GDP. In case of improvement or a slight economic downturn an automatic correction of the expenditures limit *in plus* or *in minus* will be activated [Szpringer, 2014].

Instruments concerning budgetary revenues in Poland

Apart from the instruments maintaining fiscal stability related to the budgetary expenditures, actions concerning the revenues of the budget have finally started to be appreciated in Poland by the representatives of public authorities as well as the academics.

Firstly, we would like to pay attention to the need to increase the feasibility of budget revenues planning. While in the case of implementing the revenues which are higher than it was originally planned, there are just additional revenues to spend, but serious consequences appear when the revenues forecasts were constructed with too much optimism. The effects of such estimations oblige to make important, often difficult, changes in the Budget Act during a financial year consisting of adjusting the expenditures to the state possibilities [Owsiak, 2008, p. 147].

Figure 1. shows the accuracy of the forecasts revenues in Poland in the years 2000–2013. In Poland (contrary to other countries, including France) the Budget Act is not modified every year but only when there is a special need to adapt the level of revenues and expenditures. The divergences in planning budgetary revenues in 2001, 2009 and 2013 caused such a necessity. However, these modifications were not taken into consideration to show the real data about the feasibility of revenues planning in the Budget Acts.

Figure 1: The accuracy of the budgetary revenues forecasts in Poland in the period of 2000–2013

Budgetary year	Budget Act	Execution	Budget Act	Execution	Accuracy of the revenues forecasts
	(in millions PLN)		(in millions USD)		
2000	140 909	135 663	46 303	44 579	- 3,7%
2001	161 065	140 526	52 926	46 176	- 12,8%

Budgetary year	Budget Act	Execution	Budget Act	Execution	Accuracy of the revenues forecasts
	(in millions PLN)		(in millions USD)		
2002	145 101	143 519	47 680	47 160	- 1,1%
2003	155 697	152 110	51 162	49 983	- 2,3%
2004	154 552	156 281	50 786	51 354	+ 1,1%
2005	174 703	179 772	57 407	59 073	+ 2,9%
2006	195 282	197 640	64 170	64 945	+ 1,2%
2007	228 952	236 367	75 234	77 670	+ 3,2%
2008	281 892	253 547	92 630	83 316	- 10,1%
2009	303 034	247 183	99 577	81 224	- 18,4%
2010	249 006	250 302	81 823	82 249	+ 0,5%
2011	273 144	277 557	89 755	91 205	+ 1,6%
2012	293 766	287 595	96 532	94 504	- 2,1%
2013	299 385	279 151	98 378	91 729	- 6,7%

Source: Own study based on data from the Budget Acts and reports on its execution in the years 2000–2013 available on the website of the Ministry of Finance: www.mf.gov.pl.

In the analysed period the most important divergences between planning and execution of budgetary revenues took place in 2001 (–12,8%), 2008 (–10,1%) and 2009 (– 18,4%)[4]. In 2001 poor quality of revenues planning was due to the deterioration of the economic situation in Poland, while in 2008 and in 2009 (after the period of intensive economic growth) the impossibility of realistic planning was due to financial crisis. It should be added that in the analysed period of 14 years, revenues forecasts were marked 8 times by an excessive optimism.

The main obstacles to the realistic planning of budgetary revenues result from:

---

4 What is interesting, in the first lines of the official report on the execution of the state budget in 2009 prepared by the Ministry of Finance there is a following information: "State budget revenues in 2009 amounted to 274,183,500 thousand PLN. In relation to the Budget Act for 2009, revenues were lower by 28,851,305 thousand PLN, i.e. by 9.5%". However, based on the official data of the Ministry of Finance, by subtracting the planned amount of income from the realised one, we get the amount of 55,851 million PLN (and not 28,851 million PLN), which indicates that the planned revenues were higher by 18,4% and not by 9,5% (!), as it is indicated in the report.

a) The legal nature of revenues which constitute only forecasts of tax and non-tax sources of financing state tasks. The revenues planning does not constitute the legal basis for its execution.
b) The impact of macroeconomic factors on the revenues planning, such as GDP, inflation, profits of enterprises and natural persons. Forecasting budget revenues is more accurate in a stable financial situation, as opposed to the uncertain one and periods of crisis.
c) The instability of tax system and inefficiency of tax collection by the tax and custom administration.
d) The multiplicity of tasks to realise from the public funds and the impact of the political factor influencing the shape of both sides of the budget structure (revenues and expenditures). On the one hand, government must realise state functions and, on the other hand, it has to care about the financial stability and strive to correct the excessive deficit.

For these reasons, in order to ensure the state financial stability it is necessary to improve the quality of budget revenues planning by: resigning from planning based on historical basis and restructuring financial system planning based on multiannual programming; strengthening the supervision of financial management in all public sector entities, taking into account risks such as hidden ("grey" or "black") economies, tax frauds and tax evasion, tax administration efficiency improvement so as to enable tax officers to timely realise planned revenues, strengthening the position of the Minister of Finance in the management of public finances [Kosikowski, 2011, p. 31–32, 334; Ruśkowski, 2013, p. 124–132].

Currently in Poland, in order to increase the level of collected revenues, the reform of tax and custom administrations is prepared. In 2013, the Ministry of Finance, having made the diagnosis of the most important problems related to the compliance with tax legal provisions by the taxpayers and tax administration efficiency has prepared a set of about 50 actions to implement [Ministerstwo Finansów, 2014, p. 1–4]. The planned measures aim at streamlining the process of strengthening the enforcement of tax debt by influencing the attitudes of taxpayers and they comprise, e.g.: the creation of the Central Register of Debtors, diversification of interest rates for tax arrears, coordination of investigations and controls aiming at the fight against organised fraud concerning VAT, introduction of provisions on tax evasion, modernisation of existing information systems and databases. It is estimated that the implementation of all planned measures will result in an increase in revenues at least by 6.2 billion PLN in the period of 2014–2017 [Rada Ministrów, 2014, p. 63–64].

Next to the tax administration reform, the reform of custom service is planned, also aiming at the creation of "the single settlement point" as a result of the centralisation of custom administration, simplification of audit procedures, corruption prevention and improvement of human resource management [Uzasadnienie, p. 1].

Conclusion

The chapter has presented different instruments of promoting fiscal sustainability in France and in Poland. The aim of this study did not consist of detailed presentation of instruments ensuring the sustainability of public finances in the analysed countries, but emphasised multiplicity and variety of possible instruments. As we have indicated, in both countries they concern expenditures as well as revenues of the state budget. Even if actions concerning securing and mobilising public revenues started to be introduced later, the actions on public spending, and therefore generally, are less developed, there is no doubt that these two kinds of instruments should be used jointly to ensure the sustainability of public finances.

On the basis of the instruments already implemented or planned to be introduced in both countries analysed in this chapter, some general conditions of fiscal sustainability ensuring the economic security can be formulated:

1) expenditures should be planned, executed and controlled using the effectiveness and efficiency criteria and not only the criterion of legality;
2) information about the appropriate directions of reforms should be constantly gathered thanks to the detailed process of public policies evaluation;
3) credible revenues and expenditures planning in annual and multiannual perspective should be established thanks to modern programming techniques;
4) effective deficit, debt and expenditures rules concerning all public sector should be applied;
5) effective instruments of combating tax frauds and tax evasion should be applied to convince taxpayers of the justice and equality of tax system and to motivate them to pay taxes voluntarily;
6) tax and custom administration should possess modern and effective instruments to realise their tasks, it should be composed of competent and motivated officers whose activity would guarantee the inevitability of paying taxes.

Even if there is no universal set of instruments providing financial sustainability that could be implemented in every country and at once, the implementation of such an effective system adapted to the specificity of a country is necessary and constitutes the condition *sine qua non* of the economic security.

Bibliography

Arthuis, J. (2010), La création de la DGFiP: une réforme attendue, *Revue française des finances publiques,* Vol. 110.

Council Decision No 2003/487/EC of 3 June 2003 on the existence of an excessive deficit in France—application of Article 104(6) of the Treaty establishing the European Community (Official Journal of the European Union 3.7.2003, L 165/29).

Council Decision No 2005/183/EC of 5 July 2004 on the existence of an excessive deficit in Poland (Official Journal of the European Union of 9.3.2005, L 62/18).

Council Decision No 2007/154/EC of 30 January 2007 abrogating Decision 2003/487/EC on the existence of an excessive deficit in France (Official Journal of the European Union of 8.3.2007, L 68/3).

Council Decision No 2008/622/EC of 8 July 2008 abrogating Decision 2005/183/EC of on the existence of an excessive deficit in Poland (Official Journal of the European Union of 29.7.2008, L 200/22).

Council Decision No 2009/414/EC of 27 April 2009 on the existence of an excessive deficit in France (Official Journal of the European Union of 30.05.2009, L 135/19).

Council Decision No 2009/589/EC of 7 July 2009 on the existence of an excessive deficit in Poland (Official Journal of the European Union of 4.08.2009, L 202/46).

Décret n° 90-82 du 22 janvier 1990 relatif à l'évaluation des politiques publiques (Journal Officiel de la République Française n° 20 du 24 janvier 1990 page 952).

Fiscal Sustainability Report (2012), European Commission, *European Economy,* no 8/2012.

Konstytucja Rzeczypospolitej Polskiej z dnia 2 kwietnia 1997 r. (Dziennik Ustaw 1997 vol 78 item 483).

Kosikowski, C. (2011), Naprawa finansów publicznych w Polsce (przyczyny, metodologia, kierunki i propozycje), Białystok, Temida 2.

Loi constitutionnelle n° 2008-724 du 23 juillet 2008 de modernisation des institutions de la Ve République (Journal Officiel de la République Française n° 0171 du 24 juillet 2008 page 11890, texte n° 2).

Loi n° 2012-1558 du 31 décembre 2012 de programmation des finances publiques pour les années 2012 à 2017 (JORF n° 0001 du 1 janvier 2013 page 10, texte n° 2).

Loi n° 2013–1117 du 6 décembre 2013 relative à la lutte contre la fraude fiscale et la grande délinquance économique et financière (Journal Officiel de la République Française n° 0284 du 7 décembre 2013 page 19941, texte n° 4).

Loi organique n° 2001–692 du 1 août 2001 relative aux lois de finances (Journal Officiel de la République Française n° 177 du 2 août 2001 page 12480, texte n° 1).

Loi organique n° 2012–1403 du 17 décembre 2012 relative à la programmation et à la gouvernance des finances publiques (Journal Officiel de la République Française n° 0294 du 18 décembre 2012 page 19816, texte n° 1).

Loi organique n° 2013–1115 du 6 décembre 2013 relative au procureur de la République financier (Journal Officiel de la République Française n° 0284 du 7 décembre 2013 page 19939, texte n° 2).

Lotko, E. (2014), Wybrane aspekty państwowego długu publicznego w Polsce w świetle ostatnich zmian ustawy o finansach publicznych, [in:] Z. Ofiarski (editior), *XXV lat przeobrażeń w prawie finansowym i prawie podatkowym - ocena dokonań i wnioski na przyszłość,* Szczecin, Wydawnictwo: Uniwersytet Szczeciński Wydział Prawa i Administarcji.

Marini, P. (2011), Rapport d'information fait au nom de la commission des finances du Sénat sur les allègements de prélèvements obligatoires, May.

Migaud, D. (2008), Rapport d'information fait au nom de la Commission des finances, de l'économie général du plan sur les niches fiscales, July.

Migaud, D. (2010), Rapport du Conseil des prélèvements obligatoires, les entreprises et niches fiscales et sociales. Des dispositifs dérogatoires nombreux, October.

Ministerstwo Finansów. (2013), Strategia zarządzania długiem sektora finansów publicznych w latach 2014–2017, Warszawa.

Ministerstwo Finansów. (2014), Działania zwiększające stopień przestrzegania przepisów podatkowych i poprawiające efektywność administracji podatkowej w latach 2014–2017, Warszawa.

Owsiak, S. (eds.). (2008), *Planowanie budżetowe a alokacja zasobów*, Polskie Wydawnictwo Ekonomiczne. Warszawa.

Parini, P. (2010), *La Direction générale des finances publiques: une réforme emblématique, Revue française des finances publiques,* Vol. 110.

Perrotin, F. (2010), *Les niches fiscales et sociales des entreprises, Petites affiches*, Vol. 216.

Rada Ministrów (2014), *Wieloletni Plan Finansowy Państwa na lata 2014–2017*, Warszawa.

Report on Public finances in EMU (2013), European Commission, *European Economy*, no 4/2013.

Ruśkowski E. (2013), *Correct planning of budget revenueas an essential condition for securebusiness transactions*, [in:] K. Raczkowski and F. Schneider (eds.), *The Economic Security of Business Transactions Management in business*, Oxford, Chartridge Books Oxford.

Szpringer, Z. (2014), Recent developments in public finances in Poland, www.ec.europa.eu.

Tyniewicki, M. (2013), Commentary to Article 86 of Public Finance Act, [in:] E. Ruśkowski and J.M. Salachna (editors), *Finanse publiczne. Komentarz praktyczny*, Gdańsk, ODDK.

Ustawa z dnia 26 lipca 2013 r. o zmianie ustawy o finansach publicznych (Dziennik Ustaw 2013 item 938).

Ustawa z dnia 27 sierpnia 2009 r. o finansach publicznych, (Dziennik Ustaw 2009 vol 157 item 1240 with amendments).

Ustawa z dnia 8 listopada 2013 r. o zmianie ustawy o finansach publicznych oraz niektórych innych ustaw (Dziennik Ustaw 2013 item 1646).

Uzasadnienie do projektu ustawy z dnia 13 maja 2014 r., o zmianie ustawy o Służbie Celnej, ustawy o urzędach i izbach skarbowych oraz niektórych innych ustaw.

Zawadzka-Pąk, U.K. (2013), The latest changes in the French tax evasion policy and its influence on economic and financial security, [in:] K. Raczkowski and F. Schneider (eds.), *The Economic Security of Business Transactions Management in business*, Oxford, Chartridge Books Oxford.

Zawadzka-Pąk, U.K. (2014b), Polish Financial Law, Białystok, Temida 2 (in printing).

Zawadzka-Pąk, U.K., (2014a), Konstrukcja prawna, wdrażanie i realizacja budżetu zadaniowego we Francji i w Polsce, Kraków, edu-libri.

The paper was prepared as a part of the scientific project financed by the resources of the Polish National Science Centre granted by decision No DEC-2012/05/N/HS5/02527.

Izabela Andrzejewska-Czernek[1]

Interpreting European Union tax law: Practice of Polish tax authorities

Introduction

This paper presents how, in fact, the Polish tax authorities interpret EU tax law. This study shows a variety of approaches Polish tax authorities use to "cope" with EU law. These approaches are hereby categorized and supported by numerous examples. It is also examined whether the situation is evolving and in which direction the changes are going.

It should be noted that, despite Poland's decade-long membership of the EU, Polish tax authorities still show little respect for the supremacy of EC law. In general, not only is EU law not accepted as a source of law but it is frequently contradicted.

Over the past few years, the attitude of Polish tax authorities towards EU tax law has slightly changed. EU tax law is more often "used" (however, in my opinion, only "used" rather than "applied"). The Polish Ministry of Finance does not claim directly that EU law is not a source of law in Poland in binding tax rulings and other letters, which was common practice just a few years ago. Unfortunately, this change is merely superficial and binding rulings containing the correct interpretation of EU law are still rare.

It is worth noting that Polish tax authorities do not have a particularly negative image in comparison with tax authorities from other EU countries. Tax authorities in many member states have a similar attitude towards EU tax law.

At this point let me remind, that European Union tax law is a part of the domestic legal order in Poland. National tax authorities of the EU Member States are obliged to apply and interpret it [Brzezinski 2013, p. 185][2]. Interpretation of EU tax law is necessary when the scope of domestic law coincides with that of EU law. At that very moment, the tax authority is left to its own devices; it may not seek the assistance of the Court of Justice of the European Union (further: CJEU) or any other court or national authority.

---

1 Ph.D., Legal Counsel, email: izabelaandrz@poczta.onet.pl.

2 This obligation results from European Union tax law (in particular Art. 4 paragraph 3 tirets 3 and 4 of the Treaty on the European Union and Articles 288 tiret 3 of the Treaty on the Functioning of the European Union and, prior to 1 December 2009, from Article 10 and 249 tiret 3 of the Treaty Establishing the European Community).

Polish administrative courts[3] often make references to the obligation to apply EU law by tax authorities in their judgements. The following statement, contained within hundreds of judgements of district administrative courts and the Supreme Administrative Court, is particularly worth quoting: *"(...) application of Community law in tax matters is the responsibility not only of the administrative courts, but also the state authorities, i.e. the tax authorities. As indicated above, this is due to the fact that tax authorities have a duty to obey the law and act within its limits, which means also within the limits of the Community law"* [DAC Gliwice, 2011, SAC, 2009, A].

Why bother to mention these basic obvious issues? The analysis below of the "achievements" of the Polish tax authorities in the field of interpreting EU tax law should justify this lengthy introduction.

Scope of the study and research method

It should be emphasized that research possibilities as regards the activities of the Polish tax authorities are very limited.

The main obstacle is the nature of the proceedings before tax authorities; in particular the secrecy of tax proceedings (tax proceedings are not open to the public). For this reason, the question of how the Polish tax authorities interpret EU tax law is answered on the basis of the so-called binding rulings of the Minister of Finance ("MF") issued on request of taxpayers.

The Polish Minister of Finance supervises other national tax authorities. According to the Polish Tax Ordinance, the MF shall endeavour to ensure uniform application of tax law by tax authorities and tax inspection authorities, particularly by means of interpretation and taking into account the case law and judicial decisions of the Constitutional Court and the Court of Justice of the European Union [Dz. U. 2012, item 749, item 1054]. To fulfil this obligation, the MF issues a *"written interpretation of the provisions of tax law at the written application of an interested party in an individual case (individual interpretation)"*. The MF issues such interpretations in person (by issuing general binding tax rulings) or through authorised Directors of Tax Chambers (by issuing individual binding tax rulings) [Filipczyk, 2011]. All binding tax rulings must be published[4].

---

3 Supreme Administrative Court (Naczelny Sąd Administracyjny, SAC) and district administrative courts (*wojewódzkie sądy administracyjne*, DAC).

4 According to Art. 14i of the Tax Ordinance, general and individual tax rulings must be published without unnecessary delay in the Bulletin of Public Information.

One can expect that the standpoints expressed in binding tax rulings would be respected by subordinate tax authorities. Conclusions of such view should therefore be relevant with respect to all decisions of the Polish tax authorities.

The applied research method is based on empirical analysis of binding tax rulings published on the website of the MF[5], while focusing on most recent examples.

Interpretation of EU tax law – general remarks

Polish tax authorities present a diversified approach to EU law. Unfortunately, it seems that their attitude towards EU tax law depends mainly on the particular effects of its application in a specific case.

Taking into account such binding tax rulings upon issuance of which it was necessary to apply the provisions of EU law, one could distinguish several ways of "coping" with such a situation.

Approaches adopted by tax authorities include: (1) simply ignoring EU law, (2) interpreting EU law *contra legem*, (3) applying an extensive interpretation when not authorised to do so, (4) interpreting EU law ostensibly in the correct way and (5) interpreting it correctly.

Disregard of European Union tax law

Situation where EU tax law is not applied by Polish tax authorities despite the fact that it should be, is very common. In my opinion, although ignoring provisions of law can hardly be called "interpretation", this phenomenon needs to be addressed within this study. Frequent occurrences of such cases highlight the negative attitude towards EU legal solutions of the Polish tax authorities, especially when these solutions are favourable for taxpayers. It becomes apparent that, when the application of EU tax law is advantageous to Polish taxpayers, disregard of its provisions by the tax authorities becomes quite a widespread practice.

Tax authorities do not take into account EU legislation and CJEU jurisprudence even if Polish taxpayers cite the issue of EU law (or even lack of EU-compliance)

Unfortunately, there are often serious delays and rulings are published on different sub-sites of the website of the MF: http://www.finanse.mf.gov.pl/pl/strona-glowna. Most binding rulings of the MF are available on the database of the official website of the MF http://sip.mf.gov.pl/sip.

5 The basis of the binding tax rulings researched here covers the period from 2007 to the present.

directly within the application for issuance of a binding ruling. Answering such a reasonably justified written application, tax authorities issue their decision based solely upon the provisions of Polish law, frequently and obviously inconsistent with EU law. EU-law-based arguments of the taxpayer are ignored or put off with such a statement: *"(…) it should be noted that the provisions of the tax law in force in the European Union are applied in the Member States through implementation, i.e. transposition of EU legislation into domestic law. It should be noted that, although the Polish legislator has a duty to implement the provisions of law contained in the directives, binding the Member States as to the result to be achieved, the EU allows the national authorities the choice of form and methods of attaining that result."* [Director of the Warsaw Tax Chamber in 2009, A].

This is a common response to a series of arguments raised by the taxpayer proving, for instance, incompatibility of the provisions of Polish law with EU law. It is hard to guess what the benefits are of such a statement when it comes to the justification of a specific interpretation of tax law. In my opinion, this is merely a set of truisms without a logical connection to the line of reasoning.

The fact that EU legal acts are not treated as a source of Polish law is now and again directly indicated in binding rulings of the MF. In his letter dated November 1st 2009, the Director of the Warsaw Tax Chamber stated simply that *"(…) according to Article 14 b Section 1 of the Tax Ordinance of 29 August 1997, the tax authority issuing the individual a binding ruling interprets provisions of tax law, which, according to Article 3 Section 2, may be tax acts, double taxation agreements ratified by the Republic of Poland and other tax-related international treaties ratified by the Republic of Poland, as well as executive regulations issued on the basis of tax acts. Provisions of Community law are not a source of domestic law as long as their content is not transferred to the national legal act. Thus, provisions of EU law do not automatically become domestic law which the tax authority is obliged to apply."* [Director of the Tax Chamber in Warsaw, 2009, C]. In all these cases, EU law is completely disregarded.

Contra legem interpretation of EU tax law

Examples of an interpretation completely contrary to the wording (even in cases where there is no margin for misinterpretation) of a provision of EU law are also found in the practice of Polish tax authorities [Litwinczuk 2011, p. 355.]. Moreover, it even takes place when the correct interpretation has been indicated by the European Commission, as evidenced in the case concerning Council Directive of 27 October 2003 restructuring the Community framework for taxation of energy products and electricity [Excise Directive, O.J. EU L 283,

31 September 2003, p. 51–70]. The Director of the Warsaw Tax Chamber interpreted Article 21 sec. 5 of this Directive in his binding ruling [Director of the Warsaw Tax Chamber, 2008, A].

The provision reads as follows: *"For the purpose of applying Articles 5 and 6 of Directive 92/12/EEC, electricity and natural gas shall be subject to taxation and shall become chargeable at the time of supply by the distributor or redistributor. Where the delivery to consumption takes place in a Member State where the distributor or redistributor is not established, the tax of the Member States of delivery shall be chargeable to a company that has to be registered in the Member State of delivery".*

According to the related Article 6 paragraph 5 of the Polish Excise Duty Act: *"In case of electric energy the tax liability arises on the date of supply"* [Dz. U. 2004, N° 29, item 257].

Clearly, these provisions are inconsistent. The national legislation imposes an obligation to pay excise duty at the moment of release of the energy (by the supplier), while EU regulations require payment of excise duty only up on its delivery to the end user.

In this case, the applicant asked if it was correct to pay excise duty in the case that energy is delivered to the distributor, not the end user.

At the time this binding ruling was issued, it was already known that Poland had not implemented the Excise Directive on time and that proceedings against Poland in this respect had been brought before the European Commission.

According to the Polish tax authority, all these circumstances were no obstacle to applying the provision of Polish law in its standard meaning based on strict interpretation. After citing the Polish and EU regulations, the tax authority stated that: *"Directives do not specify all the issues raised here and should be further clarified and supplemented by the member States. Member States are obliged to implement the provisions of the directives to domestic law within the prescribed periods. Application of the directives is possible on condition that they are implemented into domestic law".*

This introduction, in which the tax authority presented its obviously wrong standpoint regarding the application of EU directives in Poland, is followed by promising statements such as: *"(...) there are some special circumstances in which the Directive can be applied directly. (...) It is therefore necessary to assess the regulation contained in Art.21. sec. 5 of the abovementioned directive, taking into account its purpose and result which the EU legislator intended by introducing this provision, and then to consider whether its introduction means at the same time that charging excise duty on other entities than those listed in this provision is therefore banned".*

From the content of the binding tax ruling it does not follow, however, that this provision of EU law has been examined in terms of the possibility of direct application as mentioned in the excerpt quoted above. The tax authority argued only that it does not matter if the electric energy is taxed at the moment of being issued by the producer or when received by the final consumer because, in simple terms, energy is not like a cord; it does not have a beginning or an end.

Further findings of the tax authority are even more interesting and hence worth quoting in all their glory: *"Article 21 sec. 5 of the abovementioned directive in its direct effect* [sic! – ed. author] *does not mean that entities other than distributors and redistributors indicated therein, cannot be taxed with excise duty and, moreover, that other entities, including electric energy producers, are entitled to a refund of the excise duty paid when a Member State has failed to implement Article 21 sec. 5 of the Directive 2003/96/EEG after the transitional period had expired and in so far as the distributors and redistributors are not charged with the excise duty"*.

Further arguments supporting this conclusion are so vague and unfounded that their citation here is superfluous. Finally, the tax authority claims: *"Article 21 sec. 5 of the Directive cannot become a tool to withdraw from application of a provision of domestic law in the form of Article 6 paragraph. 5 of the Polish Excise Duty Act. Application of the provision of domestic law cannot be excluded; hence it is not inconsistent with the provisions of the abovementioned Directive. That being so, it must be held that Article 21 sec. 5 of the Directive does not grant electric energy producers any right to refund of excise duty"*.

At the end of the ruling it was stated that the unfavourable case law of district administrative courts, relied upon by the taxpayer in their application, concerned specific cases embedded in specific facts and therefore cannot be considered generally binding. Such statements concerning case law in general (including CJEU case-law) are common for binding tax rulings issued before 2013 [Andrzejewska-Czernek, 2012, p. 282].

Consequently, the entity producing electric energy was unduly considered to be liable for payment of excise duty due to the sale of electric energy to the distributor. In this way the law was violated and the violation concerned substantive EU law as analysed above, as well as the pro-EU interpretation of the provisions of domestic law which, in turn, influenced the final outcome of the binding ruling [DAC in Gliwice, 2008].

When the act of law being the basis of the analysis in this binding ruling and extensive passages of which were quoted there is interpreted *contra legem*, it cannot be regarded as a mistake. It looks rather like a deliberate action; adapting the justification to the binding ruling to conclusions assumed in advance.

It is worth noting that the CJEU issued a judgment concerning this exact matter. The Court, in a simple manner, revealed the contradiction between provisions of Polish and EU law:

> *"(...) Article 21 sec. 5 first paragraph first sentence of the directive 2003/96 explicitly provides that for the purpose of applying Articles 5 and 6 of Directive 92/12/EEC, electricity and natural gas shall be subject to taxation and shall become chargeable at the time of supply to the distributor or redistributor. The text of Article 6 paragraph 5 of the Excise Duty Act does not define precisely, clearly and transparently the moment at which tax on electricity becomes chargeable in Poland as this provision of domestic law merely states that the tax obligation arises on the date of issuing electric energy. Furthermore, from both the court file and the explanations given by the Republic of Poland at the hearing it follows that this provision is applied in such a way that tax liability arises in that member state at the time of issuing the energy by the producer and not at the time of supply to the distributor or redistributor. It can be assumed that the Republic of Poland failed to adapt its electricity taxation system to the requirements of Article 21. sec. 5 of the Directive 2003/96 as regards determining the moment at which electricity tax becomes chargeable"* [CJEU, 2009, sec. 50–53].

After the CJEU issued this judgement, the approach of tax authorities to the problem of taxing energy has changed radically. However, Polish courts are still tackling with rulings and decisions issued earlier [SAC, 2014].

Extensive interpretation of the provisions of EU tax law

Examples of interpreting EU law extensively can be easily found in the database of MF binding rulings. This tactic was applied, for instance, in a number of rulings [Director of the Warsaw Tax Chamber 2007, A, 2008, B, 2009, B] concerning interpretation of Article 90 paragraphs 2–8 of the Tax on Goods and Services Act [Dz. U. 2004, No 54, item 535] and Article 173 of the VAT Directive [2006/112/EU, O.J. EU L 347, 11 December 2006].

In a binding ruling issued on 16 April 2009, the prohibition of deduction of input tax when the proportion referred to in Article 90 paragraph 2–8 of the VAT Act did not exceed 2% was considered [Director of Warsaw Tax Chamber, 2009, C].

According to Article 173 of the VAT Directive, in the case of goods or services used by a taxable person for both kinds of transactions, i.e.:1) for transactions in respect of which VAT is deductible (pursuant to Articles 168, 169 and 170) and 2) for transactions in respect of which VAT is not deductible, only such proportion of the VAT as is attributable to the former transactions shall be deductible. The deductible proportion shall be determined, in accordance with Articles 174 and 175, for all transactions carried out by this taxable person.

Section 2 of this Article concerns measures that can be taken by Member States in this respect. In Article 173 sec. 2 e) it is stated that Member States may provide that where the VAT which is not deductible by the taxable person is insignificant, it is to be treated as nil.

The Polish legislator took advantage of this opportunity. According to Article 90 paragraph 10, subparagraph 1 of the VAT Act, where the proportion specified in accordance with subparagraphs 2 to 8 exceeds 98 percent, the taxpayer shall enjoy the right to reduce the output tax amount by the total amount of input tax referred to in paragraph 2.

However, there is also a "symmetrical" converse solution, restricting the right to deduct input tax and thus incompatible with the VAT Directive and the whole idea of the VAT system. According to Article 90 paragraph 10, subparagraph 1, where the proportion specified in accordance with subparagraphs 2 to 8 does not exceed 2 per cent, the taxpayer shall not enjoy the right to reduce the output tax amount by the amount of input tax referred to in paragraph 2.

Again, Polish and EU tax law are incompatible. Analysis of binding rulings of the Polish MF leads to the conclusion, however, that these provisions are fully consistent.

In the binding ruling, the Polish tax authority announced: *"Legislation relating to the partial deduction contained in Article 90 of the Act is not inconsistent with the provisions of EU law. According to Article 173 of the Directive, Member States may provide that, where the VAT not deductible by the taxable person is insignificant, it is to be treated as nil. Consequently, the Polish legislator determined the proportion of 2% as insignificant and concluded that in such cases a taxpayer is not entitled to deduct".*

Furthermore, the tax administration explains: *"The provisions contained in Article 90 paragraph 10, subparagraphs 1 and 2 of the Act are essentially fiscally neutral because they justly allow output tax deduction when the determined proportion is 98 percent and prevent the deduction when the proportion is 2%".*

These few sentences are practically the entire discourse regarding the provisions of EU law in this ruling. It shows that the tax authority attributes a wider meaning to EU tax law than it really should do. Adoption of such an extended meaning of the provisions of EU tax law is not justified, especially when it was wrongly implemented.

The *seemingly* correct interpretation of EU law

Imposing VAT on free of charge disposal of business goods was one of the most talked about cases in which the Polish tax authorities have applied EU law. Such free of charge disposal of goods forming part of taxable person's business assets is called "fictitious supply" [Terra, Kajus 2004, p. 43] and is taxed to ensure that the taxable person (who withdraws the goods from his business) and the "ordinary" consumer (who buys goods) are treated equally. One should mention that the provisions of EU law in this respect were tricky and repeatedly subject to analysis by the CJEU [Andrzejewska-Czernek 2002, p. 82–92, CJEU, 1992, CJEU, 2001, CJEU, 2010][6].

This manner of interpretation is called "seemingly correct". It is because the whole process of interpretation of EU law was error-free and led, taking into account only EU law, to correct results. However, taking advantage of EU law by the Polish tax authorities was not allowed in this particular case. Tax authorities may not derive negative consequences for the taxpayer because of incorrect implementation of EU law. Quoting the opinion of the CJEU Advocate General: *"It follows from the terms used in the case law and indeed from the reading of it which has been provided in legal literature that the 'deuxpôles du rapport vertical caractéristique de l'effet direct des directives' (two poles of the vertical relationship characteristic of the direct effect of directives – see Simon, D., La directive européenne, Dalloz, 1997, p. 73) - consist, as I stated previously, in the existence, on the one hand, of a 'Member State' – or of one of its subdivisions or emanations – against which the provisions of a directive which has not been implemented, or has been improperly implemented, may be relied on and, on the other hand, of 'an individual', who alone is allowed to rely on such provisions, once the period set for implementation has expired"*. [Advocate General N. Wahl, 2013].

The following binding ruling issued in 2010 is a good example of this phenomenon [Director of the Warsaw Tax Chamber 2010, A]. In the ruling the tax authority:

a) analysed domestic law (the correctness and course of this analysis will not be commented on here);
b) stated that the results of interpretation of national legislation are ambiguous;
c) noted that EU tax law should be used in this case;
d) cited the relevant provisions of EU law;
e) noted that provisions of Polish and EU law are incompatible;
f) interpreted Polish law in accordance with EU law.

Only the last of these activities is, in a way, incorrect. The tax authority did not attempt to reflect EU law if it is entitled to apply it in this case particularly if

6 This assumption concerns, in particular, the previous version of the VAT directive (388/77/EC) and its Article 5 sec. 6.

it is entitled to take advantage of the pro-EU interpretation of domestic law. It stated simply that: *"Poland is obliged to interpret law in accordance with EU law since its accession to EU on 1st May 2004. Therefore, to keep pro-EU interpretation of national legislation where, as pointed out earlier, literal interpretation of the provisions of Article 7 paragraph 2 of the VAT Act raises doubts, the interpretation consistent with the objectives of the Directives shall be applied".* [Director of the Katowice Tax Chamber 2009, A, B, C, Director of the Bydgoszcz Tax Chamber 2009, A, Director of the Warsaw Tax Chamber 2009, E, Director of the Poznan Tax Chamber 2009, A, B, C].

Such a declaration is contained in many similar rulings despite there being just as numerous contrary judgements of the courts [Kiszka, 2011, p. 349].

The fully correct interpretation of EU tax law

Of course there are binding tax rulings in which the tax authorities applied *acquis communautaire* in a way that is beyond any dispute. Very often, however, such interpretation is due to a judgement being issued by the CJEU against Poland or many judgements of Polish administrative courts in which these courts expressed the opposite to that of the MF.

It happens that the tax authority applies EU tax law without any suggestion on its own initiative. Such application occurs, however, only when EU law does not affect the essence of the ruling. Despite the lack of "real" influence on binding rulings, such application of EU law deserves praise. In most cases mentioned, the tax authority not only recognized the need for EU tax law interpretation but also made a comparison of EU and Polish provisions of law proving the result of their compliance [Director of the Poznan Tax Chamber 2009, D, E].

An example of correct application of EU law by Polish tax authorities contains binding rulings of the Director of the Poznan Tax Chamber. At first, the Director issued a ruling (unfavourable to the taxpayer) without even mentioning EU tax law provisions even though the taxpayer pointed out the relevant provisions of EU law in his application [Director of the Poznan Tax Chamber, 2008, A]. The DAC in Wroclaw repealed this ruling because of procedural defects, also without mentioning EU tax law [DAC in Wroclaw, 2011]. In the following binding ruling, the tax authority referred to EU tax law and CJEU case law presenting an abbreviated analysis of the *acquis* in relation to the case settled [Director of the Poznan Tax Chamber, 2011, A].

Another example of a correct binding ruling which was only issued following a long dispute before the courts, are rulings issued by the Director of the

Bydgoszcz Tax Chamber. The first ruling in this case being incorrect and disadvantageous was issued on 23 January 2012 [Director of the Bydgoszcz Tax Chamber 2012, A]. After three judgements [DAC in Gdansk, 2012, SAC, 2013, B, DAC in Gdansk, 2013] another binding ruling was issued [Director of the Bydgoszcz Tax Chamber 2014, A]. It was correct and contained proper interpretation of Polish law referring also to case law of the CJEU. After several years of litigation, it turned out that the taxpayer was right.

A binding ruling in which EU tax law is correctly applied by the tax authority (without external influence from the courts) having a positive impact on the final outcome of a case being favourable for the taxpayer is very hard to find. It seems that the tax authorities have not accepted EU law as a source of law in Poland [Huchla 2010, p. 413–428, Teszner 2010, p. 429–439].

Does this situation evolve?

Analysis of the most recent binding rulings gives the impression of improvement. There may be illusion that tax authorities have evolved towards a more EC-friendly tax philosophy.

Indeed, the situation has changed and this can be viewed as an improvement. Tax authorities do not declare openly that EU law is not a source of law in Poland. They often refer to the provisions of EU law and CJEU case law in their binding rulings and other letters. In my view, however, this positive phenomenon is only superficial. Reasons underlying this improvement are very prosaic.

First of all, the Polish legislator has eliminated some flagrant inconsistencies between EU and Polish law. Another large portion of errors was excluded thanks to Polish and European Union courts and tribunals. This process is really time consuming, especially taking into account the attitude of Polish tax authorities towards case law of any court [Andrzejewska-Czernek, 2012, p. 282–304][7]. Certain areas of tax law are currently arranged in such a way that opportunity for abuse by tax authorities is limited. There are more cases of correct interpretation of EU tax law but mainly for reasons indicated above (i.e. forced by case law or if it does not affect the final outcome of the ruling) because the authorities refer to it at almost every opportunity. However, most importantly, tax authorities started to use EU law against taxpayers in a more disguised way.

A perfect example of such an approach is found in recent cases concerning the VAT rate on cookies [Director of the Warsaw Tax Chamber 2013, A]. According

---

7 Generally, tax authorities often dismiss case law issued in other cases than the case pending.

to the Polish legal acts concerning VAT, "fresh" cookies are taxed at reduced rate and "non-fresh" cookies at standard rate. A cookie is "fresh" when it has to be consumed within 45 days after it was manufactured (its expiry date is 45 days or less).

In a taxpayer's opinion as presented in the application for a binding ruling, differentiation of VAT rates on the basis of shelf life (expiry date) is contrary to the principle of fiscal neutrality. The taxpayer claimed that the expiry date did not affect in any way the fact that cookies with different expiration dates can be mutually similar and competitive (please note that the application was well founded with i.e. EU-law-based arguments).

In the binding ruling, the tax authority, after citing a few provisions of Polish law:

a) stated that the EU directive is a source of law in Poland,
b) discussed the conditions for direct application of the directives in Member States,
c) described and interpreted Article 98 of the VAT directive (containing basic provisions concerning reduced rates) comparing it with corresponding provisions of Polish law and thus affirming their full consistency,
d) defined the terms of the EU Combined Nomenclature[8] and Polish (PKWiU)[9],
e) concluded that the rates for food products may be varied, as EU law allows it,
f) claimed that exceptions (e.g. provisions relating to reduced rates) have to be interpreted strictly,
g) claimed that there is no absolute ban on the application of reduced rate, e.g. for all food products,
h) claimed that none of the provisions of the VAT Directive apply to the delimitation of the application of reduced VAT rates,
i) claimed that similar regulations to the Polish law are found in many EU countries,
j) emphasised the need for setting tax rates in tax acts (cited Article 217 of the Constitution of the Republic of Poland)
k) once again cited Polish provisions concerning VAT rates,
l) stressed the need to apply Polish PKWiU,
m) cited ECJ case law: C-94/09, p. 25, 26 and 28 and C-384/01,
n) recalled several opinions of the Advocate General,

---

8 See: http://ec.europa.eu/taxation_customs/customs/customs_duties/tariff_aspects/combined_nomenclature/index_en.htm.

9 PKWiU – Polska Klasyfikacja Wyrobów i Usług – Polish Classification of Goods and Services, see: http://old.stat.gov.pl/gus/5840_2930_ENG_HTML.htm.

o) stated that cookies with an expiry date shorter than 45 days are different from cookies with longer expiry dates; the difference between these two kinds of cookies is easy to confirm. That is why the principle of neutrality and competition, as well as provisions of EU law, has not been violated.

As you can see, the ruling contains numerous arguments connected with EU law and CJEU case law. In fact, however, in the "cookie" ruling, EU law was completely ignored (leaving aside the lack of logical connections between some of the arguments). CJEU case law and the opinions of the Advocate General cited in the case were not applicable. Such an understanding of EU and Polish law has been criticised by, for example, the Polish Supreme Administrative Court [SAC 2013, A]. There are many further examples of EU tax law interpretation of this kind [Director of the Katowice Tax Chamber 2013 A, 2014].

Conclusions

Polish tax authorities do not consider EU law as a source of law in Poland. Rather it is a tool which is used only in specific cases and in a specific way. In fact, EU law is abused by tax authorities in many different ways. It is hard to qualify all such actions as *"methods of interpretation of EU tax law"*. Some authors seem to downplay this important, negative phenomenon [Bartosiewicz, 2009, p. 253–255].

Of course, isolated cases of rulings in which tax authorities have interpreted EU law correctly can be identified. In some situations, EU tax law is applied. In others it is forgotten. Worse, if the tax authorities issue erroneous interpretations in a specific kind of case, changing its approach to this specific problem can take years[10].

There are no visible signs that this situation will change in the near future. Looking at this problem from a wider perspective, there begs another question: is the Polish tax authorities' attitude towards EU tax law reflected in the overall relationships between taxpayers and tax authorities in Poland? Interesting remarks on this problem have been made by the Polish Supreme Audit Office after recent audits concerning respecting taxpayers' rights by tax offices or tax chambers in Poland [Supreme Audit Office data, 2014]. The Supreme Audit Office noticed an increasing number and, simultaneously, poor quality of binding tax rulings. The reason for this lies mainly, in the opinion of this body, in the

10 Requiring involvement of the courts of both instances and, from time to time, the CJEU.

vagueness and lack of EU compliance of Polish law. I cannot fully agree; this issue calls for further investigation.

All in all, it is also worth noting that Polish tax authorities do not have a particularly negative image when compared with tax authorities in other EU countries. Research has proven that all member states are reluctant (in the case of at least one authority) to implement ECJ rulings [Brokelind 2007, p. 13]. Problems similar to those experienced in Poland exist in many EU Member States, for example, in:

1. Finland: *"Finnish tax authorities show however a great reluctance to draw conclusions from the ECJ case law. They do not apply Community law on their own motion, and rather tend to protect the fisc's interest."* [Brokelind 2007, p. 18],
2. Scandinavian countries: *"(...) it seems to be quite common, that the tax authorities do not try to supplement the failure of the legislator to implement Community law. The conflicts seem to come quite to the judge's docket, to settle the issue on the basis of Community law."* [Brokelind 2007, p. 20],
3. Germany: *"The problem of EC law in German direct tax law practice lies somewhere else, and that is the general attitude on the part of the legislature and the tax authorities. It may even be said, that this attitude ranges from sheer ignorance or mere indifference to (sometimes rather even aggressive) countermeasures and there are no visible signs that this situation will change in the near future."* [Cordewener, Brokelind 2007, p. 155].

Bibliography

Andrzejewska-Czernek I. (2002), *Opodatkowanie prywatnego użytku towarów w świetle przepisów VI Dyrektywy VAT*, Kwartalnik Prawa Podatkowego, No ¾.

Andrzejewska-Czernek I. (2012), *Wykładnia prawa podatkowego Unii Europejskiej*, Wolters Kluwer, Warsaw.

Brzezinski B. (2013), *Wykładnia prawa podatkowego*, ODDK, Gdansk.

Bartosiewicz A. (2009), *Efektywność prawa wspólnotowego w Polsce na przykładzie VAT*, Oficyna Wolters Kluwer Polska, Warsaw.

Brokelind C. (2007), *Towards a Homogeneous EC Direct Tax Law: An Assessment of the Member States' Responses to the ECJ's Case Law*, IBFD, Amsterdam.

Filipczyk H. (2011), *Indywidualne interpretacje prawa podatkowego – prawo i praktyka*, Oficyna Prawa Polskiego, Warsaw.

Huchla A. (2011), *Prawo podatkowe Unii Europejskiej w interpretacjach Ministra Finansów*, in: Litwińczuk H. (ed.), *Prawo europejskie – 5 lat doświadczeń w polskim prawie finansowym*, Chairs and Institutes of Financial and Tax Law Congress publication, Warsaw.

Kiszka J. (2011), *Wykładnia prowspólnotowa jako element interakcji prawa krajowego ze wspólnotowym i jej obecność w procesie sądowego stosowania polskich regulacji podatków pośrednich* [in:] Litwińczuk H. (ed.), *Prawo europejskie - 5 lat doświadczeń w polskim prawie finansowym*, Chairs and Institutes of Financial and Tax Law Congress publication, Warsaw.

Terra B., Kajus J. (2004), *A Guide to the European VAT Directives. Commentary on the Value Added Tax of the European Community*, IBFD, Amsterdam.

Teszner K. (2011), *Wykładnia prowspólnotowa w interpretacjach przepisów prawa podatkowego dokonywanych przez krajową administrację podatkową* [in:] Litwińczuk H. (ed.), *Prawo europejskie - 5 lat doświadczeń w polskim prawie finansowym*, Chairs and Institutes of Financial and Tax Law Congress publication, Warsaw.

Przestrzeganie praw podatników przez wybrane urzędy skarbowe i izby skarbowe (2014) [Information of the Supreme Audit Office 2014] of June 3rd, 2014, Najwyższa Izba Kontroli, Warszawa, http://www.nik.gov.pl/plik/id,6783,vp,8611.pdf.

Judgement of 6 May 1992, Pieter de Jong v Staatssecretaris van Financiën, case C-20/91.

Judgement of 17 May 2001, Finanzamt Burgdorf v Hans-Georg Fischer and Finanzamt Düsseldorf-Mettmann v Klaus Brandenstein, joined cases C-322/99 and C-323/99.

Judgement of 12 February 2009, Commission v Republic of Poland, Case C-475/07.

Judgement of 30 September 2010, EMI Group Ltd v The Commissioners for Her Majesty's Revenue and Customs, case C-581/08.

Judgement of SAC, April 2, 2009, I FSK 4/08.

Judgment of SAC of 28 January 2013, No I FSK 697/12 [A].

Judgement of SAC of 23 July 2013, IFSK1396/12 [B].

Judgement of SAC of 13 May 2014, I FSK 884/13.

Judgement of DAC in Gliwice August 29, 2008, III SA/Gl 105/08.

Judgement of DAC in Wroclaw, January 19, 2011 r., l SA/Po 866/10.

Judgement of DAC in Gliwice, March 11, 2011, III SA/Gl 2688/10.

Judgement of DAC in Gdansk of 3 July 2012 r., I SA/Gd 473/12.

Judgement of DAC in Gdansk of 14 November 2013, I SA/Gd 1249/13.

Binding ruling of 5 December 2007 issued by Director of the Warsaw Tax Chamber, No IPPP1-443-334/07-7/AB, [A].

Binding ruling of 17 March 2008, issued by Director of the Warsaw Tax Chamber, No IPPP1-443-21/08-5/JF, [B].

Binding ruling from 21 October 2008, issued by Director of the Warsaw Tax Chamber, No IPPP1/443-1416/08-2/GD [A].

Binding ruling from January 26th, 2009, issued by Director of Warsaw Tax Chamber, No IPPP1-443-2018/08-2/JL [A].

Binding ruling of 10 February 2009 issued by Director of the Warsaw Tax Chamber, No IPPP1-443-2116/08-2/JB, [E].

Binding ruling of 16 April 2009 issued by Director of the Warsaw Tax Chamber, No IPPP1/443-78/09-3/IG, [B].

Binding ruling of 1 November 2009, issued by Director of the Warsaw Tax Chamber, No IPPB2/436–307/09–4/MZ, [C].

Binding ruling of 11 January 2010 issued by Director of the Warsaw Tax Chamber, No IPPP1-443-1099/09-4/MP [D].

Binding ruling of 14 June 2013 issued by Director of the Warsaw Tax Chamber, No IPPP2/443-341/13-2/DG, [A].

Binding ruling of 18 March 2009 issued by Director of the Katowice Tax Chamber, No IBPP2/443-5/09/ASz, [C].

Binding ruling of 15 April 2009 issued by Director of the Katowice Tax Chamber, No IBPP2/443-63/09/ASz [B].

Binding ruling of 15 May 2009 issued by Director of the Katowice Tax Chamber, No IBPP2/443-206/09/RSz [A].

Binding ruling of 22 November 2013 issued by Director of the Katowice Tax Chamber, No IBPP2/443-776/13/KO, [A].

Binding ruling of 10 April 2014, issued by Director of the Katowice Tax Chamber, No IBPP1/443-1230/13/MS.

Binding ruling of 23 January 2012 issued by Director of the Bydgoszcz Tax Chamber, No ITPP1/443-1464/11/TS [A].

Binding ruling of 20 February 2009 issued by Director of the Bydgoszcz Tax Chamber, No ITPP1/443-1077/08/KM [A].

Binding ruling of 27 March 2014, issued by Director of the Bydgoszcz Tax Chamber, No ITPP1/443-1464/11/14-S/BS [A].

Binding ruling of 14 October 2008 issued by Director of the Poznan Tax Chamber, No ILPP2/443-650/08-2/MR [A].

Binding ruling of 14 January 2009 issued by Director of the Poznan Tax Chamber, No ILPP2/443-980/08-2/EN [C].

Binding ruling of 9 February 2009 issued by Director of the Poznan Tax Chamber, No ILPP2/443-1073/08-3/EWW [A].

Binding ruling of 9 February 2009 issued by Director of the Poznan Tax Chamber No ILPP2/443-1073/08-2/EWW [B].

Binding rulings of 18 September 2009 issued by Director of the Poznan Tax Chamber, No ILPP2/443-844/09-2/EWW [D].

Binding ruling of 18 September 2009 issued by Director of the Poznan Tax Chamber, No ILPP2/443-844/09-3/EWW [E].

Binding ruling of 28 June 2011 issued by Director of the Poznan Tax Chamber, No ILPP2/443-650/08/11-S/MR [A].

Ustawa z dnia 29 sierpnia 1997 r. Ordynacja podatkowa, Tax Ordinance, Journal of Laws 2012, item 749, as amended.

Ustawa z dnia 23 stycznia 2004 o podatku akcyzowym, Excise Duty Act of 23 January 2004, Journal of Laws 2004, No 29, item 257, as amended.

Ustawa z 11 marca 2004 r. o podatku od towarów i usług, VAT Act, Journal of Laws 2004, No 54, item 535, as amended.

Council Directive 2003/96/EC of 27 October 2003 restructuring the Community framework for the taxation of energy products and electricity, O.J. EU L 283, 31 September 2003.

Council Directive 2006/112/EC of 28 November 2006 on the common system of Value Added Tax O.J. EU L 347, 11 December 2006.

Elżbieta Klamut[1]

Tax management in small business entities – Poland case study

'Views of the government over the economy can be summarized shortly: if it is alive, impose a tax on it. If it is still well, regulate it. If it stops working, introduce subsidies'

– Ronald Reagan

Introduction

Any entrepreneur, even the most honest, tries to reduce the size of burdens on their business activity. Comparing the loads from a few years before with the current ones, one can discover they are not as high as 10 to 15 years ago. They were declining each year leading to a faster development of small business activities, thus, to stimulate the economic growth.

Stimulating the economy is followed, among others, by reducing tax burdens. The aim is to achieve greater savings, which are converted into investments, which, in turn, increase production and consumption. The phrase: 'sly loses twice' has proved to be true on recent introduction of the increase in excise tax or the earlier increase in VAT tax by 1% (carried out by the government). Budget revenues from VAT tax have decreased. Excessive encumbrances do not favour budget revenues or investments; therefore, according to the rules of the Laffer curve too high taxes cause decreasing budget revenues.

In Poland almost every citizen holds a widespread belief that you must avoid paying even 'the proverbial buck.' Taxpayers use all sorts of ways to optimise tax burdens. Some of them remain consistent with the law while others are contrary to it. These types of activities undertaken include, among others, tax avoidance, evading tax law and tax evasion as well as tax savings.

Optimisation performed by enterpreneurs means either using the existing loopholes in tax law and opportunities created by law makers or illegal activities like fraud or extortion. Can small businesses optimise their tax burdens?

1 Ph.D., Institute of Economics, University of Social Sciences (Poland), emai: eklamut@spoleczna.pl.

Tax system and budget

In general, there are three key acts on the tax law in Poland. Personal Income Tax Act of 26 July 1991, Corporate Income Tax Act of 15 February 1992 and Goods and Services Tax Act of 11 March 2004. Certainly, there are others like Excise Tax Act, Property Tax Act and Agricultural Tax Act as well as many others, but the importance of these taxes for public finances is much smaller, perhaps with the exception of the excise tax.

The greatest income to the public finances is generated on the goods and services tax which flows directly to the state budget (120. 832,0 m PLN in 2011, 120. 000, 07 m PLN in 2012 and 114. 715, 6 m PLN in 2013). Second biggest income generates the excise tax (57. 963,7 m PLN, 60. 449,9 m and 60. 653,1 m respectively). Income taxes are a slighlty smaller share of the state budget (table 1) but they hold the 3rd and 4th position after VAT tax and excise tax accordingly. [Budget receipts, folder: 2011, 2012, 2013].

Table 1: Share of revenue from income tax in total revenues (in million PLN)

Specification	2011	2012	2013
CIT revenue	24.861,9	25.145,7	23.075,3
in relation to total revenues	11,67%	10,13%	8,27%
PIT revenue	38.074,9	39.809,4	45.298,1
in relation to total revenues	17,86%	16,03%	16,23%

Source: own analysis based on data from the Ministry of Finance [Budget receipts, folder: 2011, 2012, 2013].

Comparing revenues from income tax in the years 2001 to 2003 [Gołębiowski 2004, p. 8], in relation to the income of the budget they have a similar share with relation to personal income tax (2001 – 16.7%, 2002 – 17.8 %, 2003 – 19.9%) and corporate income tax (9.4%, 10.6%, 9.3% respectively). While personal income tax revenues have decreased slightly, the corporate income tax downward trend in the examined period is a continuous process. Despite the reduction in tax rates, tax revenues are high at almost the same level as in the years 2001 to 2003.

Income tax revenues grow from year to year despite the fact that companies use illegal ways to minimize the tax burdens. Regrettably, one cannot say that about the revenues from VAT tax, since in this case the value of VAT fraud has been rising year by year (chart 1). In recent years, tax services and law enforcement authorities have revealed increasingly newer dealings of VAT tax extortion.

Chart 1: Value of disclosed false invoices (in billion PLN)

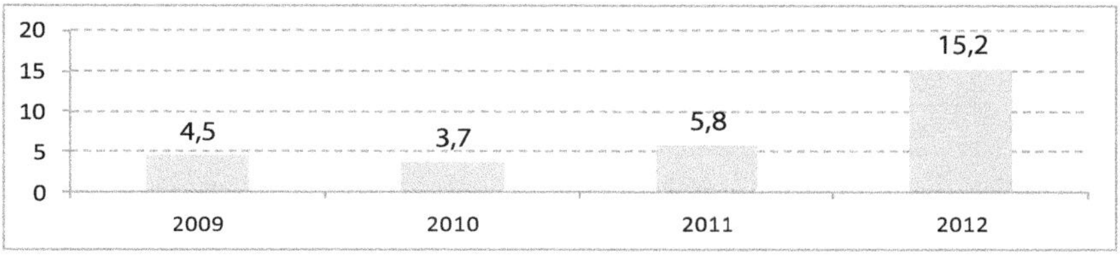

Source: 'Gazeta Prawna' of 29 Jan 2013 in: 'False invoices flood the market. State and honest taxpayers loose.'

Such factors as: excessive fiscal policy [Sokolowski 1994, p. 143] complicated tax system, poor economic situation of the country after 2007, double taxation of certain income and presence of gaps in tax law, non-complying with the principles of equality of taxation by the law makers and finally negligible legal awareness as well as the low level of business ethics are the main reasons for minimizing the tax burden, especially with illegal means. Looking at the amount of fraud in individual provinces the impression is that either there are regions in which particular business units specialized in illegal tax optimization operate on large-scale or only in those regions tax authorities work smoothly (table 2).

Table 2: Value of disclosed false invoices in 2012

No.	Province	Value of extortion (million PLN)
1.	Dolnośląskie	1 397
2.	Kujawsko-pomorskie	1 792
3.	Lubelskie	3 247
4.	Lubuskie	114
5.	Łódzkie	187
6.	Mazowieckie	2 681
7.	Małopolskie	388
8.	Opolskie	35
9.	Śląskie	1 882
10.	Świętokrzyskie	150
11.	Podkarpackie	267
12.	Podlaskie	223
13.	Pomorskie	1 649

No.	Province	Value of extortion (million PLN)
14.	Warmińsko -mazurskie	413
15.	Wielkopolskie	485
16.	Zachodnio -pomorskie	306

Source: Gazeta Prawna, z dn. 29.01. 2013, '*False invoices flood the market. State and honest taxpayers loose.*'

To sum up, high tax burdens do not favour budget revenues, as well as savings and investments.

Tax optimization in theory

There is no such term as tax optimization defined in the provisions of tax law. Practitioners who try to find ways of reducing tax burdens affecting business activity have coined it.

Tax optimization is: "the choice of lawful means to achieve particular economic result assuming minimization of accompanying tax encumbrances" [Kudert, Jamroży, p. 58, 2013].

Optimization is often referred to as a suitable choice to accomplish a specific economic purpose through minimizing the tax encumbrance. It is therefore a process of such activities that will lead to a pre-established effect, which will be achieved through analyzing possible variants of a solution bringing it to a planned purpose. The effect of such actions is maximized profit and tax burden minimized to the highest degree.

Any entrepreneur seeks maximizing profits, and as a result, financial resources, as minimizing tax burdens means reducing the outflow of funds from the company. Many tax advisers argue that tax optimization is possible to use, due to the fact, that the rules on legally permissible possibilities of economic turnover are established separately for each of the forms of that turnover. The Civil Code, in turn, [Dz.U. z 2014, poz.121. art.3531] allows taxpayers to use any legal relationships and choose appropriate solutions in the relations of private law, which enable the reduction of tax burden.

Should we equate optimization with the tax evasion or rather the tax avoidance? Looking at the definition of optimization it can be regarded as being the same, but with one exception: optimization uses only legal solutions to minimize the burdens. Somewhere between the optimization and the tax evasion we would settle the tax avoidance. It means measures to reduce the tax burden that are not activities prohibited by law, but at the same time they are not by the law indicated for application.

Evading payment of taxes means that the taxpayer exercises some activities that cause failure to pay or reduce the tax burden, and which do not comply with the applicable law[2]. Such activities cause the taxpayer to expose himself intentionally to the consequences of his decisions. Any illegal activities are covered by the sanctions set forth in both legal statutes, as well as the Fiscal Penal Code [Dz.U. z 2013, poz.186].

In economic reality the actions of taxpayers are often not possible to ambiguously assign to one of these categories, but in such cases the tax authorities always try to apply or interpret the act in favor of the state budget. Tax evasion is usually considered illegal and unethical and is generally regarded as a tax fraud.

The reasons for the tax evasion are due to moral (high taxes suggest the sense of injustice, nonpayment is not something reprehensible, a sense of satisfaction on carrying out an effective fraud), economic (problems with liquidity) or technical (the complexity of the tax system, complicated and unclear provisions of the tax law).

Tax avoidance suggests such activities of the taxpayer where he attempts to take legal tax avoidance or its reduction through the use of dissimilarity effects of business operations, while maintaining the same economic and legal effect[3].

The literature [Gaudement, Molinier 2000, p. 585] sometimes mentions saving taxes (tax savings), which consists in lowering the tax burden, but one that is generally neutral from the perspective of the tax law. This means not performing any activities, which give rise to the necessity of paying the tax. Such events are rare in the economic reality, as they would mean the abandonment of any activities of the business entities and this stands contrary to the essence of the freedom of economic activity.

Optimization is being widely discussed. Some narrow the understanding of tax avoidance arguing this is an indirect tax law infringement, while others argue this is an illegal circumvention of that law. In business there is a significant number of situations (operations) not prohibited, then permissible, but not desired by the law makers, who are trying to introduce legal instruments which prevent exercising the abovementioned. Loopholes in the law are a common phenomenon in Polish legislation, so their use is considered a legal action.

The problem of ambiguity of provisions and their interpretation and even the lack of uniform code of conduct of the tax authorities must also be added to

2 compare: Iniewski R., Nikończyk 2011, p. 16, Głuchowski 2005, p. 150.
3 compare: Munnich M., Zdudenk A., 2012, p. 35, A. Gomułowicz, J. Małecki 2004, p. 251.

these deliberations. The lack of clarity and difficulty in interpretation are caused by the fact that certain concepts are defined differently in both the tax law and the civil law. One should also take a closer look at judicial decisions on tax optimization, and as matter of fact, the circumvention of the law.

Many publications [Kudert, Jamroży 2007, pp. 18–21; Głuchowski, 2005 p. 146; Iniewski, Nikończyk, 2011, pp. 14–16] mention two streams of ideas for optimizing taxes by taxpayers:
unacceptable conduct which is treated as a circumvention of the tax law and which exploits the fact that the action consistent with law and the the one circumventing it are not strictly defined and can be interpreted differently,
proceedings, which does not affect the tax liability, but is a free exercise of the right to optimize the tax burden.

The case law of the Supreme Administrative Court of 18 November 2009 (file No I FSK 1135 to 1108), so refers to the foregoing: "In the case of tax law, the circumvention of the law (containing the concept of "abuse of rights") is associated with the abuse of the civil law structures, where application leads to the realization of facts from which the tax law does not bind any obligation. In other words, the circumvention of law exists if the conduct (of a person) is going to a specific, different than typical, formation of legal relationships arising from the provisions of law, in order to achieve beneficial result of a legal case which, under the tax law, in effect, causes the obliged to avoid paying a due tax or reduce the amount of it[4]. The term "circumvention of the law" occurs in several provisions of generally applicable law. The most fundamental is the Article 58 paragraph 1 of the Civil Code, which sets forth that an action contrary to the law or intended to circumvent the law shall be deemed null and void, unless the relevant provision provides for a different result, in particular, thet ineffective provisions of a legal action are replaced by the relevant provicions of the Act" (file No I FSK 1135 to 1108).

The Judgment of the Supreme Administrative Court of 12 November 2010 (ref. II FSK 955/10) takes it slighlty differently in this regard: 'using a legally acceptable solution by the taxpayer, which is not only aimed at achieving an economic goal, but also contributes to the reduction of a potential amount of a tax liability must not be interpreted by the tax authorities as the circumvention of tax law, which should rather be sanctioned by the provincial administrative courts. In the situation when a legal action serves solely to avoid being liable for obligations under the public law, it shall be assumed that it is the circumvention of tax law.

4 Compare: Stanik K.J. Winiarski K. *Practical porblems of fraud and circumvention of ax law* (Unimex, Publishing Office Wrocław, 2009 pp. 18–20).

The influence of tax liablities on activity of business entities

In Poland, the Small and Medium - Sized Companies (MSP) sector comprises more than 4 million businesses with about 1.8 million economically active. The vast majority are micro-businesses operating on a business of a person or its partnerships on the basis of the Civil Code, or in the form of a company based on the Code of Commercial Cmpanies. These units account most commonly on the basis of the personal income tax or flat tax (table 3).

Table 3: Structure of Small and Medium-Sized Companies (MSP) including form of taxation.

Form of record	Type of business entitiy			
	Total	micro	Small	medium-sized
Number of active entities.	1 791 742	1 719 187	57 071	15 484
Tax card	84 581	84 281	-	-
Lum sum of recorded revenues	337 648	337 639	9	-
Register of Revenues and Expenses	1 195 181	1 174 609	20 236	336
Accounting records	174 332	122 358	36 826	15 148

Source: own analysis based on: [Płatek 2014, p. 49].

Taxation on general principles gives the taxpayer the opportunity to optimize the tax burden by allowing a settlement with a spouse as well as the use of various types of tax allowances and deductions. However, in the case of lack of deductions the high-income entrepreneurs who want to reduce the amount of tax burdens choose the flat tax. Such possibility helps optimize the amount of levies paid to the State in particular years of activity; this is not possible in the continuing fiscal year. Encumbring a high-income business activity wtih a progressive tax[5] (at low tax-deduxtible costs and lack of deductions and allowances) is not effective in this case thus a flat tax seems a better solution.

Simplified forms of taxation (tax card, lump sum of recorded revenues) have their limitations, depending on type and size of activity and lack of deductions, but they remain a popular choice for those business activities that generate low costs.

5 Rate of income tax for revenues up to 85.000 PLN at 18%; for revenues over that sum at 32%; flat tax rate at 19%. Insurance contributions are deductible.

Recent studies indicate that simplified forms of business activity register are used by over 95% of the entrepreneurs of the SM-SC (MSP) sector and only less than 5% is bound to complete full business activity register in the form of keeping accounting records (chart 2).

Chart 2: Forms of taxation choden by taxpayers in 2012

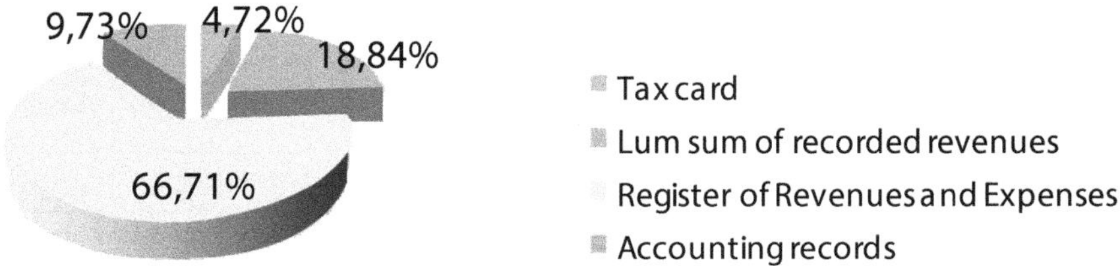

Source: own analysis based on: [Płatek 2014, p. 49].

Lowering tax rates for small business entities is a necessity. In most cases, the source of funding for these units are mainly own funds or loans from the family. Lenders are reluctant to provide loans to small size business entities. Additionaly, loan interest rates remain high, hence the need to retain the highest possible profit in the company in order to save for future development.

Table 4: Simplified forms of taxation – advantages and drawbacks

Form of taxation	Advantages	Drawbacks
Tax card	• fixed tax not dependent upon revenue, • no obligation to keep records, • no obligation to submit monthly settlement with tax calculation, • health insurance contribution tax-deductible,	• necessity to pay tax to the tax office even if no revenue earned, • obeying limit of employment, • other limitation e.g. one vehicle in transport services, • no deductions, • no possibility of tax settlement with a spouse,
Lump sum of recorded revenues	• small number of documents and records, • possibility to pay quarterly advance tax, • amount of tax dependent upon revenue, • insurance contributions deductible,	• no costs deduction, • no possibility of tax settlement with a spouse, • obligation to draw up a register

Form of taxation	Advantages	Drawbacks
Register of revenues and expenses - tax scale	• costs deductibe, • insurance contributions deductible, • possibility of tax settlement with a spouse, • allowances • tax loss deductible, • simplified form of advace tax	• large number of documents and records • complicated rules of keeping records, • tax burden higher at higher income - rate at 32%,
Register of revenues and expenses - flat tax	• one tax rate not dependent upon income - 19%, • insurance contributions deductible, • simplified form of advace tax, • tax loss deductible,	• no tax-free amount, • no possibility of tax settlement with a spouse, • no allowances and deductions,

Source: *Advantages and drawbacks of particular forms of taxation*, [podatek dochodowy.pl] (12.05.2014).

There is a large group of familiy-run companies among the SM-SC (MSP) sector which are focused on a long-term, multigenerational activity. They are reluctant to using any external sources of financing not wishing to expose themselves to a liquidity losing risk and, eventually, a bankruptcy. For these companies every penny saved is worth its weight in gold, hence the necessity to sysytematically minimize the tax burdens.

Tax management in different business entities

In the era of an increasing competition and the fight for customer, all aspects of business activity are crucial, including savings made on reduction of the tax burdens. Activities aimed at controlling these burdens are one of the symptoms of particular strategies and policies related to the optimization of these public law encumbrances.

Tax management means both planning for the tax burdens throughout the life cycle of a business entity and the tax optimization. It is about taking up such activities which are designed not only to minimize the burdens, but also to reduce the tax risk. These activities should be the entrepreneur's conscious and consistent performance. To sum up the foregoing, tax management means taking such activities that lead to ensure an adequate (correct) implementation of both tax and reporting duties [Ostaszewski, 2007, p. 56]. These activities must take into account the objectives of the company, such as the reputation, the continuation of functioning and the maximum reduction of taxation.

Tax management objectives are: seeking solutions to minimize the tax burdens as well as eliminating or minimizing the tax risk [Kunowska 2002, p. 64]. It is also a term specifying the business risks related to taxation by analyzing all the burdens of a business activity, in particular, fiscal and tax related ones.

In many countries, the optimization is treated as a normal activity both for the individuals and with business operations. Literature provides different types of taxpayers' reactions to the tax burden:
obedient paying taxes - in fear of the consequences, due to beliefs or a show,
escaping from taxes – tax avoidance (within the law) or tax evasion (violating the law)
developing tax strategies - planning tax burdens throughout the entire life cycle of an individual.

Tax strategies are a way of doing business that allows you to optimize the tax burden related to its performance. Thanks to applying certain tax strategies, companies can take advantage of the possibilities lying in the legal forms of an organisation, tax preferences, locations and fields of activity, tax havens, an appropriate costs or income management etc. Moreover, it is the means of reducing tax risk.

Every company should develop a strategy model aimed at the maximum legal reduction of taxes paid, which not only can provide the individuals a survival in crisis times but also allow a development. Maintaining tax strategies is the domain of business entities of an appropriate size and organizational capital, in fact, the majority of companies [Szymanski 2009, p. 8].

Larger companies, which want to apply the legal strategies for lowering taxes, including the income tax, have three types of concepts: the strategy of a tax capital group, the leasing strategy, the strategy with the use of a capital group.

Applying the strategy of a tax capital group involves cooperation of several legally independent entities with the aim of such 'manoeuvering' income and losses in order to avoid any liability to pay the corporate income tax. The entities within the group are taxed separately but with the use of a 'rollover of income' method, they can control the amount of the tax burden.

This solution means that the group is treated as a taxable entity and the object of taxation is the total income of the group. This means that the tax base is the excess of the total revenues of the companies of the capital group over the total costs of all the companies, i.e. the losses of some companies are deducted from the income of others. This optimization is effective when even one of the companies generate losses.

Yet, this does not function for small business entities and the vast majority of the SM-SC (MSP) sector entities are partnerships. The form of taxation that applies to them is the personal income tax. Small business entities may choose among different forms of taxation, depending on the type of business, its size, the principles of accounting, the applicability of deductions, allowances, etc.(table 5)

Table 5: Tax strategies

No.	Type of strategy	Aim
1	Cost strategy	Overvaluing tax-deductible costs to minimize taxable income
2	Income strategy	Controlling income to minimize tax burden
3	Strategies of preferences and tax exemptions	Using allowances and tax preferences
4	Domestic/foreign strategies	Using allowances and tax preferences while seeking residence for the business entity mainly to avoid double taxation. Applying international agreements
5	Strategy of legal status/ choosing form of taxation	Making use of differences between PIT and CIT
6	Strategy of legal status	Establishing tax capital group
7	Strategy of change of business type	Making use of object of a business activity to obtain preferences
8	Political/scenario strategies	Lobbying political decision-makers for construction of taxes.
9	Strategy in direct taxes bezpośrednich	Using VAT cash method and quarterly settlement to defer tax liability

Source: Walicka M. in: *Tax optimization in business activity of small entities*, Scientific Books Szczecin University, no. 708, 2012).

Is it then reasonable to talk about tax management in such small business entities? Certainly, it is. Even small entities can plan the volume of the tax burden, but only few of them do so. What is extremely important in the process of tax management is, of course, tax planning, which can be defined as the anticipation and consideration of the effects of continuous efforts to minimize the tax burden. That planning is an element of a wider financial planning including such its components as: income, expenses, etc. In the course of aforementioned process, one should also take into acount the liquidity of an entity.

Unfortunately, tax planning in small business entities seems to be treated incidentally. Polish entrepreneurs rarely decide to take advantage of the possibilities offered by tax advisory services and, by comparison with other European countries, they fall unfavourably weak. Most frequently they follow the advice of their accountants or accounting office employees, whose experience in planning or optimizing tax burdens is rather low or little satisfactory. They do not use appropriate methods to measure the tax burden, such as the effective tax rate.

Applying a progressaive tax to optimizing the tax burden is an example of a residual short-term tax planning. Entrepreneurs frequently attempt to divide their business activity into smaller ones, with each having a different form of taxation applied, the most favourable for the particular segment of the business.

Tax audit is a tool that can help in tax planning, but only at its initial stage. An external advisor can determine the status and possibilities of tax settlements, can help design and implement the tax strategy, may also indicate directions for optimization as well as the possibility of reducing and eliminating the tax risk, and finally, improving liquidity. The question is whether small business units can afford it. Only a few entrepreneurs of the SM-SC (MSP) sector are willing to seek advice from a professional and pay for it a high amount of money. Most, however, generally try to imitate their competitors, acquaintances, who have already applied optimization solutions in their units or consult various accountants, suppliers, etc. It is not that every solution appropriate for a given unit may be applied to another.

Tax planning must be a continuous process, above all including changes in tax law provisions, shifts of economy as well as plans for development of the entity. All the activites of a business entitiy should be covered in this respect.

Tax optimization in practice.

The primary goal of any business entity is to achieve a maximum profit, and in recent years one has been talking about maximizing value for the owner. Nevertheless, the income generated must be taxed for accumulating the profit or making investments in order to enlarge this value. The greater the profit, the more tax is paid by the entrepreneur. None of the entrepreneurs is willing to agree to a maximum encumbrance of the profits generated. Each of them, either legally or not, tries to reduce the amount of taxes paid. There are more and more companies seeking legal methods of minimizing taxes; however, they repeatedly attempt to apply those illegal when results are unsatifactory.

The period of transformation[6] created many opportunities for entrepreneurs to reduce the tax burden. This applied not only to those large business entities, but smaller ones as well. Exemptions from income tax helped many entrepreneurs to

6 Description of using the tax exemption is based on events from economic activity and own experiences.

develop the business activity in a fast and efficient way. Naturally, they were the activities within the law and its limits. Let us remember that the rate of encumbrances at that time was significant, reaching almost 40% of income in the case of corporate entities.

Legislation to exempt from taxation small business entities applying simplified method of a lump sum of registered revenue in the form of the Register of Revenues and Expenses allowed entrepreneurs to benefit from the exemption from income tax for a year if from the industrial sector, and for two years in the case of the food industry.

Those more foresighted and succesfull business entities benefited from the provided possibility by establishing business activities for their employees and passing maximum sales volume on the new entities within the exemption period. The mechanism was that the parent company imported the goods and then sold it with a low profit on this newly created entity, which, in turn, sold them at the maximum achievable price. After the exemption period came to an end the activity of the new units was gradually reduced.

The pattern was repeated in those business entities, this time by means of the exemption from corporate income tax. Companies with foreign capital were exempted from tax for three years from the commencement of business activity (issuing first invoice) [Business Activities, 1988, par.4]. The acquisition of such units was not difficult in the period mentioned, since the beginning of 90s introduced the commencement of the economic transformation, hence the formation of such entities.

The factor determining the choice of place of residence of a business activity and at the same time constituting the basis for the exemption from corporate income tax is a special economic zone. It is another possibility to minimize the tax burden applied by the aforementioned group.

More conscious entrepreneurs took advantage of the opportunities provided by the provisions of tax law, applying in this way the exemption from income tax, both for individuals and legal persons. Such optimization of the tax burden has allowed small business units to expand their business activities significantly at a rapid pace. The units aforementioned became, over a short period of time, large companies employing several hundred workers. With the savings on taxes the entities had a chance to develop their business activities, as most of these funds were allocated specifically for a business development.

Small business entities make use of the opportunities offered by applying different variants of simplified forms of business taxation on individuals. Starting from taxation with the tax card they apply the lump sum of recorded revenues while developing. Subsequently, they may choose between the taxation on general principles at the progressive tax scale with the possibility of settlement with a spouse and the application of numerous tax allowances and deductions. The necessity of applying the flat tax emerges as the business expands and the income rises significantly as well as the possibility of tax allowances and deductions exhausts.

Conscious business activity planning from its commencement until the maturity means also to determine an appropriate tax strategy over a particular period as to allow minimum tax burden within the whole period of the development and generated profits contribute to its maximum acceleration.

The average entrepreneur is not in the habit of using the services of tax advisors. Larger business entities merely seek help from professionals in either consulting companies or employing suitably qualified staff. Most, however, take advantage of the possibility of outsourcing, as it is both professional and cheaper.

Among the illegal forms of reducing taxes one can observe a so-called 'invoice purchasing'. These invoices have coverage neither in kind nor in services. Most are issued for the services connected with transport, consulting, advertising and construction as it is more difficult to prove they are false with these types of activities. Taxpayers attempt to limit the number of invoices of this type as well as the amount they are issued for as they are more difficult to capture by the tax authorities. Some dishonest taxpayers apply the practice of buying invoices from contractors with whom they constantly cooperate. One 'non covered invoice' is almost impossible to detect among many others.

Taxpayers exercise various ways of 'false costs' that reduce profits in the accounting books. A creative accountant always possess some appropriate methods of reducing the tax base of income tax, hence many entrepreneurs look either for accountants or accounting offices 'assisting' them in paying lower levies to the state budget. However, while using help of the creative accountant the entrepreneur should note whether greed makes a criminal out them or not. The accountants being under constant pressure to reduce taxes may decide to tackle a more risky and illegal solution just for the sake of satisfying the entrepreneur.

Conclusions

Entities of SM-SC (MSP) sector and basically Small and Micro Companies (MMP) sector finance primarily with their own capital. Generated funds are allocated for both current operations and the development. The more of these funds the unit retains and allocates for investments, the better for it and for the state as their development stimulates the economy.

Having the desire to retain the majority of the generated profits the entrepreneurs attempt to minimize the amount of the tax burden. Some of these activities lie within the law; unfortunately, they are frequently illegal activities too. Optimization efforts are still perceived as negative, illegal activities, which not necessarily is always accurate. The legislator often provokes methods allowing reduction of tax liabilities. "Shaping the tax burden by means permitted by tax law arises from: the right to choose, the discretionary freedom, the stimulus standards, the development of factual and legal state and changes in legal provisions" [Iniewski, Nikończyk 2011, p. 16 et seq.].

When stimulating the economic growth, it is not the change of tax law provisions that is of greater importance, but the reduction of costs, in principle, the tax expenditures. Yet, the question remains unanswered: what amounts of encumbrances will discourage the entrepreneur from seeking the illegal ways of reducing the tax expenditures? Despite the substantial tax cuts over several years (rate of corporate income tax from 40% to 19%) tax authorities continue to come across the cases of illegal ways to reduce the amount of tax burden. More and more frequently, fraudsters successfully offer the tax optimization[7] to clients; this means that entrepreneurs are convinced that the amount of the tax burden is constantly excessive.

Optimization aims at maximizing the net profit by reducing the amount of tax. The boundary between the tax optimization and tax cheater is not possible to identify precisely. Optimization activities, which remain consistent with the law, cannot be regarded as an escape before taxation or circumvention of the law and they must not be hidden. Any illegal activities, on the other hand, that is the tax evasion, should be condemned.

Any taxpayer, even the small one, should consciously and responsibly manage the taxes by taking any such activities that would allow him to optimize the amount of taxes; yet, these activitiesshould always fall within the limits of the law, therefore they will not be exposed to the consequences due to an economic crime.

Bibliography

Gołębiowski G. (2004), *Attempt to analyze the system of income taxation of MSP* [Small and Medium Sized Entities] in Poland (Studia i Prace KZiF Warsaw School of Economics, Warsaw, Book No 42.

7 Entries such as: 'selling costs', 'selling invoices', 'tax optimization' are easily fund on the Internet.

Capital group: tax strategy for business entities, www.egospodarka.pl.

Gaudemet P.M., Molinier J. (2010), *Public finance*, PWE, Warsaw.

Gomułowicz A., Małecki J. (2004), *Taxes and the tax law*, Lexis Nexis, Warsaw.

Głuchowski J. (2005), *Polish tax law*, Lexis Nexis, Warsaw.

Iniewski R., Nikończyk A. (2011), *Conscious taxpayer. Guidebook* (Tax Council, Lewiatan, Warsaw.

Kudert S. Jamroży M. (2013), *Tax optimization of business entities income* (ABC Wolters Kluwer Business, Warsaw.

Kunowska K. (2002), *How Small and Medium-Sized Companies can control tax burdens in: Tax management in Small and Medium-Sized Companies* (Scientific Book. Finance, Banking and Insurance No 1.

Mazur Ł. (ed.). (2012), *Tax optimization*, Lex and Wolter Kluwer Business, Warsaw.

Munnich M. Zdunek A. (2012), *Establishing and applying tax law in Poland. Tax optimization and circumvention of tax law*, KUL Publishing, Lublin.

Olesińska A. (2013), *General clause against tax avoidance*, Wydawnictwo Dom Organizatora, Toruń.

Ostaszewski J. (ed.). (2007), *The new tax order in Poland, SGH Publishing*, Warsaw.

Płatek A. (2014), The activities of non-financial companies in 2012 (Central Bureau for Statistics, Warsaw.

Rosiński R. (2010), *Polish tax system Seeking optimal solutions*, Difin, Warsaw.

Dictionary of Polish Language. (2012), PWN Scintific Publishing, Warsaw.

Sokołowski J. (1994), *Tax strategy of a company. How to reduce tax burdens*, Warsaw.

Stanik K.J. Winiarski K. (2009), *Practical porblems of fraud and circumvention of ax law*, Unimex Publishing Office, Wrocław.

Szymański W. (2009), *Tax strategies for legal persons in European Union*, C.H. Beck Warsaw.

Goods and Services Tax Act of 11 Macrh 2004 (Journal of Laws 2012, No. 177, item 1342).

Personal Income Tax Act of 26 July 1991 (Journal of Laws 2012, item 361).

Business Activities with foreign Entities Act of 23 December 1988 (Journal of Laws 1988, no. 41, item 41).

Corporate Income Tax Act of 15 February 1992 (Journal of Laws 2012, no. 74, item 1540).

Advantages and drawbacks of particular forms of taxation, www.podatekdochodowy.pl.

Walicka M. (2012), *Tax optimization in business activity of small entities*, Scientific Books Szczecin University, no. 708.

Budget receipts, Finance, The Ministry of Finance www.mf.gov.pl.

Alicja Tołwińska[1]

Use of systemic analysis in the managerial process of fiscal control bodies

Introduction

The Fiscal Audit as a specialized body mostly appointed to disclose and counteract fiscal crimes and offences is an element of the state institutional system charged with fulfilment of tax liabilities[2]. Broad powers of these authorities largely result from possibilities of obtaining information, processing data, conducting inspection proceedings and auditing EU funds.

Adequate use of information resources by fiscal audit bodies may, to a large extent, contribute to multi-objective optimization of measures taken as well as rationalization of all processes taking place in this system "Such optimization is viewed as an assessment of the problem in terms of the selected criterion, used as experts' experience, a method to determine a scope and scale of the phenomenon examined, through which, due to various aspects and specifics of information, it requires designing comprehensive methodology of research" [Piech, 2007, p. 8]. Effective processing of available data may also prompt an increase in economics of the operations across the control system, interpreted as striving to enhance effectiveness of administration in this domain [Raczkowski, 2012, p. 85]. Specifically, this applies to the methodology and forms of the analytical activities conducted as well as decision-making aspects at the level of the managing staff. This paper provides an insight into the methodological relevance of the system analysis as well as the subject and area for its application in the fiscal audit. The paper also addresses the issues regarding organizational and technical requirements likely to be essential for effective system analysis while identifying areas of tax irregularities prevailing across the economy. The barriers defined in the paper, having an adverse impact on the quality of the system analysis appear

---

1 Fiscal Control Office in Bialystok, email: alicja.tolwinska@gmail.com.

2 Fiscal audit is a concept used to define the institution of the relevant minster responsible for public finances, General Inspector of the Fiscal Audit together with subordinate heads of the fiscal audit offices as well as organizational units (i.e. fiscal audit offices) which enable to perform tasks seeking to mostly protect interests and property tights of the State Treasury. These tasks were specified by the act of 28 September 1991 on the fiscal audit (Journal of Laws of 2004, No. 41, item 214 as emended).

to be a major constraint for achieving satisfactory effects by fiscal audit authorities, both from the viewpoint of the society as well as a state. The paper seeks to describe the role of analytics employed in organizational units of the fiscal audit, the scope of their powers and required analytical competencies. Moreover, the study examines the issues of effectiveness of operations run by the fiscal audit, and criteria for selecting entities used by the bodies appointed for tracing tax irregularities in their analytical and controlling activities conducted.

Significance of the system analysis in its role in the fiscal administration

The system analysis in the fiscal administration involves investigating the correctness of taxpayers' settlements with the state budget using manifold methods and tools. Specifically, it includes identifying areas for tax irregularities risk, selecting entities to be inspected, disclosing tax abuses as well as preventing such practices in the years to come. Its primary objective is to shore up the decision-making process in choosing the entities to be controlled, and to appropriately determine and indicate the direction for operations by audit units. The application of the system analysis in the fiscal audit should directly lead to ensuring tax revenues.

By referring to the methodological meaning of the concept of the analysis, we may assume that it implies research involving breaking down the whole into its components and examining them separately [Szarucki, 2010, p. 52]. It may also be ascertained that the analysis is a process of certain reasoning, or even a specific type of speculation. Clearly, the analysis may be associated with deduction, observation, measurements as well as assessment, criticism, inquiry and deliberation. Additionally, it boils down to an estimate [Fuller, 1987, p. 10]. An analysis is the final product of analytical work which, despite description of information, should contain a forecast and identification of any ramifications produced by current and future events [Aleksandrowicz, 1999, pp. 26–27]. In essence, it should be regarded as a fundamental tool underpinning the making of business decisions. Analytics, thus, as an analysis of information is a capability of building the picture of the whole based in separate fragmented pieces, interpreting data, drawing conclusions, developing forecasts and scenarios for for future events [Aleksandrowicz, 1999, p. 7]. In the age of intelligent[3] organizations, a critical strategy to accomplish targets appears to be the deployment

3 Intelligent organization is understood as the one possessing and using knowledge in a modern manner, seeking for new opportunities, value, undergoing development phase.

of the methods for bolstering the quality, organizational culture and learning based on experience in the operations across various scientific disciplines such as: philosophy [Raczkowski, 2010, p. 262]. Narrowing the analysis process to one single technique runs a risk of overlooking significant aspects stemming from for instance: the trend, scale, etc. in assessment of the given phenomenon. And this is the result of taking wrong decisions or inadequate interpretation of results from the surveys accomplished.

When defining the concept of the system analysis, it is necessary to refer to the meaning of the term *system* which is defined as a set of interactive and interrelated units forming and modelling an integrated whole [Whittington, 2013, p. 45]. As noted by Stanisław Piaseckia system is "an entity being an organized collection of elements with definite features and relations, constituting one entirety with purpose". While making a synthesis of analytical activities, it is noticed that the same collection of elements – converting into a system, becomes then a team, and ultimately an element of another larger system [Piasecki, 1999]. Essentially, it should be highlighted that terms: *a system* and *an element* are relative concepts; and an object initially viewed as an element becomes a team, and next a system as a degree of analysis accuracy grows. Jerzy Rokita in the publication *Myślenie systemowe w zarządzaniu ogranizacjami [Systemic thinking in management of organizations]* brings focus into the fact that within a system, despite its particular part, relationship networks between its individual elements as well as the manner in which these relationships spring up perform a significant role. A system as identification of its particular parts reveals a certain entirety which is hardly recognizable [Rokita, 2011, p. 13]. A system analysis is a complex process which should integrate the impact of correlations between particular elements and a major phenomenon examined.

The Encyclopaedic definition of the system research suggests that they are a method for addressing problems through specifying and examining issues; they are intended for formulating and practical solving decision-making problems. This analysis is a research approach across social sciences which see a concept of the system as the key to understand social phenomena [Kaczorowski, 2004, p. 237]. Therefore, in situations marked by uncertainty, operations carried out by persons responsible for making strategic decisions are formally and openly supported. "A systemic approach to the surrounding environment, both natural and technical was established as a social necessity and a result of manifold trends in science and fulfilment of needs in advance of technique and technology" [Cempel, 2004]. Certainly, broad use of certain large collections will facilitate identification of those principal in the given research problem provided that appropriate techniques and tools are utilized.

An objective of the system analysis is to determine required actions or conduct phases through recognizing and considering available options, and compare their foreseen implications. Nevertheless, the boundaries of the system surveyed and its components should be clearly specified. Every person involved in research may interpret the system, being also a certain structure, in a varied manner and discern entirelydifferent elements in it [Gacparski, 1987, p. 696]. Mariusz Kudełko argues that the system analysis, alongside intensely developed scientific apparatus in the form of multifarious mathematical models allows to be reliable and unbiased in assessment of available measures, and to choose the most beneficial ones [Filipkowski, 2005]. Hence, this is a tool ensuring application of a broad spectrum of techniques and research methods.

Due to changes occurring in market economies, dynamics of economic processes, structural shifts as well as globalization a systemic approach is central to the analysis of these processes. The advance of technology including computerisation, science and surrounding economic and social processes triggered an urgency of assessment of the given phenomenon from the systemic perspective, through which a new perspective may be shown. However, due to the fact that a system analysis may cover the entirety of processes occurring in the social, economic, political or legal life – there is a shortage of ready and universal tools sets. Accordingly, this encourages their individual selection and construction depending on the source information possessed, the system in which it should function and its needs with regard to fuelling decision-making processes with information. Thus, this poses a risk of inappropriate selection of resources analysed or choice of applicable tools, or hypotheses being erroneously formulated and wrong interpretation of findings.

The role of system analysis within the fiscal audit is principally maximization of effects brought by control operations, through eliminating activities which fail to yield positive outcomes for both the interests of the State Treasury as well as society. The use of resources in the analysis, particularly the ones created to complete tasks imposed on the fiscal audit authorities in relation to other information available in the commercial environment, and combining them with scientific domains, e.g. statistics, economy or law, undoubtedly will produce efficient and effective system research. The utilization of solutions produced by the system analysis with regard to both knowledge as well as tools, allows for mitigating the areas of uncertainty. Acquisition of good quality materials, ahead of starting inspection proceedings as a result of the analysis conducted, enables better efficacy of inspections prepared, guiding them exactly where they are required, and thereby decreasing costs and enhancing effectiveness of the fiscal audit authorities. The system analysis makes it possible to gauge the strength of interdependencies occurring and the drivers affecting them. Therefore, assessment of efficacy of inspections to be carried out in the future may lead to continuing effective operations as well as changing their direction when expenditures prove to be unsatisfactory or excessively costly by exceeding potential tax revenues from tax proceedings accomplished. Though, it cannot be supposed that it is reasonable to eliminate analytical examinations focused on the specific issues or individual entities. Overall, disclosure of undesired practices within even a small group of taxpayers as well as honest entrepreneurs by inspection authorities may encourage the launch of systemic measures for eliminating such types of behaviour across the whole economy. Systemic actions may also aim at eradicating exclusively isolated behaviours or major participants in the given malpractice or organizers selected by means of analysis, which may protect the economy from further expansion of these phenomena.

The areas where the system analysis is used in the fiscal administration should largely concern tax pathologies. At present the term may be limited to, among others, activities by unfair competition having an impact on the public and legal amounts due declared and paid, intentional understating of tax liabilities, use of tax optimization which *de facto* breach the applicable law, transferring income outside of Poland as well as malpractice which is most hazardous for the interests of the State Treasury, i.e. fraudulent VAT refund claims. An organization and varied schemes of extortions being international in their character compel the launch systemic activities with regard to both, collaboration between various bodies, information exchange, techniques used for disclosing entities being in this risk area as well as methodology of inspection activities conducted.

Requirements for possibilities of using the system analysis within fiscal audit authorities

Possibilities and quality of system analyses conducted mostly depend on the standards applicable in subsystems of the fiscal inspection, which were displayed compared to the theory of the systems (Fig. 1), as well personnel competencies tools and IT resources. An important requirement for ensuring successful operations within system analyses is the policymaker's approach to the aspects related to organization of skills and tools possessed by analytical staff, reception of content produced by them, as well as perception of the analysts' role within an unit. A fundamental principle to be considered in the fiscal inspection should be the fact that analytics not to be associated exclusively with collecting data, establishing databases and operating IT systems. Responsibility for acquiring and preparing information essential for conducting analyses, as well as setting up and safeguarding technical facilities should be placed on competency departments rather than analytical ones.

Functioning of the fiscal audit system and an impact of its particular subsystem of the analyses

According to Janusz Gierszewski a system is defined as a collection of resources (methods) of operations, performance of complex activities as well as entirety of organizational principles, the body of standards and rules applicable in the specific domain as well as complete and structured set of tasks [Gierszewski, 2013]. The author emphasizes that a superior system existing in the given area modifies the structure of the remaining subsystems, whereas application of the systems theory allows for identification of mutual impact between elements. The systems theory enables to approach the problem in a comprehensive manner with the simultaneous use of interdisciplinary analytical methods. Based on that theory and the security model designed by the above-mentioned author, the model of the fiscal control from the system perspective was illustrated below:

Figure 1: A model of the fiscal control from the system perspective

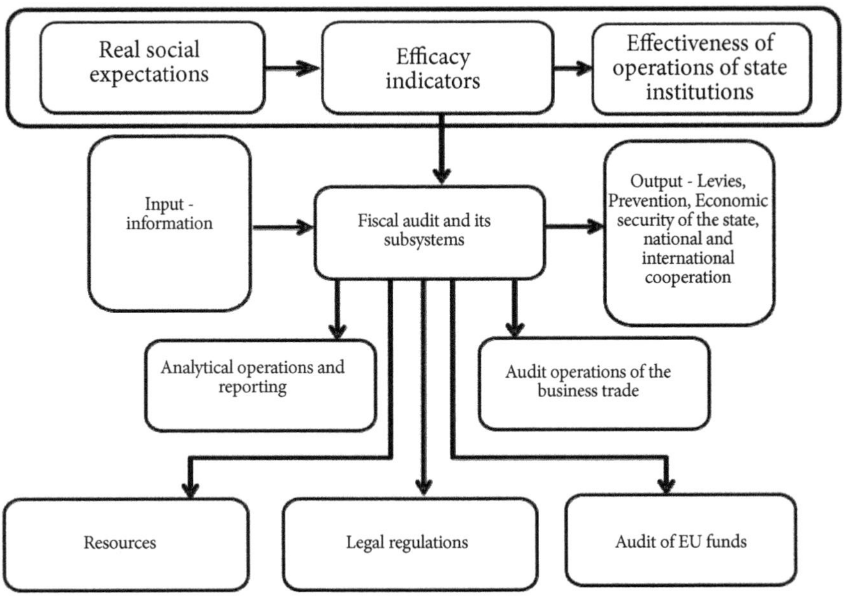

Source: own study.

Functioning of the fiscal control system is directly dependant on its subsystems comprising legal regulations, material and human resources as well as statutory operations to which this institution was appointed, with specification of controlling, analytical and forecasting activities as well as EU finds audit. Performance indicators for the system affect both the society and interests of the State Treasury alike. The backbone of the fiscal control system is information, whereas the effect – understood as an objective – levies, security of public finances, prevention as well as national and international collaboration with public institutions intended to protect the state as well as social interests. Operations within every system tend to be exposed to the risk of disruption. To eliminate threats or mitigate the risk it is necessary to accomplish an analysis covering individual subsystem and its interaction with the whole system. Major threats identified within the fiscal control system include: unclear and incoherent tax law, legislative restrictions, scarcity of tools and sufficient IT resources, insufficient collaboration with other bodies, including law enforcement authorities, disproportionate numbers of employees in relation to inspection needs, negative social perception, etc. Determination of threats is facilitated by the analysis of data with regard to employment across fiscal control offices, the number of inspection proceedings conducted by these units within a given calendar year or number of applicable legislative acts regulating taxes. Based on information obtained from controls executed by the Supreme Audit Office in the Ministry of Finance in respect of implementation of the state budget in 2011, in the chapter 19 - "Budget, public finances and financial institutions" it was found that the fiscal control offices employed 5,367 employees[4]. The report on performance ofthe fiscal control offices reveals that in 2013 10,177 audit procedures and 5,392 audit activities[5]. were carried out. Additionally, drawn upon the legislative acts website "LEX" it was found that at the end of May 2014 the following were applicable with regard to the tax law: 533 acts published inthe Journals of Laws and the Polish Monitor (Official Gazette of the Government), 92 ministerial acts, 85 acts of the European Law, and 31,000 municipal acts of law. Overtly wide spectrum of legislative norms may create serious barriers for conducting effective and swift audit activities, whereas a number of audit proceedings may suggest considerably increased needs for initiating fiscal inspections in specific areas of operations by business entities.

---

4 The Supreme Audit Office, http://www.nik.gov.pl/kontrole/wyniki-kontroli-nik/pobierz,kbf~p_12_027_201205231143331337766213~01,typ,k.pdf.

5 Ministry of Finance, report on performance of the fiscal audit in 2013 http://www.mf.gov.pl/documents/764034/1424099/Sprawozdanie+z+dzia%C5%82alno%C5%9Bci+kontroli+skarbowej+za+2013+rok.pdf.

The biggest risk posed for fiscal control operations seems to be failure to deliver on the targets specified in Art.1 of the Fiscal Inspection Act, namely: protection of interests and property rights of the State Treasury and ensuring effective payment of tax liabilities and other amounts due constituting the state budget revenue[6], and hence lack of revenue income to the budget, fluctuations of the economic security system of the state defined as: "such a state of the advance of the national economic system that ensure a high efficacy of its operations – though adequate application of internal development factors – and capacity of effective opposing external pressures likely to trigger developmental disorders" [Stachowiak, 1994, p. 189].

The standards valid in every subsystem mostly affect opportunities of using system analysis. Therefore, the quality of the reporting has direct implications for the quality and interpretation of results from the statistical analyses. Effectiveness of control determines the theme-oriented analyses, and human resources – not only the number of audit proceedings but also the number of entities selected as a result of analytical operations. Finally, the norms and legal regulations govern the entirety – i.e. possibility of gaining data, using them ahead of and in course of audit proceedings.

Structure of organizational analytical units and competencies of analysts employed in fiscal audit units

Under the powers conferred on head of the fiscal control offices[7] arising from Art. 11 of the Fiscal Audit Act the following are specified: conducting analytical and forecasting activities in relation to negative phenomena occurring within the fiscal audit and presenting findings from these activities to the government administration authorities. This task is performed through the supervision of the head over analytical and planning units as well as preparation of information, reports, studies and analyses in conformity with the needs of the top body and managing staff of the office [Zalewski, Melezini, 2011, p. 178].

The extract *Tasks of the fiscal audit offices for 2014* shows that priority activities in 2014 include: preventing irregularities through, among the other schemes: streamlining the system for analysing areas being particularly

6 Act of 28 September 1991 on the fiscal audit (Journal of Laws of 2004, No. 41, item 214 as amended).

7 Head of the fiscal audit office as a body of the fiscal audit, appointed and dismissed by the relevant minister responsible for public finances at the request of the General Inspector of the Fiscal Audit.

vulnerable to irregularities remaining in the spotlight of the fiscal control as well as enhanced innovativeness in operations carried out by the fiscal control and analytical works[8]. In the fiscal audit offices the units charged with analytical activities include departments/divisions or analysis and planning branches and revenue intelligence units. Establishment of organizational units is regulated by the Regulation of the Minister of Finance of 4 January 2011 on seats and organization of the fiscal control offices and in accordance with Art. 9(2) of the Fiscal Audit Act. The foregoing regulation shows that within these units the following may be set up: departments – comprising at least 20 employees, divisions – comprising at least 10 employees, branches – comprising at least 5 employees, multi-position workplace (sections) – comprising less than 5 employees[9]. Based on the analysis of the organizational regulations within the fiscal audit offices it may be noticed that the structure of the units committed to analytical operations fails to be uniform (Table 1).

Table 1: Structure of analytical units across the fiscal audit offices

	Seat of the fiscal audit office/province	**Structure of analytical units**		
		Department	**Division**	**Branch/Section**
1	**2**	**3**	**4**	**5**
1	Wrocław/ dolnośląskie	Analytical-Planning Department	Analytical-Planning Division within the Department	3 Analytical-Planning Sections: Jelenia Góra, Legnica, Wałbrzych within the Department
2	Bydgoszcz/ kujawsko-pomorskie	Analysis and Planning Department	lack	Analysis and Monitoring Business Trade Section within the Department, and Analysis, Identification and Monitoring Areas Exposed to Tax Frauds Section outside the Department

8 Excerpt from the tasks of the fiscal audit offices for 2014, Ministry of Finances, Fiscal Audit Department: KS/8500/5/JRS/2013, http://www.mf.gov.pl/documents/764034/928259/Wyci%C4%85g+z+zada%C5%84+urz%C4%99d%C3%B3w+kontroli+skarbowej+na+rok+2014.

9 Regulation of the Ministry of Finances of 4 January 2011 on seats and organization of the fiscal audit offices (Journal of Laws of 2011, No 13 item 62).

	Seat of the fiscal audit office/province	Structure of analytical units		
		Department	Division	Branch/Section
3	Lublin/ lubelskie	Analysis and Planning Department as well as Identification and Monitoring of Areas Exposed to Tax Frauds	lack	Reporting and Statistics Section within the Department
4	Zielona Góra/ lubuskie	Lack	Analytical and Planning Division	Analytical-Planning Section in GorzówWlkp. Within the Division
5	Łódź/ łódzkie	Analysis and Planning Department	lack	lack
6	Kraków/ małopolskie	Lack	Analysis and Programming Fiscal Audits Division, Registry Audit Proceedings and Reporting Division	lack
7	Warszawa/ mazowieckie	Analysis and Planning Department	Risk Analysis Division and Division for Planning and Reporting within the department	lack
8	Opole/ opolskie	Lack	Analysis and Planning Division	lack
9	Rzeszów/ podkarpackie	Analysis and Planning Department	lack	Analysis and Planning Section within the Department, Analysis, Identification and Monitoring Areas Exposed to Tax Frauds Section within the Department
10	Białystok/ podlaskie	Analytical Department	Analytical Division within the Department	E-trade Analysis Section within the Department

	Seat of the fiscal audit office/province	Structure of analytical units		
		Department	Division	Branch/Section
11	Gdańsk/ pomorskie	Analysis and Planning Department	lack	Analysis and Designation Section and within the Section: Analysis and Designation in Słupsk
12	Katowice/ śląskie	Analysis, Planning and IT Department	lack	IT Section within the Department
13	Kielce/ świętokrzyskie	Lack	lack	Planning and Analysis Section
14	Olsztyn/ warmińsko-mazurskie	Lack	Analysis and Planning Division	lack
15	Poznań/ wielkopolskie	Analysis and Planning Department	lack	lack
16	Szczecin/ zachodniopo-morskie	Lack	Analytical-Planning Division	lack

Source: Own study based on the data from the Public Information Bulletin of individual fiscal audit offices (as of 13.03.2014).

The analysis of organizational regulations across all fiscal audit offices indicates that within their structures there operate: 9 analysis and planning departments, 1 analytical department, 5 independent analysis and planning divisions, and 1 planning and analysis section. It was found that in one office of the fiscal audit supervision is performed by the chief director, in the remaining ones – a deputy director of one of the departments. Such a diverse structure of the units tasked with analysis may also indicate diverse approaches of policymakers to the role of analytics within the office. Having made the assumption that analytical-planning units handle operations with regard to analyses as well as planning and reporting, it may be stated that not all employees in these units perform the role of analysts. Some of them may hold the position of the planners, statisticians or IT specialists. Information presented (Table 1) suggests that the number of persons involved in conducting analyses as compared to negative practices in business transactions ranges from 5 up to 15 persons within a given province. Drawing on the data illustrating economic potentials (Table 2) within given provinces an explicit conclusion may be formed that the number of analysts within the fiscal audit is fairly low in relation to the number of entities running registered business activities.

Table 2: Economic potentials within specific provinces

No.	Province	State enterprises	Companies in total	including				Co-operatives	Individuals	In total
				commercial	joint-stock	limited liability	private partnership			
1	dolnośląskie	12	57 742	31 314	827	26 362	26 367	1 380	235 458	347 811
2	kujawsko-pomorskie	6	27 067	13 583	356	11 317	13 269	960	143 034	191 220
3	lubelskie	5	20 694	10 727	253	8 470	9 813	1 157	128 739	169 670
4	lubuskie	2	15 066	8 978	160	7 737	6 053	473	78 187	109 691
5	łódzkie	3	34 103	17 319	445	13 906	16 596	995	180 270	237 458
6	małopolskie	21	57 732	29 650	747	23 306	27 728	1 126	261 484	351 162
7	mazowieckie	69	174 060	117 820	3 682	100 769	55 929	3 115	493 118	725 828
8	opolskie	2	12 912	6 351	137	5 303	6 496	476	72 347	99 964
9	podkarpackie	2	19 962	9 585	243	7 467	10 233	802	120 807	159 564
10	podlaskie	1	10 696	5 601	111	4 034	4 969	483	74 840	96 387
11	pomorskie	6	43 950	26 599	826	22 824	17 252	1 035	196 157	271 791
12	śląskie	10	77 230	41 098	1 202	33 809	35 981	1 150	337 699	460 063
13	świętokrzyskie	3	13 197	5 665	221	4 382	7 482	502	84 992	109 692
14	warmińsko-mazurskie	3	13 937	7 346	146	5 993	6 534	727	87 373	122 018

No.	Province	State enterprises	Companies in total	including				Co-operatives	Individuals	In total
				commercial	joint-stock	limited liability	private partnership			
15	wielkopolskie	14	62 593	37 067	892	30 136	25 349	1 935	299 591	398 000
16	zachodniopo-morskie	6	30 192	16 560	275	14 287	13 592	1 112	163 924	219 453
17	In total	**165**	**671 133**	**385 263**	**10 523**	**320 102**	**283 643**	**17 428**	**2 958 020**	**4 069 772**

Source: own study based on the date provided by the Central Statistical Office: Tables concerning the national economy entities without individuals running exclusively individual agriculture holdings as of 31.01.2014 – entities by provinces, sub-regions, districts and communes: http://www.stat.gov.pl/bip/389_5685_PLK_HTML.htm.

From the data presented (Table 1, Table 2) it is clear that there is no correlation between the number of employees in analytical units within specific fiscal audit offices and the fact that some of these units operated outside their provinces (Table 3). It should be underlined that the number of entities specified in Table 2 refers to registered companies. As noted by Konrad Raczkowski estimates by the Central Statistical Office reveal that active entrepreneurs in 2013 totalled 1.8 million [Raczkowski, 2014, p. 30]. Basically, this confirms existence of big discrepancies in data caused by entrepreneurs neglecting their obligations related to deregistering their companies as well as possibilities of using inactive entities for operations other than business, e.g. performing certain transactions, building an "artificial, false" track record of the company, etc. Companies having a legal personality are frequently the subject of sale performed by entities dealing with such operations. The discrepancies may be interpreted as an instance of organizational ineffectiveness of the state institution being responsible for the quality of the data.

Jurisdiction over the venue of the fiscal control offices is governed by the Regulation of the Minister of Finance of 29 November 2010 on determining the territorial scope for operations carried out by directors of fiscal control offices[10]. Information contained in appendix to this regulation, demonstrating a territorial scope for operations performed by directors of fiscal control offices, shows that only 5 offices operate exclusively within the boundaries of its province, whilst the remaining 11 encompass districts and towns/cities with district forming a part of another province.

Table 3: Territorial scope for operations performer by a director of the fiscal audit office

No.	Name of the director of the fiscal control office	Territorial scope for operations performer by the director of the fiscal control office
1	Director of the Fiscal Control Office in Warsaw	Province: mazowieckie, except for the following districts: białobrzeski, ciechanowski, garwoliński, gostyniński, grójecki, kozienicki, makowski, miński, mławski, lipski, łosicki, ostrołęcki, ostrowski, płocki, płoński, przasnyski, przysuski, pułtuski, radomski, siedlecki, sierpecki, sochaczewski, sokołowski, szydłowiecki, węgrowski, wołomiński, wyszkowski, zwoleński, żuromiński, żyrardowski, the city having the rights of the district: Ostrołęka, city having the right of the district: Płock, city having the right of the district: Radom andcity having the right of the district: Siedlce

10 Journal of Laws of 2013, item 257.

No.	Name of the director of the fiscal control office	Territorial scope for operations performer by the director of the fiscal control office
2	Director of the Fiscal Control Office in Białystok	Province: podlaskie, as well as districts being a part of mazowieckie province: ostrołęcki, ostrowski, sokołowski, węgrowski, wołomiński, wyszkowski, and the city having the right of the district: Ostrołęka
3	Director of the Fiscal Control Office in Bydgoszcz	provincekujawsko-pomorskie, as well as districts being a part of mazowieckie province: gostyniński, sierpecki, płocki, płoński, andcity having the right of the district: Płock
4	Director of the Fiscal Control Office in Gdańsk	Province: pomorskie
5	Director of the Fiscal Control Office in Katowice	Province: śląskie
6	Director of the Fiscal Control Office in Kielce	Province: świętokrzyskie, except for the following sandomierski district, as well as districts being a part of mazowieckie province: białobrzeski, lipski, przysuski, radomski, szydłowiecki, zwoleński, and the city having the right of the district: Radom
7	Director of the Fiscal Control Office in Kraków	Province: małopolskie
8	Director of the Fiscal Control Office in Lublin	Province: lubelskie, as well as districts being a part of mazowieckie province: garwoliński, kozienicki, miński, łosicki, siedlecki, and the city having the rights of the district Siedlce
9	Director of the Fiscal Control Office in Łódź	Province: łódzkie, as well as districts being a part of mazowieckie province: grójecki, sochaczewski, żyrardowski
10	Director of the Fiscal Control Office in Olsztyn	Province: warmińsko-mazurskie, as well as districts being a part of mazowieckie province: ciechanowski, makowski, mławski, pułtuski, przasnyski, żuromiński
11	Director of the Fiscal Control Office in Opole	Province: opolskie
12	Director of the Fiscal Control Office in Poznań	Province: wielkopolskie, except fot districts: międzychodzki and wolsztyński
13	Director of the Fiscal Control Office in Rzeszów	Province: podkarpackie, as well as sandomierski district being a part of świętokrzyskie province
14	Dyrektor Urzędu Kontroli Skarbowej w Szczecinie	Province: zachodniopomorskie, except for myśliborski district

No.	Name of the director of the fiscal control office	Territorial scope for operations performer by the director of the fiscal control office
15	Director of the Fiscal Control Office in Wrocław	Province: dolnośląskie
16	Director of the Fiscal Control Office in ZielonaGóra	Province: lubuskie, as well the myśliborski district being the part of zachodniopomorskie province, as well as the districts being the part of wielkopolskie province: międzychodzki andwolsztyński

Source: Territorial scope for operations carried out by directors of fiscal control offices – appendix to the regulation by the Minister of Finance of 29 November 2010 on determining territorial scope for operations carried out by directors of fiscal control offices.

According to the list of clerical positions, positions within specific groups and professional qualifications required for performing works on clerical positions in fiscal control offices, there is no work position for the analyst[11]. Legal regulations do not regulate the form/course of the qualification proceedings or the requirement for specialist competencies or professional competencies useful for performing work on that position. The fiscal audit act specified specialist requirements for recruitment for the fiscal intelligence units and implementation units[12]. Recruitment for an analytical unit may, thus, proceed in a routine manner. There are no regulations in terms of requirements for a candidate to have a job seniority to a similar position. In the course of the recruitment process no psychological examinations cannot be carried out, which help to identify predispositions for performing work on such job position in other services or business. As a result of such recruitment it is hard to verify whether a candidate without any tenure in fiscal audit or a person employed in a given office on a position other than analytical will effectively perform the role of the expert or decision-maker's consultant to a satisfactory degree. It may be acknowledged that an employee tasked with analysis is a knowledge worker – well-organized and competent expert appreciating its skills and expertise, being also a specialist

11 Regulation of the Prime Minister of 9 December 2009 on determination of civil servants positions, required professional qualifications, official ranks of civil servants, multipliers for determining remuneration and detailed principles for determining and paying other performances to which the civil service corps is entitled (Journal of Laws of 2009, No. 211, item 1630 as amended).

12 An implementation units possesses special powers with regard to legitimizing, detaining, searching through means of coercion and firearms, whereas an intelligence unit conducts activities in the form of preliminary investigation allowing for preserving traces in an undercover manner.

in the industry, seeking for unconventional possibilities of tackling a given problem. In view of the specifics inherent to the work it should require to be treated individually within a flexible work time system as well as collective confrontation of views and formulation of ideas [Raczkowski, 2010, p. 75]. At present, legal norms regulating the employment relationship of these persons in the fiscal audit do not stipulate distinguishing them as an expert group or they do not provide an opportunity of working in flexible work time system. It would be reasonable to consider establishment of a knowledge management department within the fiscal control offices made up of knowledge-workers having individual work conditions suitable for performing activities related to analyses.

Thomas H. Davenport in the publication *Competing on Analytics. The New Science of Winning* emphasizes that it is difficult to find a person possessing business intelligence and analytics knowledge as well as interpersonal and IT skills. He underlines that an analytical talent at the beginning of the 21st century was equally required by the market as a software developer profile at the end-90s. Personnel scarcity of analytically talented persons occurs on the American market as well as the European market. Companies pursuing strategies rested on analytical skills are unquestioned leaders in their fields. To fully harness analytical resources it is not enough to possess qualified analysts. They should be a part of the business team, become involved in the decision-making process and participate in discussions about what is most important and while presenting complicated issues they should be treated as active and crucial co-founders of the success of the business entity [Davenport, 2011, p. 109].

Despite analytical competencies, prominence was given to management of analytical teams characterized by certain specifics. As described by Tomasz Aleksandrowicz, the chief of the analytical team should be a major analyst himself, be familiar with principles of analytical work, professionally manage in the bureaucratic realm, be a "filter" between a recipient of analysis and an analyst, which protects an employee from attempts to influence the analysis by a recipient. Furthermore, he underscores that a person managing an analytical group should ensure intellectual autonomy for the analytical team, and not to force analysts to corroborate his own concepts or those of policymakers. An author accurately placed emphasised the significance and the role played by supervisors of analytical employees by citing Sherman Kent's words: "an analyst must be so close to the decision-making centre so as to have an access to as many guidelines as possible in respect of the policymaker's needs and resources of his previous knowledge, and at the same time to be sufficiently far away so as not be exposed to his impact, thereby posing a risk of losing impartiality and adequate assessments" [Aleksandrowicz, 2013, pp. 14–15, 20–22].

Clear frameworks for recruitments for a position of crime analysts employed in state agencies are in operation for police. A candidate is subject to psychological examinations intended to verify matching to the required profile. The profile includes, among others, a certain level of intelligence, memory and perception; moreover, at least 3-years' experiencein crime intelligence or investigation department is required. On top of that, such a person has to possess a definite level of IT and database knowledge [Maciejczyk, Klonowska-Senderska, 2012, p. 5]. The first course of crime analysis at Polish police took place in 2001, whereas its mainstay relies on the Anglo-Saxon system with regard to visualisation, presenting intricate data in the form of diagrams and synthetic conclusions corroborated by presumptions. Because of cross-border and multidisciplinary character of organized crime in the 1960s in the USA, a scientific programme ANACAPA was designed which to date has constituted a basis for analytical activities used throughout the world by a majority of public institutions.

The qualification profile for a given work position includes a list of worker's skills that seem to be precious and vital. On the whole, two categories may be identified: traits needed to fulfil certain tasks, i.e. knowledge, experience, practical skills, personality attributes and traits attuned to the company's specifics, its organizational culture and position, i.e. psychological traits [Stefański, 2007, p. 101]. Artur Stefański in the publication *Rolakwalifikacjianalityków w zarządzaniuryzkiemkredytowym w bankach [The Role of Analysts' qualifications in management of the credit risk across banks]* details numerous traits useful for the position of the credit analyst, including self-motivation, intelligence, honesty and impartiality, capability of taking decisions, consistency in operations, psychological resilience, sense of institutionalism, sense of responsibility [Stefański, 2007, pp. 103–104].

Tomasz Aleksandrowicz brings a spotlight into three areas of operations carried out by persons employed in the position of analyst. They include: analysis of information, use of expertise and consultancy. The author highlights that analytical-advisory teams gained nowadays in importance so that they may be called the "fifth element of power" – alongside legislative, executive, judiciary and press. An analyst should be equipped with expertise, skills for distinguishing useful information and acquiring it from reliable sources, quick learning of operating IT devices, capabilities of convincing policymakers as to validity of conclusions from an analysis, presenting correlations between various facts [Aleksandrowicz, 2013, pp. 14–15, 20–22]. An important aspect is also preparation of materials by analysts at their own initiative as well as readiness to show an unbiased standpoint to policymakers – not necessarily consistent with their superior's expectations. An analysis should reflect the autonomy of the person drawing up, as it cannot solely boil down to simple confirmation of policymaker's arguments or assumptions, which proves to be beset by partiality and violates an analytical cycle [Aleksandrowicz, 2013, p. 16].

Powers conferred on analytical units are defined in Art. 11(2)(6) of the Fiscal Audit Act as analytical and forecasting activities in relation to negative phenomena occurring within the fiscal audit. Despite analytical and planning units, these activities are performed by the fiscal intelligence providing information about adverse practices disclosed as a result of these operations. Activities by fiscal intelligence strive to acquire, collect and process information about entities being examined; information is repeatedly obtained within operational activities [Kulicki, 2012, p. 2]. Principally they refer to identification and disclosure of tax frauds in cooperation with law enforcement authorities and the General Inspector of Financial Information. Frequently, industries with a heightened risk of tax irregularities draw the biggest interest.

IT resources as fundamental tool for executing systemic analyses while selecting entities to be controlled

System research may be conducted based on information collected and IT tools making it possible to process data across a broad range. Pinpointing of entities takes place on the basis of the risk areas already specified in the Tax Discipline Plan as well as a variety of data attained pursuant to Art. 7 of the Fiscal Audit Act or data acquired through audit proceedings by agencies. A crucial part of analyses is the processing of information outside the Ministry of Finance as well as gathering data by tax authorities.

As noticed by Dariusz Ćwikowski [Ćwikowski, 2011, p. 287] increasing computerization of the state institutions fosters attaining, processing and systemizing of data by the state authorities. For that reason an effective analysis may be accomplished, which is a result of combining various facts and information. Currently state authorities possess statutory powers to collect, process and getting access to specific data. Many varied central registries and records were set up across public institutions, for instance: the National Business Registry (REGON), Polish resident Identification (PESEL), Central Land and Mortgage Register, Central Vehicle and Driver Register (CEPiK), National Court Register (KRS), Central Insurant Register. Overall, these databases contain information about financial transactions, personal data and other facts in respect to business entities or private individuals. The possibility of unrestrained use of this information allows for effective identification of taxpayers and family members, and even foreign entities carrying out business directly or indirectly on the territory of Poland.

A system analysis applied for designating entities for audit enables to determine potentials and benefits resulting from future operations conducted by tax authorities.

At present the most negative phenomena with regard to fiscal control are low revenues to the budget from the goods and services tax. This is defined as the VAT gap, being the difference between actual and projected revenues. Its growth clearly suggests an increase in tax abuses. It is also perceived as difficulties of tax administration in tacking this problem while using currently available resources [33, 2014, pp. 4–5]. The policy pursued does not guarantee minimization of the gap or constraint of dishonest entities involved in the malpractice of fraudulent tax refund claims.

As displayed in the follow-up document of the Supreme Audit Office of 20 December 2013 drawn up following the control completed in the Ministry of Finance with regard to "combating VAT frauds", the General Inspector of the Fiscal Audit[13] launched measures designed for clamping down on the tax gap. He commissioned the fiscal audit agencies to widely use the risk analysis in specific areas as well as to deploy optimal available investigation techniques and methods so that investigation tasks are accomplished in the most effective manner. He put an emphasis on stepping up collaboration and information exchange between bodies appointed to combat economic crime, and tightening collaboration with relevant foreign bodies, thereby clamping down on tax crime[14] in a comprehensive way. The recommendation given by the General Inspector of the Fiscal Audit may indicate a shift in previous techniques used, their expansion or adoption of the systemic approach. Meanwhile, a further decline in VAT revenues may show that even boosted actions seeking to curb that practice fall short of the goals. The applicable fiscal policy may also adversely affect the outcome of analytical operations conducted as their results are directly subject to its form.

Specific criteria determine designation of entities to be audited by fiscal agencies. According to information published on the website of the Ministry of Finance as to the selection of taxpayers to be controlled by tax authorities[15] the following areas were identified (Table 4):

---

13 Pursuant to art. 8(1)(2) of the act on the fiscal audit the General Inspector of the Fiscal Audit is an office superior over directors of the fiscal audit offices.

14 Supreme Audit Office, Follow-up document no. KBF-4101-07-01/2013 P/13/042, http://www.mf.gov.pl/documents/764034/3794865/23122013_NIK_zwalczanie_oszustw_w_podatku_od_towarow_i_USLUG.PDF.

15 Tax body understood as an institution of the fiscal office head, fiscal chamber director and relevant minister responsible for public finances.

Table 4: Criteria for designating entities in the risk areas for 2013

No.	Criterion
1.	ENTITIES DISCLOSING SUBSTANTIAL VAT REFUNDS OR FREQUENT SURPLUS IN INPUT TAX OVER TRANSFERABLETAX DUE
2.	ENTITIES DISCLOSING SUBSTANTIAL REVENUES AND AT THE SAME TIME LOW INCOME OR LOSSES FOR BUSINESS ACTIVITIES OR MAKING DEDUCTIONS FOR LOSSES FROM PREVIOUS YEARS
3.	TAXPAYERS OR PAYERS OF INCOME TAX FAILING TO PAY TAX DUE OR ADVANCES FOR PARTICULAR MONTHS OR QUARTERS
4.	ENTITIES FAILING TO REPORT BUSINESS OPERATIONS, THOSE DISSAPEARING, CEASING TO SUBMIT TAX RETURN OR SUSPENDING BUSINESS OPERATIONS
5.	PERFORMING BUSINESS TRANSACTIONS THROUGH INTERNET

Source: Ministry of Finance, Tax Administration Department, CRITERIA FOR DESIGNATING ENTITIES IN RISK AREAS FOR, Warsaw 2013, http://www.is.waw.pl.

According to preliminary assumptions to the foregoing criteria, designating should take place with the use of the module labelled "Group analysis" within the subsystem Control which should be activated at least twice a year and should cover the period of at least 5 quarters. In spite of general criteria, detailed criteria were defined in order to assess the risk. Based on this information we may draw a clear conclusion that the module certainly fulfils its role as an ancillary tool in the process of selecting entities to be controlled, though it fraught with risk of limiting the analysis to risk areas designated which fail to encompass all fraud schemes exploited nowadays by dishonest taxpayers and criminal groups operating on the market exclusively to make fraudulent tax refund claims.

The unsatisfactory level of tax revenues undoubtedly suggests hardships faced by fiscal audit authorities as well as tax agencies in combating tax crime. Essentially, they may originate not only from legal restraints but also from technical aspects. The issues addressed by JacekMatyszczak in relation to functioning of the telecommunication system within the administration illustrates its standing and the impact of potential threats to telecommunication infrastructure [Matyszczak, 2008]. The author demonstrated that numerous communication and IT systems tend to be implemented in the administration, yet there is not always an opportunity of their mutual exchange between specific departments. Typically, the form, type and application of data gathered in individual organizations is tailored to accomplishment of tasks within specific institutions, and therefore there is often no option for utilizing these systems by other units. In view of independent and diverse infrastructures, interfaces, protection of classified data, it is highly unlikely to implement uniform mechanisms for managing and processing these data through a national integrated system. Hence, the lack of a common system for all entities across public administration may be one of the primary reasons behind inefficient fulfilment of tasks across Poland, thereby running a risk of eroding telecommunication and IT security. This may be exemplified by the systems operating in the Ministry of Finance intended exclusively for tax authorities and those separate put into operation across the customs administration or fiscal audit units.

A technical aspect of the public administration systems and their state is repeatedly addressed in publications by CzesławJędrzejek. Principally he brings focus to inconsistency of IT systems implemented across the administration. He claims that IT systems operating today across the fiscal administration prevent from making effective use of information collected (resulting from inconsistent data types, lack of uniform dictionaries, labels, lack of adequate management of data at all levels). The author underlines the problem of semantic coherence between the data model underlying applications, and an inventory formed by the database [Jędrzejek, 2007, p. 54]. This means that analytical tools fail to correspond to possessed data with certain quality and variety. According to CzesławJędrzejek central to effective operations is an analysis prepared on the basis of various IT systems which include diverse data in large quantities [Jędrzejek, Bąk, Cybulka, Martinek, 2006, p. 276]. Dispersed individual databases, incoherent data types, shortage of possibilities of generating questions (e.g. in SQL) is a serious barrier hindering effective functioning one of the fiscal audit subsystems which are IR resources. External assessment of the commercial setting (including press environment/business entities, scientists) completed or analyzed by the fiscal administration revealed ineffective operations by law enforcement, judicial and fiscal authorities. The authors of the publication *Skalafinansowejprzestępczościzorganizowanej w Polsceidlaczegojejzwalczanie jest taknieefektywne [The scale of financial organized crime in Poland and why its combat is so ineffective]* argue that the reasons for that state are manifold, among them are legal obstacles, lack of collaboration between bodies and low analytical capacity of the state bodies [Więckowski, Jędrzejek, 2014, p. 460]. They claim that stable law, effective operations of the state, standards, collaboration between institutions and suppliers of IT solutions are critical for integration of the systems [Jędrzejek, 2007, p. 239]. Meanwhile, despite varied projects in this field, no integrated IT system embodying data from diverse departments across the Ministry of Finance has been established to date. Ineffectiveness of the fiscal apparatus may directly be a key cause of threats to effective functioning of the state.

In the opinion of Wojciech Filipowski, widespread use of computer technologies also engenders threat of not discerning the magnitude of processes, e.g. structures of criminal groups which evolved from monolithic, highly hierarchical forms towards networks [Filipkowski, 2006, p. 68]. So, an aspect of possessing data is not so significant as their skillful processing and pinpointing the most important ones. At this juncture it should be stressed that business entities are very familiar with possibilities and powers of the audit or tax authorities. The specifics and scheme for extorting VAT refunds frequently point out the high awareness among criminal groups with regard to limitations of the fiscal administration resulting from the territorial extent, manners in which information flow between specific bodies or length of potential audit and opportunities for using the means, i.e. securing bank accounts/withholding the tax refund. This leaves the bodies appointed for enforcing the tax dues helpless against increasingly endemic tax crimes.

A system of tax administration called e-Declaration seems to provide a chance for partial and initial tackling IT problems. They partially replaced manual introducing data to the tax authorities systems, being a source of knowledge for the fiscal audit bodies. The news published on the website of the Ministry of Finance show that from the beginning 2014 there was a significant surge in the number of documents reported electronically through the system e-Declarations.

Figure 2: Dynamics for using applications e-Declarations by taxpayers

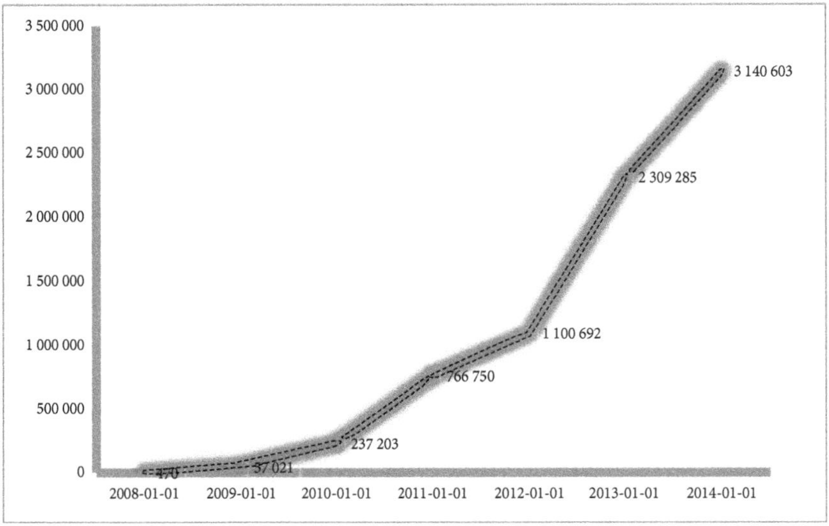

Source: own study based on the data of the Ministry of Finance.

Statistics (Fig. 2) imply that handling the affairs with the fiscal authorities through internet increasingly grow. The system activated in 2008 was scarcely popular because solely 470 persons decided to use this form of settlement. Subsequent periods brought successive increase in individuals using electronic declarations PIT – at the end of January 2014 as many as three million documents were submitted in that form[16]. The foregoing settlement system undoubtedly leads to quicker processing tax data and making them available to the finance departments. However, there is no information whether this form of settlements has any implications for the quality of IT subsystems and whether it provides any chance for establishing a uniform system in this respect for the whole administration within the departments of the Ministry of Finance.

Achieving satisfactory effects from the operations executed by the fiscal audit authorities in the aftermath of system analyses produced

Efficacy of analytical operations based on the information available seems to be difficult to determine. In the wake of analyses completed audit proceedings initiated in the fiscal audit – as key mechanisms counteracting negative tax practices – could have reflected a level of effects produced by operations of the whole system. This indicator is characterized by certain deficiency – due to diversified character of activities undertaken by the fiscal control, performing a vast variety of other tasks, it would not fully mirror efficacy of these units. Based on the system theory it may ascertained that an assessment indicatorof the quality or effectiveness of the analysis conducted in the fiscal audit offices may be, on the one hand, a level of meeting interests of the State Treasury, and on the other, a level of competitiveness security of entrepreneurs who discharge appropriately their levy liabilities towards the state. According to Ryszard Bełdzikowski, efficacy of the fiscal audit mostly rely on professional designation of entities and competence of those auditing, and it should not be solely associated with measurement-based decisions, fines or other financial sanctions [Bełdzikowski, 2011, pp. 144–14].

The Canadian tax services in its model designed for examining their performance assumes that a performance level reflects an indicator of dynamics for discharging tax and registry duties, and not investigation of increase in abuses

16 Consolidation and centralization of customs and tax systems http://www.kic.gov.pl.

and irregularities[17] traced. In countries where a level of public services provided is fairly high, quarterly, weekly or frequent analysis of effectiveness of operational activities across the tax administration is executed [Dohrmann, Pinshab, 2009]. Whereas the department of finance publishes annual information about results of the fiscal audit and accomplishment of tasks commissioned to its units.

In 2012, to enhance effectiveness of designating entities to be controlled, the General Inspector of the Fiscal Audit obliged selected fiscal audit offices to carry out analytical activities "allowing for identification of entities suspected of tax frauds in selected areas[18]. While deploying specialized IT tools, an analysis of data from available databases was completed and the monitoring through Internet was effected. Lists of entities with high risk of VAT irregularities selected as a result of these measures were transferred and used by relevant fiscal audit offices having territorial jurisdiction. In the process of designating the following were taken into consideration: results from analysis of data from the Polish Application VIES[19] concerning discrepancies between purchase of goods and services from EU countries declared by Polish taxpayers and supplies to Poland declared by EU partners, information about entities suspected of involvement in tax frauds are detailed within the network Eurofisc[20], information received from other EU states at the requests of the Polish administration submitted on the basis of the Council Resolution no. 904/2010 on administrative cooperation and combating fraud in the field of value added tax".

With regard to combat with tax frauds, systemic solutions are implemented, chiefly through bolstered cooperation with the UE states within multilateral controls, VIES exchange, information exchange based on SCAC documents [Krukowski, 2012, p. 387].

17 Canada Revenue Agency, Annual report to Parliament 2012–2013, http://www.cra-arc.gc.ca/gncy/tp/rprts/menu-eng.html.

18 Supreme Audit Office, Follow-up documents no. KBF-4101-07-01/2013 P/13/042, http://www.mf.gov.pl/documents/764034/3794865/23122013_NIK_zwalczanie_oszustw_w_podatku_od_towarow_i_uslug.pdf.

19 Information Exchange System on intra-community transactions and entities registered for the purposes of VAT UE between EU member states.

20 Network operating on the basis of the Council Regulation No. 904/2010 on administrative cooperation and combating fraud in the field of value added tax; its objective is efficient exchange of information between EU member states, facilitate multilateral cooperation with regard to combat VAT frauds.

The structure of audits findings (Fig, 3) split into specific tax titles shows that in 2012 share of VAT irregularities disclosed topped the list – in relation to its level over 2010–2013 and in relation to other tax titles. Clearly, this testifies to strengthened investigation operations with regard to disclosing abuses in goods and services tax, and, on a negative tone, it may imply upturn in extortions which thus brought about fall in VAT revenues to the budget.

Figure 3: Structure of proceedings conducted by the objective scope of audits over 2010–2013.

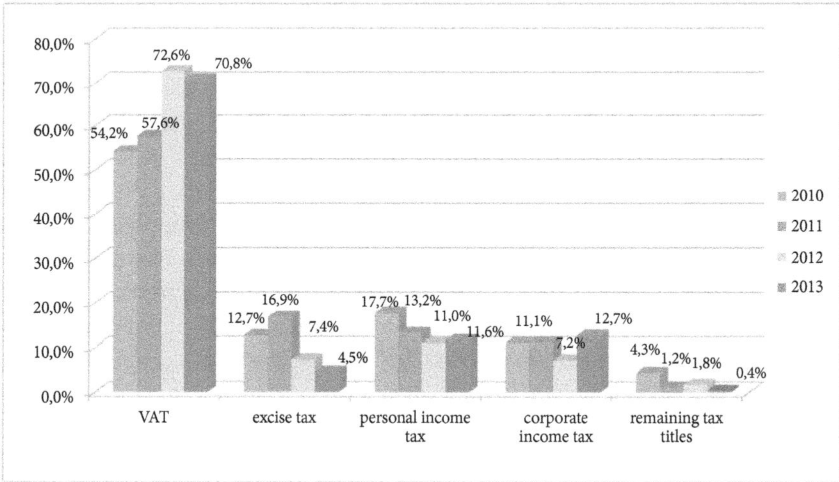

Source: own study based on the data provided by the Ministry of Finances: Report on performance of the fiscal control for 2013: http://www.mf.gov.pl/documents/764034/1424099/Sprawozdanie+z+dzia%C5%82alno%C5%9Bci+kontroli+skarbowej+za+2013+rok.pdf

As claimed by Dariusz Ćwikowski effective elimination of newly-established trends in tax frauds is made possible thanks to controls deliberately prepared, thereby having a positive impact on competitiveness principles and performance of honest entrepreneurs. It should be kept in mind the void left by eliminated illegal activities will be swiftly filled by others with distinct methods and techniques of their operations. Therefore, a process of continual analysis and audit flexibly aligned to new mechanisms may yield required effects [Ćwikowski, 2011, p. 287].

An analytical process preceding audit operations in such institutions such as: organizational units of fiscal audit, constitutes a backbone and thus it should be continuous in its character, embracing past and future periods in its scope.

Though, previous observations of operations taken by the fiscal audit agencies impels to state that mechanisms of tax avoidance or tax evasion occurring in the economy are frequently a consequence of the analysis, accomplished by taxpayers and teams of business advisors, of tax law, powers conferred on tax and fiscal audit authorities, including in particular weak points of the systems where these institutions operate. In effect, this leads to uncovering tactics, schemes of activities (frequently criminal) by the fiscal administration take place not at the initial phase but at the development phase of such mechanisms. An analysis conducted as well as identification of entities involved in such a scheme enables to designate a certain group of taxpayers to be controlled, whilst leaving a certain percentage (often a significant percentage) of entities that will never be subject to audit. That's why establishment of experts' teams comprising auditing units, analysts, IT specialists as well as legal counsellors across fiscal audit agencies would enable exposure of future or potential threats to tax revenues. Preventing them at the initial phase would signal satisfactory outcomes from such systemic activities. In essence, a toolkit essential for comprehensive analysis include tax knowledge, results of conducted controls exposing irregularity mechanisms as well as, on occasions, ambiguity in applying law and all data attained from tax authorities and cooperating institutions. An approach of systemic designation makes it possible to bring to light not only current and past, but also future untypical behaviors among entities aimed at avoiding and evading taxation through continually changing organizational forms of such malpractices, as well as enables to assess possibilities of exploiting such mechanisms against the background of binding legal regulations.

The Agreement concluded between the Ministry of Internal Affairs, Ministry of Finance and General Prosecutor on 30 January 2014 on cooperation in respect of designing systemic solutions to counteract and combat economic crime lends legitimacy and confirms the need for systemic actions. These bodies intend to compile a catalogue of principal activities, proposals, legislative amendments to reduce the level of economic crime, techniques fostering effective registering and managing of secured assets acquired through criminal activities, as well as to develop programmes and agenda for specialist trainings for employees of these departments[21]. The Minister of Internal Affairs, Bartłomiej Sienkiewicz claims that cooperation with regard to establishment of legal and organizational

21 Ministry of Internal Affairs, Agreement on cooperation in combatting "white collars" frauds: https://www.msw.gov.pl/pl/aktualnosci/11769,Porozumienie-o-wspolpracy-w-zwalczaniu-przestepstw-bialych-kolnierzykow.html.

system likely to effectively curb and eradicate this type of economic crime, and "experience of the Ministry Of Finance, General Prosecutor Office and Police collected into one team, being able to launch collective actions within the government and parliament so as to narrow such phenomenon in Poland, will deliver effects"[22]. The Ministry of Finance, Mateusz Szczurek, on that occasion, defined economic crime acknowledging that this is "not only decline in state revenues or decrease in tax owned to the state, but it means that all honest Poles are forced to pay higher tax", putting an emphasis on the fact that economic crime also causes unequal functioning of the economy, also within the area of unrestrained competitiveness[23]. The positive result of the systemic actions sought by these bodies will be a situation where economic crime will be effectively tackled while maintaining possibilities of running unrestrained business operations by honest taxpayers. This objective is well encapsulated in the opinion held by Konrad Raczkowski who claims that "it is institutions that should set up frameworks for varied actions taken by both the government as well as the private sector, whereas legislators should pursue a sensible structural policy approaching entrepreneurs through willingness to cooperate, cooperative attitude, balance of powers" [Raczkowski, 2014, p. 524].

Conclusions

Efficient and effective use of information possessed by the fiscal audit may significantly contribute to increasing tax revenues as well as economic security of the state. After all, management of economic securityshould be a kind of art seeking to preventively recognize current threats within the national economy, secures against the state of economic inequality, creates capacity of attaining objectives formulated [Raczkowski, 2012, p. 82]. Thus, due to systemic studies it is easier to understand certain interrelations occurring in the tax crime environment, and thereby identifying other subsystems. They may directly lead to preventing expansion of the tax dysfunctions which appear to be one of major threats to the public finance security, being a crucial element of the state economic security. Basically, strategic thinking focused in creative analytical approach is critical to mitigate the risk referring to elimination of current threats to security, [Raczkowski, 2013, p. 68]. Probably in order to intensify and continually enhance the quality of tasks performed by the fiscal audit it

22 Ibidem.
23 Ibidem.

is required to analyze the risk of these activities and to make legislative alterations. BogusławSzlachcic in this study *Analizaryzyka w zarządzaniukryzysowym [Analysis of risk in crisis management]* states that "conducting a detailed analysis for all systems is often overtly costly, whereas superficial handling of serious threats may be ineffective. Without the analysis of the risk it is unlikely to determine the risk value. Therefore, it is not obvious whether time, money and human resources allocated to the analysis are higher than losses generated by the risk subject to the analysis" [Szlachcic, 2013, p. 105]. It should be noticed that broad/ systemic approach provides an opportunity of identifying networks of criminal groups set up exclusively to commit tax extortions. The fiscal audit authorities enjoy broader powers than fiscal offices with regard to obtaining information or carrying out tax proceedings beyond their territorial jurisdiction. The act on freedom of business activities compelled investigation bodies to prepare analytical material, and even evidence ahead of starting the proceedings. Overall, an in-depth and wide-ranging analysis, updated on an ongoing basis, proves to give a chance to curtail some inconveniences stemming from, among others, limited investigation time. Its methodology should be adapted to any change occurred in the scheme of tax extortions or tax evasion. In sum, to ensure adequate revenues to the state budget, and at the same time to provide business entities with fair competition on the market, it is necessary to take care of the quality of data collected, IT tools designed for processing, as well as personnel support for persons employed on analytical positions, because these drivers mostly affect the results produced by systemic operations taken by the fiscal audit.

Bibliography

Aleksandrowicz T. R. (2013), *Analityk informacji w administracji rządowej* [in:] *Analiza informacji w zarządzaniu bezpieczeństwem*, ed. K. Liedel, P. Piasecka, T. R. Aleksandrowicz, Difin, Warszawa.

Aleksandrowicz T. R. (1999), *Analiza informacji w administracji i biznesie*, Wyższa Szkoła Handlu i Prawa w Warszawie, Warszawa.

Bełdzikowski R. (2011), *Kontrola skarbowa, uprawnienia, struktura, skuteczność*, Difin, Warszawa.

Canada Revenue Agency, *Annual report to Parliament 2012–2013*, http://www.cra-arc.gc.ca/gncy/tp/rprts/menu-eng.html.

Cempel Cz. (2004), *Teoria i inżynieria systemów: zasady i zastosowania myślenia systemowego*, Instytut Mechaniki Stosowanej Politechniki Poznańskiej, Poznań, http://neur.am.put.poznan.pl/is_2005/tis_2005.pdf.

Ćwikowski D. (2011), *Konstrukcja opodatkowania nieujawnionych źródeł dochodów jako jeden z elementów walki z przestępczością*, [in:] *Przepadek przedmiotów i korzyści pochodzących z przestępstwa*, ed. E. M. Guzik-Makaruk, Wolters Kluwer, Warszawa.

Davenport T. H. (2011), *Zdolności analityczne jako broń konkurencyjna*, [in:] *Sztuka łączenia technologii ze strategią*, [tł. ZespółTłumaczy Harvard Business ReviewPolska] *org. HBR on Aligning Technology with Strategy*, Harvard Businness School Publishing Corporations, Harvard.

Dohrmann T., Pinshaw G. (2009), *The Road To Improved Compliance. A McKinsey Benchmarking study of tax administrations - 2008–2009*. http://www.mckinsey.com/~/media/mckinsey/dotcom/client_service/public%20sector/pdfs/road_improved_compliance.ashx.

Filipkowski W. (2006), *Przestępczość zorganizowana – ujęcie prawne i kryminologiczne*, „Prokuratura i Prawo", no. 12.

Fuller R. J., Farrell J. L. (1987), *Modern Investments and Security Analysis*, McGraw-Hill Book Company, New York.

Gacparski W. (1987), *Teoria systemów*, [in:] *Filozofia a nauka. Zarys encyklopedyczny*, ed. Z. Cackowski, J. Kmita, K. Szaniawski, Ossolineum, Wrocław.

Gierszewski J. (2013), *Model bezpieczeństwa społecznego na tle teorii systemów*, „Kwartalnik" 2013, nr 2, Colloquium Wydziału Nauk Humanistycznych i Społecznych Akademii Marynarki Wojennej, Gdynia.

Jędrzejek Cz., Bąk J., Cybulka J., Martinek J. (2006), *Aspekty narzędziowe w projekcie systemu do analizowania naruszeń prawa*, XII Konferencja PLOUG, Poznań.

Jędrzejek Cz. (2007), *Logiczna i informatyczna semantyczna reprezentacja danych finansowych* [in:] Z. Gilowska, P. Pogonowski, I. Sobczy (eds.), *Przyjazna Administracja Skarbowa*, Difin, Warszawa.

Jędrzejek Cz. (2007), *Semantyczny opis danych finansowych*, [in:] *Nowoczesna Administracja Skarbowa*, Z. Gilowska, R. Tadeusiewicz, J. Tchórzewski (eds.), Difin, Warszawa.

Nowa encyklopedia powszechna PWN. (2004), ed. B. Kaczorowski, volume I, Warszawa.

Krukowski A. (2012) *Podatki i ich pobór a bezpieczeństwo ekonomiczne*, [in:] K. Raczkowski (ed.), *Bezpieczeństwo ekonomiczne. Wyzwania dla zarządzania państwem*, Wolters Kluwer, Warszawa.

Kryteria typowania podmiotów w obszarach ryzyka na 2013 rok: http://www.is.waw.pl.

Kudełko M. (2005), *Znaczenie analizy systemowej w prognozowaniu rozwoju sektorów paliwowo-energetycznych*, „Polityka Energetyczna", volume 8, Zeszyt specjalny, Wydawnictwo IGSMiE PAN, Kraków.

Kulicki J. (2012), *Formy prawne działań kontrolnych organów skarbowych w sprawach zobowiązań podatkowych* [in:] „Analizy BAS" 2012, no. 1(68).

Maciejczak P., Klonowska-Senderska I. (2012), *Analiza kryminalna - skuteczne narzędzie, ale nie panaceum na brak myślenia*, Kwartalnik Policyjny, no. 4, Centrum Szkolenia Policji, Legionowo.

Matyszczak J. (2008), *Funkcjonowanie systemu telekomunikacyjnego administracji publicznej*, Bezpieczeństwo Narodowe, no. 1/2.

The Supreme Audit Office, http://www.nik.gov.pl/kontrole/wyniki-kontroli-nik/pobierz,kbf~p_12_027_201205231143331337766213~01,typ,k.pdf.

The Supreme Audit Office, Follow-up Document No. KBF-4101-07-01/2013 P/13/042: http://www.mf.gov.pl/documents/764034/3794865/23122013_NIK_zwalczanie_oszustw_w_podatku_od_towarow_i_uslug.pdf.

Piasecki S. (1999), *Analiza systemowa a teoria organizacji* [in:] K. Mańczak (ed.), *Analiza systemowa i zarządzanie*, PAN, Warszawa.

Piech H. (2007), *Wielokryterialna optymalizacja na bazie wiedzy niepewnej*, Wydawnictwo Politechniki Częstochowskiej, Częstochowa.

Raczkowski K. (2014), *Strategiczne zarządzanie wiedzą w systemie gospodarczym a teoria racjonalnych oczekiwań*, „Marketing i Rynek" 2014, no. 5, Warszawa.

Raczkowski K., Sienkiewicz-Małyjurek K. (2013), [in:] K. Raczkowski, K. Żukrowska, M. Żuber, (eds.), *Interdyscyplinarność nauk o bezpieczeństwie*, Difin, Warszawa.

Raczkowski K. (2010), *Zarządzanie wiedzą w administracji celnej w systemie bezpieczeństwa ekonomiczno-społecznego*, Difin, Warszawa.

Raczkowski K. (2012), *Percepcja bezpieczeństwa ekonomicznego i wyzwania dla zarządzania nim w XXI w.*, [in:] *Bezpieczeństwo ekonomiczne. Wyzwania dla zarządzania państwem*, K. Raczkowski (ed.), Wolters Kluwer, Warszawa.

Raczkowski K. (2010), *Pożądany model zarządzania wiedzą w administracji celnej*, [in:] K. Raczkowski, *Zarządzanie wiedzą w administracji celnej w systemie bezpieczeństwa ekonomiczno-społecznego*, Difin, Warszawa.

Raczkowski K. (2014), *Współczesny model tetrarchii zarządzania a bezpieczeństwo ekonomiczne obrotu gospodarczego*, [in:] K. Raczkowski (ed.), *Bezpieczeństwo ekonomiczne obrotu gospodarczego. Ekonomia. Prawo. Zarządzanie*, Wolters Kluwer, Warszawa.

Raport PwC. (2014), *Luka podatkowa w VAT – jak ją zwalczać?*, Warszawa.

Rokita J. (2011), *Myślenie systemowe w zarządzaniu organizacjami*, Wydawnictwo Uniwersytetu Ekonomicznego w Katowicach, Katowice.

Regulation of the Minister of Finance of 4 January 2011 on seats and organization of the fiscal control offices (Journal of Laws of 2011, No. 13, item 62).

Regulation of the Prime Minister of 9 December 2009 on determining civil servants' positions, required professional qualifications, official ranks of civil servants, multipliers for determining remuneration and detailed principles for determining and paying other performances to which the civil service corps are entitled (Journal of Laws of 2009, No. 211, item 1630 as amended).

Stachowiak Z. (1994), *Bezpieczeństwo ekonomiczne*, [in:] W. Stankiewicz (ed.), *Ekonomika obrony*, AON, Warszawa.

Stefański A. (2007), *Rola kwalifikacji analityków w zarządzaniu ryzkiem kredytowym w bankach*, Wydawnictwo Wyższej Szkoły Bankowej, Poznań.

Strona internetowa: http://www.kic.gov.pl.

Strona internetowa: https://www.msw.gov.pl/pl/aktualnosci/11769,Porozumienie-o-wspolpracy-w-zwalczaniu-przestepstw-bialych-kolnierzykow.html.

Report on the fiscal audit for 2013 http://www.mf.gov.pl/documents/764034/1424099/Sprawozdanie+z+dzia%C5%82alno%C5%9Bci+kontroli+skarbowej+za+2013+rok.pdf

Szarucki M. (2010), *Metodyka analizy porównawczej w badaniach międzynarodowych*, Zeszyty Naukowe, no. 827, Uniwersytet Ekonomiczny w Krakowie, Kraków.

Szlachcic B. (2013), *Analiza ryzyka w zarządzaniu kryzysowym*, [in:] K. Liedel, P. Piasecka, T. R. Aleksandrowicz (eds.), *Analiza informacji w zarządzaniu bezpieczeństwem*, Difin, Warszawa.

Act of 28 September 1991 on the fiscal audit (Jpurnal of Laws of 2004, No 41, item 214 as amended).

Whittington J. (2013), *Ustawienia systemowe w coachingu zasady. Praktyka i zastosowanie*, [tł. Anna Niedzieska], Co&MePublishing, Warszawa.

Więckowski J., Jędrzejek Cz. (2014), *Skala finansowej przestępczości zorganizowanej w Polsce i dlaczego jej zwalczanie jest tak nieefektywne*, Instytut Automatyki i Inżynierii Informatycznej, Politechnika Poznańska, Warszawa.

Excerpt from the tasks of the fiscal audit offices for 2014, Ministry of Finances, Fiscal Audit Departament KS/8500/5/JRS/2013: http://www.mf.gov.pl/documents/764034/928259/Wyci%C4%85g+z+zada%C5%84+urz%C4%99d%C3%B3w+kontroli+skarbowej+na+rok+2014.

Zalewski D., Melezini A. (2011), *Ustawa o kontroli skarbowej, Komentarz praktyczny, stan prawny:1 lipca 2011 r.*, C.H. Beck, Warszawa.

Zenon Stachowiak[1] and Bartosz Stachowiak[2]

Institutional perception of unofficial economy in Poland – Contribution to the reflections on its positive effects

Introduction

The economic security of every country is a result of undergoing social reproduction processes, and these are an effect of human activities marked by varied levels and characteristics of entrepreneurship, which on one hand bolsters the level of economic security of the country or on the other it may decrease it. It is widely held that actions taken by people to make gains in an unofficial economy have features of crime. Such an approach is not wholly accurate in view of the broad range of forms engendering significant and diverse consequences. This implies the need to thoroughly examine the essence of the "unofficial economy", to pinpoint these structural elements which despite negative connotations may be regarded as permissible economic activities, yet remain unreported to the authorities, that is those labelled as the "grey market" and to explore areas of its occurrence and threats triggered by it; to outline its obscure and positive aspects in economy and, against that background, its relative size within the Polish economy, and finally to attempt to indicate and validate positive aspects of its functioning

Perception of the essence of the "unofficial economy"

Understanding of the specifics of unofficial economy is unlikely without referring to comprehension of its institutional social-economics [Kołodko, 2004, pp. 199–201]. This concept in the practice of social-economics, likewise in reference literature and statistics emerged relatively recently. Over many years the concept of the *grey market* has been raised in colloquial discussions as well as in scientific investigations. As it did not fully allowed for understanding the specifics of the these economic activities taking place outside the *official*

1 Professor, Ph.D., National Defence University, Domicile address: 04–447 Warsaw, ul. Roty 5, e-mail: zenstach@wp.pl.

2 Ph. D., Cardinal Stefan Wyszyński University in Warsaw, Domicile address: 05-092 Dziekanów Polski, ul. Asnyka 28, e-mail: bartosz.stachowiak@onet.eu.

economy, the term of *unofficial economy*, currently cited, is a more suitable category. Such an approach enables to not only specify the remaining definitions depicting these phenomena but also to indicate its areas and structure, and to conduct their analyses and assessments.

The *unofficial economy* appears under numerous synonyms such as: second trade, second economy, informal economy, shadow economy, parallel economy, unobservable, immeasurable, black economy or fourth sector. Frequently other designations are attributed to it such as: adverse, alternative, concealed, autonomous, unregulated, confidential, dual, marginal, parallel, peripheral, underground, shadow, unregistered, untaxed, informal, unofficial, black, subordinate, twilight, counter cash, or unrecorded [Gładek, 2008, pp. 12–13; Kozłowski, 2004, p. 14; Rajewski, Zienkowski, 1995, p. 13]. The multitude of synonyms enumerated reveals that there is no single widely accepted definition of the unofficial economy, yet we deal with the concept to which various descriptions and sense is assigned. A multitude of views also prevails in Poland.

As argued by P. Williams, an unofficial economy is not accidental side effect of long-term tendencies, but this is "…. rather an inevitable consequence of activities run by organizations which deny the state right to legally justified monopoly on violence, corrupt state institutions, pose threat to integrity of financial and commercial society's sectors, and those which typically ignore or violate legal and social standards at both levels: state and international" [Williams, 1997, p. 377].

The unofficial economy as one of the forms of social management occurs in both the national as well as the international arena. Such perception of this management form implies its complexity and multidimensional determinant factors for its causes and effects. Based on the institutional approach (a paradigm of so-called new institutional economy) requiring to view the issue from numerous standpoints and within a broad context of circumstances, it should be noted that in the entire spectrum of economic activities carried out by the state alongside official economy (national) we deal with – as claimed by F. Schneider and K. Raczkowski – an unofficial economy – illegal (called black economy or black market) ; and semi-legal economy designated as a grey market [Schneider, Raczkowski, 2013a, pp. 1–2, Schneider, Raczkowski, 2013b, pp. 3–31].

The first, that is the unofficial illegal economy covers such activities as: theft, corruption, bribery, organized crime, paid protection, manufacture and sale of prohibited goods, terrorism, smuggling, or fictitious transactions. They typically have criminal foundations generating manifold threats against legal activities, thereby curbing or impeding its development. It should be also seen as threat against economic security of the state[Schneider, Raczkowski, 2013a, pp. 1–2, Schneider, Raczkowski, 2013b, pp. 3–31].

The second, that is the unofficial semi-legal economy, which is related, perceiving through the prism of resources emigration, to optimization of taxes in compliance with applicable laws (that is to say tax avoidance) and tax evasion at the same time. Though, it should be highlighted that insofar as tax avoidance may bear the veneer of legality, tax evasion may take on the form of activities inherent to the unofficial illegal economy. The unofficial illegal economy embraces: unregistered activities of households, providing services and production without registering (authorization) and permits (license) and their inappropriate reporting, speculative transactions, use of insider information to perform beneficial transactions by persons having privileged access due to specific functions performed or being employed in the given institution. It is motivated by the account of unlimited profits and predicted costs [Schneider, Raczkowski, 2013a, pp. 1–2, Schneider, Raczkowski, 2013b, pp. 3–31].

A list of activities incorporating both types of unofficial economy is far more extensive. On a national scale it points out a wide scope of activities and a variety of forms, both at the national alike international level.

The unofficial illegal economy at the national level includes: car theft, robberies, group burglary, crimes connected with privatization, stock exchange and banking crimes, crimes in foreign trade, illegal production and trade of drugs, tax and customs frauds, banking extortions and stock exchange embezzlement, forging trademarks, abuses in public works. These activities increasingly entail commissioned murders, racketeering, crimes connected with debt collection and financial settlements, or crimes between rival criminal groups. In addition, this covers activities that involve illicit manufacturing and selling of goods, as well as providing services by entities having no qualifications (e.g. medical, construction, etc.). An example illustrating the practice is e.g. the production and trade of drugs or illegal abortion. In essence, activities aimed at illegally generating income – both money as well as in-kind from bribery, extortions or thefts are similar in their character. Such operations are frequently defined as "black market" or "black economy". Whereas on the international scale the following should be detailed: money laundering, arms smuggling, drug trafficking, child trafficking, prostitution, as well as illegal border crossing as well as trafficking in human beings and goods.

Meanwhile with regard to the unofficial economy it should be underlined that it involves manufacturing of goods or providing services which are not prohibited by the state, yet its size in whole or in part are hidden from state administration bodies (tax, customs, national insurance or statistical). This type of hidden activities is principally labelled as "grey market" and defined as economic activities by persons not registered by statistics, namely hidden earnings, hidden financial and in-kind transfers as well as production and services operations within the domain of households[Schneider, Raczkowski, 2013a, pp. 1–2, Schneider, Raczkowski, 2013b, pp. 3–31].

While depicting an unofficial legal and illegal economy, it should be stressed that in the social and economic life we experience their mutual penetration, because an urge to refrain from paying taxes fosters criminal behaviour.

The approach to the concept of *grey economy* currently presented is slightly distinct from that prevailing in the past. In this respect the views held by the Western economists specializing in these issues may be cited, namely F. Schneider, D. Enste and S. Vaknin. According to F. Schneider and D. Enste grey economy in economy refers to both legal as well as illegal activities. The first will shift into grey economy provided that it entails tax avoidance resulting from failure to report income from self-employment and from work unregistered with legal economic activities; and exploitation of tax gaps to minimize tax liabilities – manifested in discounts for employees or neighbour's help. Whereas the second – illegal activity – relies on monetary transactions in relation to trade in stolen goods, drug dealing and manufacture, prostitution, gambling, smuggling and financial frauds, and on non-monetary transactions in relation to barter of drugs, stolen or smuggled goods; production and cultivation of drugs for own use or theft for own use [Schniedr, Enste, 2002]. Similarly, S. Vaknin discerns and identified two types of grey economy: illegal activities unreported to the state, and in consequence untaxed: and legal activities not registered in the tax bodies where income is unreported and untaxed [Vaknin, 2000].

The definitions displayed and understanding of the "grey economy" suggest its certain explicitness in relation to illegal activities. It seems that most adequately "grey economy" should encompass all legal activities, yet concealed because of failure to pay taxes by entrepreneurs or other business entities or individuals intended to generate additional income, that is profits, through intentional failure to pay money considerations in favour of the state. Essentially, this means activities in the grey sphere always breach the interest of the state as a political and economic institution.

The Russians labelled the "grey economy" as "tieniewaja ekonomika", the Americans "underground economy or second economy", the Germans "Schattenwirtschaft", the Italians "lavorno nero", and the French "travail an noir" acknowledging that it made up of all types of economic activities which contribute to creating the state's value in the scale of entire national economy, though they are not considered in the social-wide balance, and therefore they are also not considered in social accounting.

Due to the vast divergence in labels assigned to the grey economy, it seems reasonable to use the terms "unofficial economy" or "informal economy" which would allow for establishing a more coherent conceptual apparatus for these issues [Raczkowski, 2013, p. 353]. In its wake the "grey economy" in economy should refer to an unofficial legal economy and in the context of all correlations between both realms of the economy.

With regard to each entity involved in the unofficial economy, diverse motives are in operation. Referring to an individual (a household) it should be indicated that it will predominantly be a quest or even a necessity to ensure livelihood for oneself and one's family. While for enterprises it will mainly be a drive to survive on the market.

Activities in an unofficial economy imply the need to perceive traits of offences (misdemeanours) or crimes. They are the result of a wide spectrum of prerequisites to dysfunctions engulfing economic life. They stem from the fact that people at the moment of possibility of committing such actions, commit them until eased by social, economic, political and legal circumstances. They heavily depend on the approval of the state for such a character of business activities, whether more or less intentionally it will leave legal, supervision, organizational and managerial gaps. In practice it means the prevalence of illegal actions over legal ones as the first one yields bigger gains [Janik, 2010, p. 41–51].

Areas and size of the "unofficial economy" in the Polish economy

In Polish economy there are numerous diverse forms and platforms in which the unofficial economy occurs, both illegal as well as legal, may be identified. Specifically, a combination of these two activities tends to be particularly hazardous for public order and state finances. The following should be detailed in the collection:

a) sale of liquid fuels frequently leading to organized crime with a mafia structure manifested in failure to pay taxes due (excise and VAT) to the budget, which are then legalized in various forms (e.g. money laundering);
b) sale of liquid gas at LPG petrol stations without declaring income instead of selling it for heating purposes which are released from the excise duty;
c) sale of ethyl tainted alcohol likely to be used for producing alcohol products after disinfection as well as for manufacturing products intended for consumption;

d) sale of tobacco products from countries over the Eastern border and China to be introduced into the Polish market (as well as the EU) and sold at attractive prices without payment of excise duty to the state budget;
e) illicit trafficking and gambling on the Internet having a character of unregistered trade of goods and services, and consequently untaxed.

A crucial area where the unofficial economy thrives are transfers of proceeds abroad manifested by performing transactions on grossly unfavourable conditions or concluding fictitious agreements, thereby leading to a diminished taxable base.

Illegal employment is a significant area where the unofficial economy, having attributes of grey, has held sway. This is a widespread practice generally accepted by society as such. Basically, it covers almost all ages and professional groups. As paid work performed without establishing an employment relationship is not encumbered by taxes, national insurance contributions and other financial liabilities of the state.

Another area of the unofficial economy with innumerable shades of grey is unregistered sales of goods and services largely incorporating: conducting business operations without registering, failure to report a tax obligation, gaining proceeds not corresponding to disclosed sources or coming from undisclosed sources; establishing fictitious entities, issue of fictitious invoices as well as abuse tax reliefs and allowances.

The magnitude of phenomena comprising the unofficial economy is difficult to gauge. Estimating its scale and size in the national economy presents many problems. In view of paucity of a coherent methodology designed for its identification and assessment, the methods[3], being reliable to a limited extent, are applied. A certain remedy was modification of the social accounts system

3 The primary methods used for gauging the size of the unofficial economy include: questionnaires allowing for assessing the size of the grey economy; labour force factor – determining an estimate size of shadow employment based on the declined share of the labour force in registered economy; demand for cash – informing about the increased demand as a basic transaction form for the grey economy; hidden variable approach – regarding the size of the grey economy as a function of variables observed (such as: tax burdens, burdens resulting from the government regulations, amount of cash in circulation, official work time, level of unemployment,…) having an impact on the grey economy and allowing for depicting both the causes as well as effects; and physical factors (e.g. electricity consumption as a physical indicator of the overall economic activity) Cf. *Shadow Economies: Size, Causes and Consequences*, in: “The Journal of Economic Literature” 2000.

(national) of the UN by the organization in 1993. This system (SNA – 93) imposes on the state statistical bodies a duty to assess the size of the grey economy. That means that GDP currently published contains a value of effects delivered by official economy activities as well as unofficial legal economy (the one from the grey economy). Nevertheless, that does not suggest that the estimate of the scale of size does not create many problems to the unofficial economy.

When limiting the discussions to the part of the unofficial economy having a legal character (designated as the *grey economy*) it should highlighted that in the opinion of economic experts linked to international economic organizations, there is currently no single country devoid of the unofficial economy. Countries with a marginal scale of the phenomenon are a rare exception. They estimate that this area generates from 10% up to one third, or even 40–50% of the world GDP. Though there is no pattern supporting the evidence that it is low in developed countries and high in underdeveloped countries.

From among the OECD countries over 1999–2007 only the United States of America (8.6%) and Switzerland (5.5%) stood out with a low level of the unofficial legal economy – standing below 10%. For the remaining countries the figure was two-digits. However, a trend to marginally decrease its level became apparent in most countries.

Across Europe in the EU states – based on the data from 2013 an average size of the unofficial economy is estimated at 18.5% of GDP, and ranges between 7.5% and 31.2% of GDP across the group. The member states may be divided, by the size of the unofficial economy, into four groups: below 10% (5 countries); from 10% up to 20% (10 countries); from 20% up to 30% (12 countries) and above 30% (1 country).

Having assessed the unofficial legal economy in Poland it should concluded that its share in the Polish economy is large when compared to other states across Europe. Yet they vary by the manner in which they are perceived and sources of its information. According to the Polish Central Statistical Office in 2011, the grey economy generated (production and services) equivalent to the 12.6% of official GDP (this is around USD 60 billion), while the value resulting from concealing the portion of the activities from the tax authorities by registered business entities accounted for 71% was, and undeclared work accounted for 29%. Such a value generated was concealed from the tax authorities.

Prof. F. Schneider, University of Linz, an international expert committed to investigating the unofficial economy, revealed a larger scale of unregistered economic trade across Poland. He argues that unregistered economic trade was equivalent to 23.8% of official GDP in 2013 versus 27.4% in 2004 [Schneider, Raczkowski, 2013b]. Moreover, he also lists, based on his research conducted, the determinants affecting growth of the unofficial legal economy such as: high tax rates and national insurance contributions (35–38%), low tax morality (22–25%); low quality of state institutions (10–12%); stringent regulations on labour market (7–9%) and low quality of public services.

According to another source – the Polish Confederation of Private Employers – unofficial activities in the first decade of the 21st century in the Polish economy was assessed at over 20.5% of GDP, while around 80% was generated by legal activities, and 20% by illegal operations. However, unofficial activities were diversified in particular sectors of the national economy. The highest share is reported in construction, retail and transport, and a slightly lower portion in production and health care.

As argued by the Institute for Market Economics, however, the size of the unofficial legal economy in Poland stood at 19.5% of GDP. Overall, it implies that Polish economy refrains from paying for the state over two months [Cieślak-Wróblewska, 2014, p. A1].

The size of the unofficial legal economy in Poland is substantially larger than the average across most of the EU states. F.Schneider reckons that over 2004–2012 across 27 EU states the size on average stood at 18.5%, from 21.9% in 20014 down to 18.9% in 2012. In 2013 the following countries outstripped Poland in terms of the size of the unofficial legal economy: Bulgaria (31.2%), Romania (28.4%), Croatia (28.4%), Lithuania (28.0%), Estonia (27.6%), Latvia (25.5%), Cyprus (25.2%) and Malta (24.3%). Whereas a lesser percentage calculated of GDP was posted in Greece (23.6 %), Slovenia (23.1%), Hungary (22.1%), Italy (21.1%), Portugal (19.0%), Spain (18.6%), Belgium (16.4%), Czech Republic (15.5%), Slovakia (15.0%), Sweden (13.9%), Denmark, Finland and Germany (13.0%), Ireland (12.2%), France (9.9%), Great Britain (9.7%), Holland (9.1%), Luxembourg (8.0%) and Austria (7.5%). He emphasizes that the poorer the country, the larger the magnitude of the grey economy[Schneider, Raczkowski, 2013a]. It is estimated that business transactions in the unofficial economy throughout the EU states in 2013 totalled Euro 1.9 trillion [Cieślak-Wróblewska, 2014, p. B4].

The phenomenon of the unofficial economy also comes to the fore in the countries that emerged in the aftermath of the collapse of the Soviet Union. Available information indicates that it occurs at varying levels – from relatively low in Baltic countries (Estonia, Latvia, Lithuania) to extremely high endemic in Ukraine (40% of GDP) and Russia (52.6% of GDP during 2011–2012) [Szara strefa, 2014].

Equally importantly, the unofficial economy also affects the labour market. According to data provided by the International Labour Organization, the illegal employment rate in developed Western countries is 15–20%, whereas in the underdeveloped countries 25–30%. It is estimated that around half a billion of people work in unofficial economy throughout the world. In the EU states employment stands at, depending on the method used for its determination, between 7 and 19% of the total employment which corresponds to 10–28 million of jobs. The unofficial economy with regard to employment is far more diversified in individual countries – it equalled up to: 7% in Austria, 21% in Belgium, 7% in Denmark, 4% in Finland; 14% in France; 35% in Greece; 23% in Spain; 14% in Holland; 10% in Ireland; 14% in Germany; 7% in Sweden; 13% in Great Britain and 26% in Italy [Weber, 1998].

In the EU the phenomenon of the unofficial economy is seen in few premises likely to be boiled down to the fact that on the one hand the functioning of the European Union rests on liberal rules of unfettered exchange, and on the other, fulfilment of these rules hinges on numerous and detailed laws as well as complicated deviations from them. It is reflected not only in illegal smuggling but also stealing subsidies. As such it is more cunning than violent in its character, and it is scarcely socially condemned.

In Poland the size and dynamics of the unofficial economy is mostly driven by self-employment, indirect taxes, tax morality and economic freedom.

Displayed comparisons of the unofficial economy in the international context in relation to the EU states allow for ascertaining that its larger extent takes hold in new, not old countries of the European Union as well as that within the old countries, a higher share of the unofficial economy prevails in the south of Europe.

According to the data provided by the Central Statistical Office of Poland in 2010 in Poland 730 thousand persons performed undeclared work which constituted around 5% of those employed. It was definitely less than in 1995 when 2199 thousand individuals were involved in undeclared work. A downward trend in undeclared work should be connected with emigration from Poland in the wake of acceding to the EU [Migracje, 2013]. In the views of Polish experts a more realistic figure is 1.7 million at the productive age are moonlighting.

Shift trends across the unofficial economy examined by the Central Statistical Office of Poland enable to note that this problem principally affects small and medium-sized companies. At their core are easier opportunities than in large companies, of concealing income generated. Surveys commissioned by the Polish Confederation of Private Employers found that Polish entrepreneurs suspect their competitors of hiding 20.2% of their turnover and employing 18.6% for undeclared work. Though a pattern appears evident that these processes take place in relation to practices used by a direct competitor, whereas in relation to "themselves" they often allow the possibility of executing similar activities. Meanwhile, analyses investigating the use of illegal proceeds reveal that its share in individual consumption totals 1.9% points, and around 3.1% points in investments. All in all, this suggests that they contributed to improving the living standards in some households, and in some enterprises they unofficially funded investments, thereby increasing official GDP in the future.

An unofficial economy engenders many threats. When they are recognized by the state and handled as one of the goals of the state security policy, then in relation to an individual, the level of anxiety experienced is minor.

Effects produced by operations within the unofficial economy, irrespective of its character and prevailing management method, should be seen as a manifestation of economic entrepreneurship by the entities forming it, enterprises and household members. They are achieved in a definite economic reality formed both by unofficial legal as well as illegal situations, facts and economic phenomena. On this occasion the conclusions formulated give rise to diverse reflections, doubts and assessments. They take place in all countries, under all possible economic systems and at different phases of their development. They are visible on a daily basis in a variety of countries – including Poland.

It may be assumed that the unofficial economy (second economy) includes: unreported sales with regard to unregistered production and service provision by unregistered business units (private and state) as well as private persons; unreported trade related to operations around the state enterprise; unreported transactions on the borderline of the private and state sector; unreported foreign transactions, black currency market, speculations, etc.; as well as sale of illicit goods and services. In the Polish circumstances, a country which converts its economy into the market path and adjusts it to the EU's requirements, an essential cause underlying the unofficial economy, from the viewpoint of the producer, is avoidance to pay taxes, customs and national insurance contributions, and thus minimize the manufacturing costs, while for the person employed "unofficially" – scarcity of possibilities of registered work or an intention to earn extra money to supplement low wages.

In the present day world the unofficial economy occurs in all countries, though their reasons as well as the scope and forms in which it springs up tend to be diverse. Central to its occurrence has always been an urge to quickly grow rich. Other drivers determining emergence and maintenance of the grey market in the economy are: technical revolution, struggle for a sales market, human migrations, the shift from the centralized economy to the market one, legal and institutional loopholes, incoherence of the legal system, increasing state intervention to economic life, declining employment and increasing unemployment.

Other causes underpinning its expansion also include: high tax burdens, large sums for mandatory national insurance, stringent economic policies, excessive state intervention in the labour market, a large number of small enterprises, impoverished households, rapidly increasing human resources at productive age, high levels of hidden unemployment in agriculture, extremely low levels of real wages and income, a large number of individuals entitled to obtain unemployment benefits, retirement pensions and disability pensions.

Obscure and positive aspects of the "unofficial economy" in Poland

The phenomenon of the unofficial economy, even though hard to be methodologically identified, affects the entire economies and entire territories of the state. Principally it is perceived in the economic context, though it has a profound moral, legal as well as social and political dimension. Its underlying essence, while covering several elements that prompt to approach the phenomenon in the light of critical assessments, does not enable to discern positive assessments in relation to this form of "entrepreneurship".

Despite the substantial scale of the "unofficial economy" embedded in national economies across many countries, an attempt to clamp down on it failed to be successful. In this respect a focus is brought to the conviction that its functioning in the long-run tends to be harmful to the economic growth, yet a full concentration of forces by authorities is likely to produce even more detrimental results to the economic and social growth. Hence, it is recommended to select an option of its gradual civilizing.

The unofficial activities in the economies across countries triggers not only negative but also positive assessments. Alongside numerous shortcomings inherent to its functioning, there are also specific benefits for ordinary citizens as well as for entrepreneurs. They may be clearly identified in the moral and legal, social and political as well as economic context. At the same time this means that there are adversaries as well as proponents of the unofficial economy.

If the downsides of the unofficial economy involve: threat to existing jobs, unfair competition to companies conducting legal operations and their declining profitability, and in some cases bankruptcy, obscuring a real picture of the labour market and unemployment, lack of retirement pension, disable pension and health guarantees for persons employed "off the books"; or dual financing of the unemployed "unofficially" employed and thus declined income to the state budget; these activities are coerced by the ineffective policy pursued by the state. Economic entities (households and enterprises) only adjust to them with the goal of surviving. Persons operating in the unofficial economy are aware of uncertainty caused by the failure to ensure work security. They are also conscious of lesser social security, though it is larger than in the event of being unemployed and deprived of the benefits from the state.

However, some unofficial illegal activities are always unacceptable such as: extortion of money from the bank, money laundering, or corruption. All these activities clearly reflect the threat to the economic security, thus eroding credibility of the state. Their bulk portion bears the traits of organized crime. Basically it is related to the fact the Polish financial system is exploited for laundering money coming from operations carried out by domestic criminals as well as foreign criminals. To conceal the property illegally acquired, these resources are allocated, among other ways, to: business investments, activation of business operations, expansion of an operating business entity through its financing, opening bank accounts in various banks, purchase of real estate, purchase of valuable movables, portfolio investments, purchase of currency, works of art, establishing fictitious companies faking business operations, concluding agreements by the use of fake documents; starting operations in the name of third persons, pretending to conduct legal financial transactions, excluding community property, fictitiously dissolving marriages, gifts in favour of close relatives, gifts in favour of fictitious foundations as well as transfer abroad and further investment in legal interests [Sędzicka, 2010].

The most significant implications and consequences brought by the unofficial economy is a reduced inflow of monetary resources to the state budget and national insurance. A gap in budget revenues resulting from unofficial activities is one the reasons behind the budget deficit. A the same time, it impels high taxation of recorded economy, thereby stirring further growth of the unofficial economy. Meanwhile, it should be noted that in relation to the majority of enterprises we deal with shadow activities generating income to the detriment of the revenues to the state budget, while in relation to the social group comprising unemployed performing minor works seasonally or occasionally, pensioners, annuitants as well as portions of the budget sector, the loss incurred to the state budget should be considered as relatively low. This loss is offset by activation of persons without work and proceeds from indirect taxes (primarily VAT).

Many advantages of the unofficial legal economy may be found in unrecorded employment. After all, it provides opportunities of work for persons that would stand no chance for employment in the official economy where cutting-edge technologies and innovations in production processes generate preconditions for unemployment surges. This suggests that unrecorded employment should be seen as an alternative for unemployment compelled by scarcity of workplaces within the recorded economy. Above all, it reduces unemployment and alleviates its effects. Specifically, it significantly reduces the number of real unemployed persons, and often, simultaneously, to a large extent, boosts a difficult situation of such families that due to low wages in the recorded sector possess income below the minimum level required for subsistence. The unofficial economy enables to start work exceeding the statutory number of hours or seasonal and occasional work, and thus generate extra funds for families remaining in tough living and housing conditions [Herer, Sadowski, 1995, p. 33,42]. During the downturn employment in unofficial economy constitutes a natural buffer against destitution and real unemployment.

Unrecorded work may stimulate the setting up of new workplaces which often could not be established in a legal manner owing to high social burdens. Due to failure to pay taxes and national insurance contributions, shadow enterprises may effectively compete with recorded enterprises. They contribute to creating cost advantage towards entities officially operating. Growth of the unofficial economy also diminishes overt and disguised unemployment in the non-agricultural sector, which in turn has a positive impact on the rate of GDP growth. Most workplaces in the unrecorded economy would not emerge in the official economy because of high establishment costs.

It should be also noted that the unofficial legal economy discharges the budget state from payment of benefits and allowances for those unemployed and enables the persons deprived of benefits to survive.

An importance aspect of newly established workplaces is the fact that money earned in the shadow economy returns to the official circulation and thus they are taxed by VAT. It is estimated that over two thirds of the money earned in that manner finds its way into the legal economy, thereby invigorating it and mitigating crises and recession phenomena. They enhance the standard of living for persons employed there.

In Poland, the biggest opportunities of operating in the unofficial economy are enjoyed by self-employed persons, that is individuals running sole proprietorship. In general, they have the best opportunities for tax evasion. In part, this is a result of decreased supervision by the government which, in the best general interest, encourages citizens to become their own employers, and thus cutting down unemployment.

While seeking for positives inherent to the unofficial economy, its production effects should specified as they allow for meeting the needs of the society as well as the economy. In that context, another feature should be emphasized which is its flexibility expressed by a swifter shift in structures of production of goods and provision of services as a response to changes in demand. Furthermore, it fulfils higher consumption aspirations of people whose official income falls short of meeting their needs. It is manifested, among other things, by increased access to various foreign products, e.g. through delivery of goods from abroad without customs duties and other fees. Clearly, this implies that entities operating unofficially help to better satisfy the society's needs.

Another positive aspect of the unofficial economy is giving impetus to the economic growth through investing portion of illegal proceeds by companies into company's expansion. Proceeds illegally acquired enter back to the official circulation and then are allocated to consumption purposes, bolster demand and revive the economy. Frequently money is utilized more effectively than it would be done by the budget.

On top of that, another positive facet of the unofficial economy is a shift in development macro proportions, manifested in a decreased gap between recorded and real national income without causing a rise in unemployment; increased pace of GDP growth in the recorded sector in the short-term, which will result from the shift itself in employment and other productions factors to that sector, and in the long-term shift in production factors from the grey economy to the recorded economy, which may deliver positive indirect effects stimulating quicker overall GDP growth through increased propensity to invest.

Practice of the economic life proves that combat with the shadow economy is directly proportionate to losses sustained as a result of shadow activities. The problem may be tackled in two ways: by liberalizing or tightening fiscal policy. In Poland the latter solution tends to prevail. This measure seems to bring the economy into a vicious circle. A response to high burdens is creation of new shadow areas. A certain proposal to shrink the unofficial economy level seems to be legalizing the areas where the unofficial economy holds sway and imposing lower levies for insuring them.

Having recognized a positive impact of the shadow economy in the economy and society (consumers' community) it is necessary to embrace a new philosophy which involves adopting activities for systemically combating and curbing, though not destroying, small business. According to the surveys of CASE and SMG/KRC every third Pole accepts the operations in the unofficial economy, and every fifth is indifferent. This means it has general social approval, because on the one hand, it is profitable to use benefits produced by this type of economy, and on the other, there is a conviction that public money is not spent sensibly and payment of taxes fails to bring proportionate benefits to citizens [Surmacz, 2011].

An important issue from the viewpoint of the shadow economy is the fact that it is formed by people – both as representatives of households as well as enterprises – entrepreneurial and creative persons in creating their jobs as well as flexible in their activities conducted. Typically, they stand out with a high level of innovativeness. An extensive body of research reveals that they tend to be more hardworking.

All in all, the unofficial economy yields benefits not only to basic economic entities, so from the microeconomic perspective but also from the macroeconomic perspective leading to enhanced macroeconomic indicators. This is a consequence of the fact that the statistical offices (e.g. the Central Statistical Office of Poland) incorporate its value in GDP which boosts the relations of these indicators to GDP (e.g. relation of the public debt to GDP). Advantages are outweighed by negatives. Pros and cons emerging in the unofficial economy indicate that the phenomenon is extremely complex and as such it can only be limited in its size and scope but not totally liquidated.

Conclusions

The unofficial economy perceived by the prism of the "grey economy" and "black economy" in the world economy is a moral, social and political and principally economic problem which should be recognized, assessed but also tackled by way of its civilizing. It also appears as an entrepreneurial form with various facets in the face of the broad spectrum in which the concept is viewed. It should be thoroughly specified and clearly divide the "grey economy" from the "black market".

The phenomenon of the "grey economy" is affecting all countries in today's world, irrespective of the management style, prevailing social and political regime, geographical location or development level achieved, has to be perceived through both the prism of its negative as well as positive aspects, and hence assessed in a well-balanced manner and resolved in a manner that reflects interests of all stakeholders (entities) and assessed through the prism of its defects and benefits. Therefore, because it is a phenomenon occurring across all world economies, its elimination is unlikely. However, it is necessary to make efforts seeking its constraint. The method for its reduction should be, above all, a decrease in labour costs, public levies, expenditures in bureaucracy as well as simplified administration procedures and legal regulations.

The unofficial economy exists not only in the economy but also in politics. These two spheres often overlap. After all, numerous economic decisions – as noted by many practitioners of economic life and evidenced by the social and economic reality – are made during informal meetings representing various political set-up and various interest groups. It implies that the official aspect of politics is often a tool designed for public acceptance of decisions made beforehand. In this respect, a view held by G. Kołodko appears symptomatic "... a relation of decisions made in the grey economy to those taken, from the very beginning till the very end, in the official sector is larger than the relation of trade in the grey economy to the recorded economic cycle." [Kołodko, 2004, p. 48].

Advantages underlying the unofficial economy may be found only in its legal area ("grey economy"). Its facets are frequently beneficial, yet they may be highly hazardous. It all depends on the situation in which an entity (an individual, enterprise) involved happened to be, whether its activities are driven by tax avoidance or evasion motivated by a profit and loss account, or whether they are a response to secure its living as a family viewed from the angle of the human being, or to survive on the market viewed from the angle of the enterprise.

Bibliography

Cieślak-Wróblewska A. (2014), *Dziś wyjdziemy z szarej strefy*, Rzeczpospolita, no. 59.

Gładek P. (2008), Szara strefa – zakres pojęcia i podstawowe obszary badań, (in:) E. Stawiasz (ed.) Zrządzanie wzrostem małych i średnich przedsiębiorstw w kontekście szarej strefy, Uniwersytet Łódzki, Łódź.

Janik E. (2010), Szara strefa - patologia życia gospodarczego, in: „Zeszyty Naukowe Uniwersytetu Rzeszowskiego" – Bulletin 64.

Kołodko G. (2004), *Zmiany instytucji i polityki dla szybkiego rozwoju gospodarczego*, [in:] A. Noga (ed.), Zmiany instytucjonalne w polskiej gospodarce rynkowej, PTE, Warszawa.

Migracje ludności w latach 2005–2012, GUS, Warszawa 2013,[in:] http:/WWW.stat.gov.pl/bldl/app/strona.html?p_naqme=indeks.

Raczkowski K. (2013), Gospodarka nieoficjalna w systemie zarządzania państwem, (in:) E. Gołębiewska, K. Raczkowski (ed.) Przedsiębiorczość i zarządzanie, T. XIV, Bulletin 8, Part II, SAN, Łódź.

Rajewski Z., Zienkowski L. (1995), *Szara gospodarka w systemie rachunków narodowych*, in: Szara strefa gospodarki. Wybrane problemy, Studia i Prace z Prac Zakładu B.S.-E. GUS i PAN, Zeszyt 233, Warszawa.

Schneider F., Enste D. (2002), *Hiding in the Shadows. The Growth of the Underground Economy*, International Monetary Fund, March.

Schneider F., Raczkowski K. (2013b), Size and development of the shadow economy and of tax evasion within Poland and of its neighbouring countries from 2003 to 2013: some new facts, [in:] K. Raczkowski, F. Schneider (eds.), The Economic Security o Business Transactions. Management in Business, Chartridge Books Oxford, Oxford.

Schneider F., Raczkowski K. (2013a), *Strefa nieoficjalna w gospodarce*, in: „INFOS BAS. Zagadnienia społeczno-gospodarcze“ no. 21 (158), as of 21 November.

Sędzicka M. (2010), Przestępstwo prania brudnych pieniędzy jako przejaw zagrożenia bezpieczeństwa obrotu gospodarczego, [in:] Z. Ciekanowski (ed.), Infrastruktura bezpieczeństwa publicznego. Ogólnokrajowe i lokalne wyzwania cywilizacyjne, WSzZiP, Warszawa.

Stankiewicz W. (2013), Ekonomika instytucjonalna. Zarys wykładu, Wydanie III, AON, Warszawa.

Shadow Economies: Size, Causes and Consequences. (2000), The Journal of Economic Literature.

Szara strefa w Europie, [in;] http://polish.ruvr.ru/2014.

Surmacz W. (2011), Szara strefa: Błogosławieństwo czy przekleństwo?, Wiadomości biznesowe. Newsweek, Warsaw.

Vaknin S. (2000), *The Blessings of the Informal Economy* [in:] http:/www.ce-review.org/00/40/vaknin40.html.

Williams P. (1997), *Groźny nowy świat: transnarodowa przestępczość zorganizowana w przededniu dwudziestego pierwszego wieku*, [in:] D. B. Bobrow, E.Haliżak, R.Zięba (eds.), *Bezpieczeństwo narodowe i międzynarodowe u schyłku XX wieku*, Fundacja Studiów Międzynarodowych, Warszawa.

Weber T. (1998), *Commission targets undeclared work* [in:] www.eiro.eurofund.ie/1998.

Magdalena Kowalczyk[1]

Struggle with the tax gap in Poland

Introduction

This paper seeks to provide an insight into the problem of tax gaps in Poland. The paper draws upon available data on the practice which is not sufficiently examined and analysed by relevant authorities. There is also a paucity of information about the reasons for such a state. An attempt has been made to present the phenomenon that occurred and continues to linger in Poland, having a serious effect on the country, as illustrated by selected examples based on available materials.

The issue of combating and preventing tax gaps in Poland proves to be problematic. The principal reason is instability in a law which is intricate and complicated. Analysis of tax laws reveals that they are frequently amended and modified, and perhaps should be rewritten in a simplified and clear language.

There is also no awareness among citizenry on the need to pay taxes in order to utilize them for our benefits. Thus, it is essential to persuade people of the significance of tax levies. Moreover, informing a society on the manner in which funds, coming after all from tax payers, are used and disbursed, has a great importance.

A downside of our system is the fact that exploitation of tax loopholes is not regarded as harmful or something which should be stopped. Penalties for abuse of lax law are not severe while exploitation of loopholes is widely approved which does not facilitate operations for tax authorities. Furthermore, these same authorities appear to experience overemployment. Maintaining a taxation apparatus is not cost-effective in Poland, and it fails to fulfil all necessary tasks. Employees of the tax bodies often lack the relevant expertise and skills to use all available methods and techniques for closing a tax loophole. It is required to establish collaboration at an international level in this regard.

"*The principle should be that a tax system is designed in such a way so that it is deprived of loopholes and any other defects enabling taxpayers to achieve tax benefits which are not intended by legislators and disrupt applicable principles of equal taxation*" [Olesińska, 2013, p. 357].

Various countries struggle with the problem of tax gaps. In Poland such practices are also endemic. However, there is no official data disclosing the scale of

1 Ph.D., State Vocational College in Sulechów, emai: m.b.kowalczyk@wp.pl.

the practice. It is also questionable whether the problem has been thoroughly investigated by anyone in Poland. Even the Ministry of Finance does not conduct any research on that issue and fails to publish any reports on a tax gap in Poland.

"The scale of the tax evasion is principally determined by estimating the size of budget tax revenues. Similarly to the estimate of the shadow economy, it is tremendously challenging to precisely specify the size of the tax gap, and worldwide literature lacks comprehensive in-depth analyses of the phenomenon" [Sowiński, 2009, p. 172]. More information on tax evasion may be found in various reports in the US, specifically a report issued in 2013 "Corporate tax dodgers, 10 companies and their tax loopholes" provides thorough statistics on the existing loopholes. In Poland it proves difficult to determine the scale of the tax gap because of the paucity of official information. Therefore, the application of an estimation method is likely to be the best way for analysing the phenomenon [Sowiński, 2009, p. 162].

Sources of the applicable law and available literature as well as reports published and statistical data on the subject were helpful for exploring the phenomenon. The tax gap occurring in Poland has been analysed based on accessible information and sources used. An extensive body of the materials is available through internet and other publications.

When analysing the practice in Poland, it was noted that the legal system should be more complete. The concept of completeness is closely linked to the term of the tax gap. A complete system is marked by a lack of loopholes. "The tax system should be free of redundant hindrances and at the same time it should conform to the individual's rights and the principle of equality under the law. High principles should guide the establishment of a tax system. i.e. combining numerous taxes into a certain whole" [Gomułowicz and Małecki, 2004, pp. 199–200].

Despite the above assumption, loopholes emerge in almost every legislative branch. Basically, they hamper the operations performed by the agency. A loophole is mostly seen as a "white spot" or "void". According to others this is merely a lack of legal regulation. However not every lack of provision is regarded as a loophole. The reasons behind gaps in the law are manifold. The law fails to keep abreast of changing lifestyles. A legislator enacting the laws is not capable of foreseeing all circumstances to be regulated. "That's why the tax system does not constitute a life domain; being closed in itself and for itself. It is derivative it is nature, and accordingly it is dependent on the growth and level of economic relationships as well as on political and social relations prevailing in the state. It is being honed in terms of the forms and content as the civilisation makes headway. The shifts taking place in the economy and politics affect the content and setup of taxes" [Gomułowicz and Małecki, 2004, p. 200].

The tax law system is formed by the set of norms applicable over specific time [Nowacki and Tobor, 2002, pp. 124–125]. "Only the norms appropriately enacted tend to be binding, which means that they were endorsed by the authorised body and in compliance with the procedure stipulated" [Morawski, 2009, p. 62]. These norms continue to evolve, which may ultimately trigger the occurrence of tax loopholes.

The concept of the tax gap

In essence it is hard to define the majority of concepts in the law for different reasons, e.g. because of diverse situational contexts and ambiguous language. "It suffices to look through any dictionary, or even any randomly selected pages of a dictionary to realize a wide variety of ambiguous words" [Zieliński, 2002, p. 140].

The concept of the tax loophole (tax gap) lacks any legal definition. Maybe legislators will provide clarification of the issue in the future. Furthermore, the Polish laws do not contain uniform views as to the existence (or lack) of legal loopholes. A dispute also rages around closing and removing loopholes in the law.

"We can distinguish at least three types of gaps in the tax law" [Mastalski, 2006, p. 145]. The first type is the intentional gap: where the legislator has intentionally not provided for any regulation to leave room for the development of a precedent. This kind of a legal void can be perceived more as a "general clause" or "understatement" rather than as an actual gap. The second type is the unintentional statutory gap: where the legislator could not foresee all circumstances while designing its regulation. This is a real gap. The third type is the exclusion of a sphere of economy from tax regulation, thereby creating a tax-free area [Mastalski, 2006, p. 145]. The legislator's silence on a tax obligation, whether deliberate or by mistake, creates an area exempt from taxation [Mastalski, 2006, p. 146]. In addition, there is the issue of tax avoidance – "circumventing the tax law" or tax reduction, i.e. when the tax obligation does not arise or arises to a lesser extent – "tax optimization" [Olesińska, 2013, p. 297).

For the purpose of the paper it was adopted that a concept of the gap signifies the "difference between potential tax revenues due to the state budget and actual revenues collected". A difference refers to the gap between tax owed to the budget and tax paid over specific period. Occurrence of the loophole is certainly driven by instability of the law, inefficacy of tax collection, shadow economy, tax abuse as well as tax evasion and its avoidance [Kuźmiuk, 2012].

Occurrence of tax gaps in Poland

The tax regime in Poland includes numerous loopholes that reduce the amounts owed to the state budget. A tax gap rises each year at a rapid pace. Tax frauds, in the opinion of some people, contribute to "diminished competitiveness of Polish business". A tax gap suggests a liability likely to be paid to the budget if tax collections were executed in an appropriate manner [Lewiatan, 2013].

Tax loopholes in the tax law in Poland are mostly a result of rapid changes effected in the tax law. Basically, these changes were not followed up by comprehensive solutions of all related issues. Tax loopholes and their exploitation are largely fuelled by the fact that the Polish tax law is unstable, complicated and confusing, thereby leading to abuses and diminished tax liabilities to the state budget. The situation does not improve, but continues to deteriorate. For instance, acts on income tax were amended 200 times in total and maybe they should be rewritten rather than continually corrected. It should be remembered that over 2000–2010 the corporate income tax act (i.e. Journal of Laws of 2011, N. 74, item 397 as amended) was amended at average 64 times and over 2000–2003 – 22 times. Over the recent period (2010–2014) a variety of amendments were also made. It transpires that over 10 years (2000–2010) the act was amended on average 6 times a year. In effect, these statistics look even worse with regard to the personal income tax act (i.e. Journal of Laws of 2012, item 361 as amended). In this case the Seym (Lower House of Parliament) amended its provisions on average once a month (31 amendments) over 2000–2003, and over 2000–2010 the amendments totalled almost 100. During 2010–2014 36 changes were introduced to the regulation. This is a worrisome practice as it applies to the act that affects almost every citizen. The same pertains to the Tax Ordinance Act (i.e. Journal of Laws of 2012, item 749 as amended) forming a kind of "constitution" for each taxpayer and tax authorities. This act over 2000–2010 was amended 60 times, whereas over 2000–2003 – 17 times, in other words on average every 2 months [Hussein, 2004, p. 356]. Over 2010–2014 the Tax Ordinance Act was subject to change 32 times. Moreover, a better picture is presented by the tax on goods and service (i.e. Journal of Laws of 2011, No. 177, item 1054 as amended), the Act was put in place in 20014 and until 2010 it was changed 22 times. Though recent years (2010–2014) brought as many as 19 alternations. The VAT acts together with regulations equalled around 12,000 pages. Thus, it is hard to imagine that the law is coherent. It is unlikely with such a number of "provisions" [Żaryn, 2013].

Tax acts are increasingly extensive, complex and thus unclear for an average citizen. Such a "legal jungle" facilitates divergent and frequently arbitrary interpretations of the laws, thereby leading to treating taxpayers in an unequal manner [Hussein, 2004, p. 364]. Tax laws lacking necessary precision may be exploited by many persons as proved by the practice. The law is required to be clear and precise as this is critical for protection of citizens' constitutional rights and freedoms. An addressee of the legal regulation should know what behaviour and for what reasons it has legal implications. According to the principles underlying a democratic state, a statutory regulation conferring on the state agency the rights to enter the sphere of civil rights and freedoms needs to fulfil a requirement for sufficient definition. The language used for legal regulations needs to meet particular requirements. Principally, it should be communicative so that obligations and rights will be easily understood. Complicated and unclear structures of the laws contradict clear tax law [Gomułowicz and Małecki, 2004, p. 114]. Tax regulations should be characterized by its precise definition, i.e. enacting specific norms in the tax law which prohibit definite actions while refraining from using indefinite concepts and conferring "decision-making leeway" on the agencies. The law cannot define taxpayer's actions which are based on vague criteria [Olesińska, 2013, p. 357]. "A taxpayer needs to be certain as to their duties as well as their entitlements with regard to calculation and payment of the tax (...). This all should be clear and obvious for a taxpayer. At the roots of vague tax regulations are usually structural errors in the laws implemented, extended reference systems, compound-complex sentences, unclear concepts, lack of internal coherence among legislative acts, widespread subject matters in numerous legislative acts" [Sowiński, 2009, p. 251].

The problems, mostly stirred by unclear legal regulations and ambiguous Polish tax law, may be illustrated by identifying three negative phenomena linked to diminished tax revenues in Poland. The first is escape from tax. The practice tends to a commonplace because in the states with "high" tax rates companies escape to so-called tax havens (labelled in other words as "oasis or tax shelter"). This practice is also used by Polish taxpayers. They escape to countries offering more favourable tax schemes (e.g. Monaco, Luxembourg). This is teetering on the edge of the law [Lipowski, 2002, s. 9–10]. In the view of the experts, a borderline for profitability of investment in the haven is an amount of half a million zlotys in income annually. While merely taxing a dividend in a state having no such a tax, saving may stand at PLN 95,000. This amount accounts for 19% of the dividend tax due in Poland. Some taxpayers utilise the practice as it is a legal procedure [Żaryn, 2013]. "Each taxpayer may navigate its affairs so that resultant tax liabilities be as little as possible" [Grzywacz, 2010, p. 54]. Therefore, states that refrain from imposing taxes or impose low fiscal liabilities on the specific income categories enjoy huge popularity [Grzywacz, 2010, p. 52]. The press claims that "around 10,000 entities could escape to tax havens from Poland" [Żaryn, 2013]. "It is essential to liquidate tax havens which are currently a tool for commercial and wholesale tax evasion through complicated structure of tax avoidance – which appears to be difficult in the medium term or even long term – due to increasing number of beneficiaries who have the possibilities of hampering political and organizational precautious measures through their accumulation of the capital" [Schneider and Raczkowski, 2013, p. 29].

A second negative practice triggered by a tax loophole in Poland is tax underestimation or avoidance. "Avoidance is an intentional activity and its aim, similar to tax evasion, is decreased tax liability" [Sowiński, 2009, p. 16]. Thus, companies determined to pay taxes in Poland seek opportunities for not paying them. In doing so, they pursue two strategies. At the start it should be stated that the law allows for, in particular cases, decreasing taxation (tax minimisation is not applied in Poland on a mass scale). So tax evasion is left at disposal. This way involves exploitation of legal loopholes not intentionally designed by legislators. The efficacy of these practices mostly hinges on the knowledge of the company's personnel [Żaryn, 2013]. Tax avoidance in a strict sense should be perceived as operations conducted in line with the law. This is a trade-off between taxpayer's interest and society's interest. The extent of the trade-off depends on the tax policy and financial needs of the state. It is a proven fact that specific forms of tax avoidance are permitted by jurisdiction in some countries which typically suggests no definite sanction [Lipowski, 2002, p. 35]. Accordingly we distinguish legal tax avoidance arising from agreements on avoiding double taxation. Additionally, there is unlawful tax avoidance which is almost identical to tax evasion. Distinction between legal and illegal tax avoidance is contingent on the sanctions stipulated in the law and court decisions in this regard [Lipowski, 2002, p. 40].

Below, tax gaps are illustrated based on varied examples under different circumstances.

Income tax gap

Polish income tax regime allows for circumventing tax liabilities. For instance, big retail chains in Poland are an example of exploiting tax loopholes. In recent years a wide range of retail chains sprang up in Poland. Yet, they thrived as long as they did not have to pay taxes or they avoided them. On the whole, they disappeared the moment they became subject to income tax in Poland. "When they became eligible for tax liabilities they were quickly sold to new chains hitting the market in Poland. This can be traced based on press articles and statistical data on how many retail chains disappeared over recent years" [Żaryn, 2013].

Certain tax privileges were enjoyed by employers running supported employment enterprises. "In 2000 a legislator cancelled a relief in income tax for entrepreneurs running supported employment enterprises. In accordance with regulations applicable beforehand, taxpayers with a status of supported employment enterprises were exempt from income tax" [Sowiński, 2009, pp. 214–215].

Capital gains tax gap

Tax gap involved rounding capital gains tax in line with the Belka's tax (the label comes from the name of the minister who put the tax in place). There were rules for rounding the taxation base to PLN 1 and also the tax to PLN 1. This practice was used to establish one-day deposits. They allowed for circumventing the Belka's tax. If "any deposit was charged less than PLN 2.49 of interest, so 19% of the tax from the amount equalled less than 50 groszy. By rounding down, the tax amounted to zero which resulted in no interest taxed". A change in the legal provisions is intended to round the tax accrued on the deposit gains to 1 grosz [Skwirowski, 2011].

Tax on goods and services gap

The VAT gap is a difference between an amount of tax liabilities arising from transactions concluded and actual revenues paid to the State Treasury. The reasons behind it may include: "shadow economy", extortions, tax avoidance, errors or bankruptcies. This tax generates over 40% of revenues to the state budget [Conference at BCC, 2012].

"The losses of VAT to the Polish Ministry of Finance have been investigated by a study of PwC (2013). In this study an attempt is made to estimate the size of the tax gap caused by VAT-fraud and a description of the mechanism of tax frauds in Poland and the European Union is given. Moreover, the study also gives a description of identified systematic problems which lead to abuses resulting in the increase in Shadow economy and tax evasion tax frauds on a large scale. The study also presents some proposals of systemic solutions (which could have been helpful to fight against tax offenses and consequently to decrease the tax gap or tax fraud originating from VAT)." [Schneider and Raczkowski, 2013 p. 23–24].

Table 1: Tax on goods and services gap in Poland and collation from 2010–2012 (in million PLN)

	2010	2011	2012
Minimal value	**21 503**	**27 800**	**36 450**
Average value	**30790**	**38150**	**47489**
Maximum value	*40077*	*48500*	*58527*

Source: a study based on the documents provided by PwC and Structural Research Institute, *State Treasury Losses in VAT May 2013.*

The gap in tax on goods and services, as illustrated in the above juxtaposition increases yearly. A scale of so-called VAT gap estimated in the reports by consulting companies totals around PLN 36.5–58.5 billion. Though there is no efficient manner for clamping down on the practice. Tax offices, receiving annual revenues generated by VAT less than those projected, step up inspections. They are carried out to close at least portion of the gap through: e.g. imposing financial penalties. Inspections by fiscal authorities and increased VAT rates are not the best solution. However, it may imply that some steps were taken in this regard. According to "reports of supervision agencies in the first quarter 2014 1400 inspections were conducted which led to detecting VAT extortion of over PLN 2 billion. This constitutes an increase by PLN 400 million as compared to the analogous period of the previous year. During the control over 36,000 false invoices at the total value of PLN 5 billion 700 million were revealed. The number of false invoices is almost identical to the first quarter of the previous year, whereas the amount indicated is higher by PLN 1.5 billion. The analyses conducted in the financial department show that fraudulent claim of VAT refunds generate the biggest losses for the budget" [MF: fiscal inspectors, 2014]. "Fighting tax evasion from VAT-fraud is maybe the most important policy goal. If also in the European Union all member states try to efficiently fight tax fraud by making the VAT-system more efficient with clear-cut rules and little exemptions, then his would lead to great success in reducing this type of tax fraud. Due to the lack of the common fiscal policy it is unlikely to, among others, harmonize tax rates, and therefore the EU states having the highest tax rates should expect heightened risk of the tax reclaim fraud through numerous dummy transactions and buffer companies within intra-Community trade. Thus, it may lead to elimination of some honest business entities from the market which will be unable to compete with fraudulent entities in terms of the price. Budget losses triggered by the growing tax gap because of tax refunds undue will increase the deficit (and thus the public debt), and they may translate into spending cuts in the following tax year, which may impact the rate of economic growth" [Schneider and Raczkowski, 2013 p. 29].

Shadow economy

"The grey economy (unofficial semi-legal economy) is both a deliverance and a threat to the state. Everything depends on whether the person engaged in such business, which typically applies tax optimization on purpose and, at the same time, evades taxes, is motivated by the account of unlimited profits and calculated losses or struggles to keep the company on the market" [Raczkowski, 2013, p. 360]. "On the other hand, the black market (unofficial wholly illegal economy) with its inherently criminal nature is nothing more but a threat. The existence of the black market directly undercuts or blocks the pursuits of legal business and threatens the state as an organization" [Schneider and Raczkowski, 2013 p. 5].

"Persons operating in the semi-legal unofficial economy typically undertake two types of activities: lawful tax optimization (tax avoidance) and unlawful tax evasion" [Schneider and Raczkowski, Bureau of Research Chancellery of the Sejm, 2013, p. 1]. The unofficial economy prompts an increase in the tax gap which results from undeclared business operations. In Poland the shadow economy covers practically all professions (unregistered baby sitters, construction workers, tutors are among the most typical examples). Self-employ-ment has the biggest influence on the size and development of the shadow economy [Schneider and Raczkowski, 2013 p. 16].

"In the studies addressing the question of the underlying causes behind the shadow economy an emhasis is placed on the impact of not only tax savings but also other factors such as:

a) not being subject to restrictions with regard to the labour law,
b) lack of other administrative restrictions (e.g. licence, registration),
c) sense of leeway and flexibility in shaping economic relationships,
d) easy entry to the sector,
e) lower earnings, but also lower prices of goods and services" [Sowiński, 2009, pp. 152–153].

The biggest losses for the Polish budget result from informal economy in the fuel, tobacco and alcohol sectors. The Polish Organisation of Oil Industry and Trade estimate that in 2012 the losses to the state budget as a result of the shadow economy in the fuel sector stood at PLN 3 billion. In 2013 there was a surge to the level of around PLN 4 billion. Shadow economy for tobacco products in 2012 "is estimate as over 12 billion items (6.2 billion cigarettes and 6 billion tobacco for smoking)". The above data reveals the level accounting for over 20% of the total Polish tobacco market. By using estimated data the Association of Polish

Spirit Industry Employers assess that the shadow economy for the alcohol sector generates losses at PLN 1.2 billion annually to the budget. Industry organizations provide estimate data based on statistical data, though it should be kept in mind that the shadow economy may actually be much bigger. We should remember that the shadow economy generates losses not only for one single defined industry but for interrelated industries. This involves the loss of thousands of potential jobs. Hence, curbed burdens and simpler registration procedure are intended to prevent these adverse ramifications [Article: information for the administration, 2013].

Table 2: Size of the unofficial economy in Poland over 2010–2013

year	2010	2011	2012	2013
% of official GDP	25.4	25	24.4	23.8

Basic data included in the Table come from the study by F. Schneider and K. Raczkowski, *Shadow economy in Poland and EU member states*, Bureau of Research Chancellery of the Sejm, 2013, p. 3.

Despite the shadow economy there is a phenomenon of the black market, i.e. activities entirely illegal, being crime-related practice. These activities concern, e.g. fictitious transactions, corruption, bribery, organized crime, etc. They pose a threat to the state and legal business operations which in consequence sustain sizeable losses [Schneider and Raczkowski, Bureau of Research Chancellery of the Sejm, 2013, pp. 1–2].

“The average size of the shadow economy in 27 EU-Countries was 22.3% in 2003 and decreased to 18.4% (of official GDP) in 2013” [Raczkowski and Schneider, 2013 p. 1]. “If we first consider the size and development of the shadow economy of Poland it had a value of 27.7% in the year 2003, which then steadily declined to 25.3% in the year 2008, increased slightly to 25.9% in the year 2009 and since then decreased to 23.8% for the year 2013 (forecast)” [Raczkowski and Schneider, 2013 p. 10]. “The eastern countries or the “new” European Union members, such as Bulgaria, South-Cyprus, the Czech Republic, Latvia, Lithuania and Poland have higher shadow economies than the “old” European Union countries, like Austria, Belgium, Germany, Italy; hence, one can observe an increase of the size of the shadow economy from west to east” [Schneider and Raczkowski, 2013 p. 15].

Other tax gaps

While seeking for ways of paying less tax, “gift boom” escalated at the end of the 20th century. It appeared that tax regulations contained a loophole allowing each individual to give money to their nearest relatives for the purposes widely defined. When granting a gift they could claim a gift tax allowance. "In 1996 a gift tax allowance was exploited by almost every third citizen. In total 6.3 million taxpayers transferred gifts which shrank the state budget by PLN 1.9 billion". In effect, a big portion of these gifts, if not all, were fictitious as the fiscal authorities were not capable of verifying them. When the gift loophole was closed from 1 January 1997, interest in gifts fell. In PIT Return for 2009 less than 300,000 individuals wrote off a gift tax allowance. Following gifts, taxpayers attempted to write off disability pensions and privately funded scholarships [Skwirowski, 2013].

"Until 1999 a loan agreement was subject to taxation by fiscal charges, meanwhile improper deposit agreements (storing money or things specified as to their types), similar in many respects, was not subject to tax obligation. Thus, this led to concealing loan agreements through making improper deposit agreements. Eventually, this persuaded a legislator to expand the objective scope of taxation in the act on civil law transactions tax. By the same token, a legislator put into practice exemptions for loan agreements concluded between family members in view of the common practice of not disclosing them by close members of family" [Sowiński, 2009, p. 216].

Abolition of the dog tax was forced on the legislator, as the majority widely evade paying this tax and there were no effective means of enforcing this fiscal obligation. Liquidation of the tax proved to be a suitable solution. It was replaced by an optional fee for owning a dog [Sowiński, 2009, p. 216].

Taken together, the occurrence of tax gaps in the various examples displayed above is huge. When analysing the Eurostat data and comparing them with the data provided by the Central Statistical office of Poland in terms of trade exchange between Poland and the EU, we can see an increased tax gap likely to equal "at least 28–32% of actual tax revenues". This means that "between PLN 69.5 billion and 79.4 billion were not paid to the state budget". Such amounts fail to be paid in Poland because of the applicable law and loopholes occurring in it. Closing tax gaps is likely to solve numerous financial problems in Poland, e.g. covering the budget deficit [Żaryn, 2013]. "The size of the tax gap in Poland, calculated by the cautious GUS estimates is negligibly less than the size of the budget deficit and remains at a level close to the amounts spent on the public debt service. This insight helps understand the tremendous importance of the tax evasion to the state budget. With the ideal assumption that when there is no shadow economy and maintaining public spending at the current level it would be possible to balance the state budget" [Sowiński, 2009, p. 183].

Methods and manners for clamping down on tax gaps by relevant authorities

A desire to escape a tax has, and will continue to prevail. In the situation when we face a necessity to hand over about 20% or more of our income to tax authorities, many of us begin to consider how to avoid that experience. First, we start to think about typical reliefs and allowances, and then we move on to complicated circumvention of the regulations, i.e. exploitation of loopholes. Tax authorities considerhow to combat this practice. It can be handled through tightening up the tax system to curtail possibilities of escaping tax payment. Though as shown in the history of the tax law, escapes from tax obligation have always occurred [Skwirowski, 2013].

"Reduction of the shadow economy can be achieved using various channels that governments can influence. The main challenge still is to bring shadow economy activities into the official economy in a way that goods and services previously produced in the shadow economy are still produced and provided in the official economy. Only then the government gets additional taxes and social security contributions and transfers value added from the shadow into the official economy" [Schneider and Raczkowski, 2013 p. 28].

Fiscal reform could improve the situation. Fiscal organs are characterized by inadequate division of competencies, lack of sufficient knowledge and overemployment. The Polish fiscal apparatus employs "over 65,000 persons. This suggests that the cost of over 1,600 persons from the fiscal administration falls on one million inhabitants". According to the data of the International Tax Benchmarking, Polish fiscal administration proves to be "the most ineffective across the EU" [Conference at BCC, 2012].

Analyses produced testify to the complex nature of the Polish tax system and fiscal apparatus. The recent ranking "Paying Taxes", featuring the most beneficial tax systems for business, "Poland ranked 114 (out of 183 countries). Ahead of Poland were, among others, Cambodia (66), Afghanistan (94) and Ethiopia (103). Such an outcome results from the number of payments and hours devoted to discharging tax obligations by medium-sized companies. Yet, the OECD assesses the Polish tax system as poor and costly. As provided by the report "Tax Administration in OECD and Selected Non-OECD Countries: Comparative Information Series (2010)", PLN 1.72 out of PLN 100 collected as tax revenues in Poland is spent on fiscal administration. To put that into context, Germany spends 79 eurocents out of Euro 100 from revenues. The Polish tax system distinguishes as many as 13 types of taxes, but even a simple PIT provides for 40 various types of statements in total designed to communicate between an employer, employee (taxpayer) and tax office" [Żaryn, 2013].

Therefore, recent years were expected to yield changes through taxpayer's enhanced position in its relations with fiscal authorities. Also, inspection procedures were supposed to be simplified. It was critical to eliminate flaws in the financial policy of the state. Furthermore, a struggle with bureaucracy was launched through reducing the number of documents necessary for tax proceedings. The majority of citizens feel confused in the "jungle" of continually changing regulations [Górzyńska, 2004, p. 10].

This state calls for a radical improvement, both in the public as well as individual interest. A vast number of tax regulations, their instability and the vagueness of many phrases included in them cause that "the tax law is viewed as one of the most complicated and hermetic law branches" [Pomorska, 2004, p. 301]. The specifics and complexity of the tax laws are scarcely comprehensible for most citizens. These provisions are only clear to a narrow group of specialists [Pomorska, 2004, p. 301].

A tax gap is tremendously hazardous. The struggle with a tax gap is challenging and falls short of results. There is no effective method to underpin and improve the actual state. Nevertheless, we should not remain passive and cease to make attempts. It should be kept in mind that tax frauds and tax evasion are illegal activities involving escape from tax liabilities. On the other hand, tax avoidance may be consistent with the law, yet it is inappropriate exploitation of the tax system with the goal of decreasing or avoiding tax liabilities [Report, 2013].

Thus, it is vital to handle a tax gap using diverse methods. This may be supported by the Polfisc system, among the others, put into operation by revenue bodies at the beginning of April. This is an analytical tool intended to quickly trace tax extortions [MF: fiscal inspectors, 2014]. Furthermore, two teams have been operating in the department of finance for some time. The first is committed to enhancing the effectiveness of operations performed by tax administration and prosecution of frauds. The second aims to boost the quality of handling taxpayers. They both strive to curb a tax gap. Fiscal bodies need to operate in a "uncommon and civilised" manner, principally placing an emphasis on bolstering the quality of handling taxpayers and raising awareness that it is worthwhile being honest [Będziesz uczciwy?, 2014].

"Also, Polish fiscal administration began implementation process for cutting-edge methods of tax control using IT techniques (ACL, Winldea, Ocean GenRap, CAATs)" [Sowiński, 2009, pp. 325–326]. "Meanwhile it is worth highlighting that due to IKOS system implemented by the fiscal agencies and algorithms designed to statistically analyse probability of tax evasion (in the case of the fiscal control), advanced methods of data analysis are gradually put into operation" [Sowiński, 2009, p. 318].

Moreover, the ministry of finance intends to set up the Central Debtors' Register. This is connected with a philosophy of "good and bad taxpayers". The idea involves a diverse approach by tax authorities to those with arrears and those that timely settle their liabilities. "Good taxpayers" may benefit from additional facilities, e.g. quick settlement of accounts by the revenue bodies. The register (likely to be operational from 2016) is supposed to disclose debtors with undisputable amounts due of at least PLN 500 in taxes and other contributions. They will be reported in the register following 60 days from the receipt of the notice. The register will be kept in online mode [Będziesz uczciwy?, 2014]. The Ministry of Finance also plans to establish the institution of the warning letter. Tax bodies would use the letter to inform about abuses traced in VAT in the trade of specific goods [Będziesz uczciwy?, 2014].

There is also an idea to pay a tax on goods and service on a special account, so-called "split payment model in VAT". According to that principle, a company which purchases goods pays on the seller's bank account a net amount. VAT charged on the invoice is paid on a special company's account opened at the tax office for settling solely this tax [MF: fiscal inspectors, 2014].

At the end it should be highlighted that universality of taxation arising from art. 84 of the Constitution (Journal of Laws, No. 78, item 483 as amended) required adoption of the norm making a tax obligation inevitable. These norms were included in art 24a and 24b of the Tax Ordinance Act and they were designed to closely tighten up the tax system. The measure was supposed to prevent exploiting loopholes in the tax law for tax evasion [Olesińska, 2013, p. 276]. Art. 24a contained authorisation granted to tax inspection authorities to declare legal effects from concealed legal action. Art. 24 b of the Tax Ordinance Act was a more far-reaching step setting out a legal regulation for overlooking legal effects of legal actions which delivered significant tax benefits such as decreased tax, increased loss and raised overpayment, by authorities [Stanik, Winiarski, 2013, p. 55]. This article was mainly subject to doctrinal analyses as it was not a ground for resolutions because it was operational for a short time. It entered into force on 1 January 2003 and on 7 February 2003 it was appealed against by the Constitutional Tribunal which challenged its validity in its ruling of 11 May 2004 (K 4/03 Journal of Laws No. 122, item 1288) [Olesińska, 2013, p. 282, 287]. The act amending the act of 30 June 2005 – the Tax Ordinance Act and the act amending other acts (Journal of Laws, No. 143, item 1199) repealed art. 24a and 24b. Instead another general clause was implemented – art. 199a of the Tax Ordinance Act which conferred on tax authorities power to examine statements of intent in terms of their ostensibility [Stanik, Winiarski, 2013, pp. 57–58]. "Circumventing the tax law in the context of art. 199a § 1 and 2 of the Tax Ordinance Acts should be understood as a situation when the specific meaning given to the legal action by a taxpayer is determined by its intention to achieve a favourable economic result due to fraudulent activity intended to conceal an actual business transaction" [Stanik, Winiarski, 2013, p. 72].

This regulation in the Tax Ordinance Act was believed to be a remedy for tax gaps. The clause is expected to have an impact in the form of prevention. It should be applicable to all taxes and it should pertain to occurrences related to running business operations and occurrences related to involvement in business entities [Olesińska, 2013, pp. 347–348].

Tax evasion is also regulated by international laws. "The act under the international law focused on the issues of tax evasion is the Strasburg Convention of 25 January 1988. The convention imposes an obligation of administrative assistance in tax matters on the states that ratified it. The assistance includes information exchange, simultaneous tax inspections and involvement in tax inspections abroad as well as help in enforcement and security proceedings and service of documents. Legal regulations pertaining to combating tax evasion are also contained in the European law" [Sowiński, 2009, p. 340].

"Having analysed legislators' responses to taxpayers attitudes toward taxation, it is possible to identify numerous activity forms seeking to curtail the scale of tax evasion practice. The most frequently used are as follows:

a) specifying vague or generally formulated laws to limit the possibilities of law abuse,
b) taxing entities that previously were not subject to taxation and used for tax escape – an instance of such practice is illustrated above by taxation of the improper deposit. The threat of mass tax evasion is the rationale for keeping the inheritance and gift tax,
c) setting additional requirements for tax privileges or hampering tax evasion – an example of such measures is a requirement for transferring monetary funds from the gift obtained for a public benefit institution through a bank transfer,
d) abandoning the solutions that encounter tax resistance – for instance as outlined above implementing exemption of loan agreement conducted between family members from tax on civil law transactions,
e) making sanctions more stringent,
f) conferring bigger powers to bodies responsible for controlling compliance with tax regulations by taxpayers – even by launching a special supervision

procedure with the goal of inhibiting persons paying excise tax from committing frauds,

g) imposing duties on taxpayers which fulfilment impedes tax evasion – as for instance an obligation to keep documentation for transactions between related entities or an obligation to report transactions with the means of fiscal cash registers,

h) lump-sum calculation of tax and putting simplified forms into place, being beneficial to a taxpayer due to low costs for tax collection" [Sowiński, 2009, pp. 216–217].

Guidelines and postulates for rectifying the ongoing situation

The Polish tax system tends to be conducive to searching for loopholes. "The tax system in Poland is leaky, economically ineffective and unclear for taxpayers". These leaks are correlated to efficiency of the state in devising and collecting taxes. Everything rests on the effectiveness of the authority and tax administration as well as citizen's awareness. The first step is to persuade citizens that taxes paid will be disbursed in compliance with public purpose. When acceptance for taxes rises there will be no reasons for seeking lawful tax avoidance or unlawful tax evasion. The taxes will be not accepted unless citizens are convinced that the state through its institutions fulfils collective and individual needs [Żaryn, 2013]. "An important factor determining tax discipline is a level of so-called "tax morality"." [Sowiński, 2009, p. 356].

In addition, tax privileges should be abolished to effectively clamp down on the tax gap. Comprehensive reforms should be rolled out so that the tax system becomes simple, clear and just. Tax acts should be rewritten in such a manner. Thus, at the heart is broad cooperation of the Seym with experts specialising in taxes and full use of experiences gained by countries with a stable tax system. The issue of establishing a coherent system adequate to the actual state as well as logical and correlative legal regulations are brought to the forefront [Naczyńska, 1998, p. 102]. It is vital to pursue excellence of the tax law so that it contains a minimal number of reliefs and allowances [Kulicki, 2000, p. 320]. Above all, it is necessary to organize and simplify legal and tax regulations. Marek Zuber argues that the Polish laws regulating taxes should rewritten so as "to curtail possibilities of tax avoidance and tax reduction in a manner not provided by legislators" [Żaryn, 2013].

Another problem is posed by the practice of enacting secondary legislation to acts overnight to be effective together with their publication. Irregularities produced by unstable tax law triggered progressive setbacks of the law, thereby hindering effective and efficient operations of tax agencies and compelling other unexpected amendments to laws which confines rational and lawful behaviour of taxpayers, particularly those running business operations. "In these circumstances the tax law was not applied consistently, taxpayers were handled on an unequal footing and tax rules were designed through guidelines and recommendations" [Hussein, 2004, pp. 356–357].

Taking into account the above problems in tax regulations it should be stressed that taxes should be lower and equal for everybody. This will tighten up the system and increase revenues to the budget. Besides, unilateral domestic means used for closing a tax gap appear ineffective and insufficient in many cases. This reveals the urgency to adopt a coordinated and multidisciplinary approach at a domestic and international level. It should be kept in mind that the combat with tax fraudsters, tax evasion and avoidance as well as aggressive tax planning requires definitely boosted cooperation between tax bodies across countries as well as collaboration between tax authorities and other enforcement agencies. It is essential to determine areas where regulations and administrative cooperation may be streamlined in order to rein in tax frauds through appropriate application of the programmes FISCALIS i CUSTOMS [Report, 2013].

Moreover, it is important to handle a tax gap simultaneously at a domestic and international level. It is recommended for EU member states and Poland to focus on allocating adequate human resources, knowledge and funds to a domestic tax administration. Funds should be earmarked on training audit bodies with regard to tax frauds and tax avoidance [Report, 2013]. "In the era of globalization and liberalization of principles guiding capital tranfer, running business operations abroad, international tax competeition, etc. cooperation among tax authorities across various jurisdictions proves to be critical for effective tracing, prosecuting and enforcing arrears resulting from tax evasion" [Sowiński, 2009, p. 338].

Conclusions

"The tax gap cannot be definitively eliminated, likewise crime cannot be eliminated. However, it may be substantially mitigated and thus limiting possibilities for committing tax frauds. A favourable tax system might encourage taxpayers to settle their accounts in the state where economic activities are carried out. Thus, it is imperative to decrease and simplify taxes so that they are less acute" [Żaryn, 2013]. "It should be also underscored that the complexity of the tax system causes increased possibilities for tax avoidance though the use of loopholes, abuse of multiple exemptions, allowances, etc. The more technical options for tax evasion at the disposal of the taxpayer, the bigger propensity to exploit them" [Sowiński, 2009, pp. 128–129].

The problem of tax gaps has been recognized for many years. They tend to be widespread and they inflict vast losses on the budget and society. Hence, the proposals for addressing the problem come up, yet they are not 100% efficient. The fiscal apparatus is not adjusted to the scale of tax swindles. The civil servants still lack basic knowledge on business trading, opportunities of using databases possessed or collaboration. Additionally, ideas suggesting tightening up the Polish tax system are not executed because there is no political will. Inertness of an employer and tax authorities with regard to tax holes is worrisome. The reasons behind loopholes is the fact that many lawyers serve in the Seym establishing a tremendously potent lobby [Żaryn, 2013].. "Although a postulate for simplified tax law is a staple element of almost every election manifesto, yet following the change in government, it appears that political elites are not prepared to allow any alterations in the tax law. An example illustrating this case was the appointment of the government headed by Kazimierz Marcinkiewicz in October 2005. Although the election manifesto of the Law and Justice party (PIS: Prawo I Sprawiedliwość) included a declaration to simplify the tax law – following the appointment of the government it transpired that there are no specific blueprints for accomplishing the concept – in an attempt to create the concept, taxpayers, entrepreneurs and experts were asked to display their ideas for changes" [Sowiński, 2009, pp. 266–267].

On top of that, some are not interested in changing the tax law in Poland. For them the more complicated the law, leaving room for abuses, the better [Żaryn, 2013]. This is not a positive practice as it has a direct impact on the budget. Also, another negative aspect is failure to carry out surveys on the size and extent of tax gaps because the information obtained might serve all persons, chiefly entrepreneurs [Conference at BCC, 2012].

To sum up, a vast range of diverse factors affect the practices of applying the tax law and exploiting tax loopholes. The primary drivers include: quality of tax regulations, effectiveness and efficacy of operations conducted by the apparatus charged with taxes, and state of judicial decisions given chiefly by courts. Nevertheless, it should be highlighted that court proceedings in cases against tax frauds are strenuous and lengthy. Yet, persons finally found guilty receive lenient penalties. Consequently, tax frauds become low-risk crimes. VAT frauds are more profitable than ordinary criminal activities because penalties are not so severe. As for the profitability of such activities, this is one of the most lucrative businesses [MF: fiscal inspectors, 2014]. "The ordinary crime concerned with robberies and thefts has shifted to tax crime which proved to be more lucrative".

We face erosion of the taxation base and growing shadow economy with a soaring scale of tax frauds [Będziesz uczciwy?, 2014].

In conclusion, the tax gap should be tackled, and it is essential to talk about it as well as about evasion and abuse of the tax law. The focus should be brought to the fact that the borderline between evasion (abuse) and optimization of the taxation basis, which is not prohibited, is vague and elusive. The judicial decisions of the European Court of Justice repeatedly emphasised that when one activity is subject to tax and the other is not at all or to a much lower tax, a taxpayer does not have to choose a higher tax rate. The aim is to clamp down on frauds, tax avoidance and potential law abuse, and the activities consistent with the law are permitted. After all, it is necessary to distinguish fraudulent activities from those intended for tax avoidance through abuse of powers arising from the legal norms from activities falling into the boundaries of taxpayer's rational operations [Stanik and Winiarski, 2013, p. 107–110].

Bibilography

Article information for the administartion, *Gospodarka nieoficjalna. Konsekwencje funkcjonowania szarej strefy dla gospodarki [The Unofficial Economy. Consequences of the Shadow Economy for the Economy]*, 31.12.2013 (source: http://www.eu-go.gov.pl/pl/dla-administracji/artykuly-informacyjne-dla-administracji/2298-gospodarka-nieoficjalna-konsekwencje-funkcjonowania-szarej-strefy-dla-gospodarki/).

Będziesz uczciwy? W urzędzie skarbowym będziesz VIP-em, Gazeta Wyborcza 21.04.2014 (source: http://wyborcza.biz/biznes/1,101562,15832357,Bedziesz_uczciwy__W_urzedzie_skarbowym_bedziesz_VIP_em.htm).

Corporate tax dodgers, 10 companies and their tas loopholes (2013), Raport, Tax Fairness and IPS (source: http://www.americansfortaxfairness.org/files/Corporate-Tax-Dodgers-Report-Final.pdf).4. Gomułowicz, A. and Małecki, J., (2004), *Podatki i prawo podatkowe*, Wydawnictwo Prawnicze LexisNexis, Warszawa.

Górzyńska, E. (2004), *Podatnik w urzędzie skarbowym – prawa, obowiązki, procedury*, Wydawnictwo Difin, Warszawa.

Grzywacz, J. (2010), *Pranie pieniędzy. Metody, raje podatkowe, zwalczanie*, Szkoła Główna Handlowa Oficyna Wydawnicza, Warszawa.

Hussein, A. (2004), System podatkowy w świetle badań kontrolnych Najwyższej Izby Kontroli [in:] *Polski system podatkowy. Założenia a praktyka*, ed. A Pomorska, Wydawnictwo Uniwersytetu Marii Curie-Skłodowskiej, Lublin.

Kulicki, J. (2000), *Kontrola skarbowa. Studia podatkowe*, Dom Wydawniczy ABC, Warszawa.

Kuźmiuk, Z. (2012), *Ogromna luka podatkowa w Polsce*, Stefczyk 7.11.2012 (source: http://www.stefczyk.info/publicystyka/opinie/ogromna-luka-podatkowa-w-polsce,5844308455).

Lewiatan chce pomóc w walce z luką podatkową w VAT. (2013), PKPP Lewiatan, Warszawa 15.07.2013 (source: http://konfederacjalewiatan.pl/opinie/aktualnosci/2013/1/lewiatan_chce_pomoc_w_walce_z_luka_podatkowa_w_vat).

Lipowski, T. (2002), *Raje podatkowe - charakterystyka i sposoby wykorzystania*, Ośrodek Doradztwa i Doskonalenia Kadr sp, z o.o., Gdańsk.

Mastalski, R. (2006), *Prawo podatkowe*, Wydawnictwo C. H. Beck, Warszawa.

MF: Inspektorzy skarbowi wykrywają coraz więcej oszustw w VAT [MF: Fiscal inspectors trace increasingly more frauds], Serwis Wyborcza 27.04.2014 (source: http://wyborcza.biz/biznes/1,101562,15865107,MF__inspektorzy_skarbowi_wykrywaja_coraz_wiecej_oszustw.html).

Morawski, L. (2009), *Wstęp do prawoznawstwa*, Wydawnictwo „Dom Organizatora", Toruń.

Naczyńska, J. (1998), Funkcjonowanie instytucji kontroli skarbowej, *„Roczniki Nauk Prawnych"*, No. 8.

Nowacki, J. and Tobor, Z. (2002), *Wstęp do prawoznawstwa*, Zakamycze, Kraków.

Olesińska, A. (2013), *Klauzula ogólna przeciwko unikaniu opodatkowania*, Wydawnictwo „Dom Organizatora", Toruń.

Konferencja w BCC. (2012), *Polska traci miliardy z powodu luki w VAT*, 6. 11. 2012 (source: http://m.biznes.pl/konferencja-w-bcc-polska-traci-miliardy-z-powodu-l,5297532,10735,107,news-profil.html).

Pomorska, A. (2005), Stosowanie prawa podatkowego przez aparat skarbowy – główne problemy i nieprawidłowości, [in:] *W kręgu prawa podatkowego i finansów publicznych. Księga dedykowana profesorowi Cezaremu Kosikowskiemu w 40-lecie pracy naukowej*, [in:] H. Dzwonkowska and J. Głuchowska and A. Pomorska (ed.), Wydawnictwo Uniwersytetu Marii Curie – Skłodowskiej, Lublin.

PwC commissioned by the Structural Research Institute, *Report on the State Trasury Loss in VAT May 2013*.

Raczkowski, K. (2013), Gospodarka nieoficjalna w systemie zarządzania państwem [in:] Gołębiowska, E. and Raczkowski, K. (eds.), *Zarządzanie – nowe perspektywy, Przedsiębiorczość i zarządzanie*, Społeczna Akademia Nauk, Łódź, Vol. XIV, Book 8.

Schneider F. and Raczkowski K. (2013), Shadow economy in Poland and EU member states, "*Bureau of Research Chancellery of the Sejm*", No. 21 (source: http://orka.sejm.gov.pl/WydBAS.nsf/0/7E1E8CE2D305DA2DC1257C3F003B9B68/$file/Infos_158EN.pdf).

Schneider F., Raczkowski K. (2013), Size and development of the shadow economy and of tax evasion within Poland and of its neighbouring countries from 2003 to 2013: some new facts, [in:] K. Raczkowski, F. Schneider (ed.), The Economic Security of Business Transactions. Management in Business, Chartridge Books Oxford, Oxford.

Skwirowski, P. *Podatki jak durszlak*, Gazeta Wyborcza 8.05.2013 (source: http://wyborcza.biz/biznes/1,100897,13867940,Podatki_jak_durszlak.html).

Skwirowski, P. *Zniknie luka w podatku belki. Tylko czemu zostaje podatek*, Gazeta Wyborcza 26.05.2011, (source: http://wyborcza.biz/finanse/1,105726,9671066,Zniknie_luka_w_podatku_Belki__Tylko_czemu_zostaje.html).

Sowiński, R. (2009), *Uchylanie się od opodatkowania. Przyczyny, skutki i sposoby zapobiegania zjawisku*, Wydawnictwo Naukowe UAM, Poznań.

Report of 2 May 2013 on the combat tax frauds, tax evasion and tax heavens (2013/2060 ((INI)). (source: http://www.europarl.europa.eu/sides/getDoc.do?pubRef=-//EP//TEXT+REPORT+A7-2013-0162+0+DOC+XML+V0//PL).

Stanik, K. and Winiarski, K. (2013), *Praktyczne problemy nadużycia i obejścia prawa podatkowego*, Oficyna wydawnicza UNIMEX, Wrocław.

Żaryn, S. (2013), *Podatkowe sito coraz mniej szczelne*, Gazeta Bankowa 25.07.2013 (source: http://www.bankier.pl/wiadomosc/Podatkowe-sito-coraz-mniej-szczelne-2880191.html).

Czesław Jędrzejek[1]

VAT tax fraud and its relation to the low efficiency of the Polish value added tax collection system

Introduction

Despite its GDP growth, Poland faces numerous economic issues. The budget deficit was 42.19 billion zloty in 2013 [Ministry of Finance, 2014] being 2.6% of GDP (Polish gross PKB), or over 8 billion zloty less than anticipated. This has been achieved by delaying payments or cancelling planned expenses towards the end of the year.

On 10 December 2013, the European Council issued a new recommendation for Poland under the Excessive Deficit Procedure (EDP). On 2 June, 2014, this procedure was suspended for Poland [European Commission, 2014]. This happened despite the fact that the budget deficit in 2013 was 11.8 billion zloty higher in 2013 compared to 2012 [Ministry of Finance, 2013]. The rationale was presumably a prediction of above 3% growth in GDP for Poland in both 2014 and 2015. For 2014, the budget deficit is not to exceed 47.66 billion zloty in 2014, only because private retirement funds in pension plan portfolios are being transferred to the government social security fund (ZUS).

The Polish Ministry of Finance justifies the budget deficit by a marked deterioration of the economic situation in Poland's external environment followed by a slowdown in domestic economic activity as a key factor explaining non-achievement of the 2012 and 2013 budgetary targets. As a result of that slowdown, the government revenue was much lower than expected.

Indeed, the overall GDP growth declined from 4.5% in 2011 to 1.9% in 2012 and 1.6% in 2013 caused by slowing domestic demand. Net exports were almost the only source of growth during 2012 and 2013.

1 Prof., Ph.D., Institute of Control and Information Engineering, Poznan University of Technology, Poznan, Poland, email: czeslaw.jedrzejek@put.poznan.pl.

Poland has high unemployment and low wages. In 2013, the average hourly labour costs in the Polish economy [Eurostat, 2014] excluding agriculture and public administration were estimated to be €7.2 - almost the same as in 2008 - compared to €23.7 in the EU28 and €28.4 in the eurozone (EU17). This translates into a low tax base.

The rhetoric of the Polish Ministry of Finance is followed by leading economists and Polish government institutions such as The Polish Supreme Audit Office (Najwyższa Izba Kontroli) who, despite its criticism of the Polish Ministry of Finance (MF), does support its rhetoric [also, see Namysłowski, 2014].

During the past two years, it has became obvious that the considerable economic growth slowdown of 2012 and 2013 was accompanied by a very significant increase in the scale of the shadow economy.

This situation is confirmed by MIMIC studies that estimate that the shadow economy generates 24% of Polish GDP [Schneider, Raczkowski, 2013, p. 12]. PwC estimated the tax gap as ranging from 36.5 to 58.5 billion zloty. [PwC Report, 2013, p. 14]. This number is comparable with VAT payment arrears that at the end of 2013 stood at 33.1 billion zloty. The efficiency rate of collection enforcement was 21.8 % [NIK, 2014, p. 3].

The MF does not use the concept of tax gap as is the case with the Research Office of the Chancellery of the Polish Parliament. At the same time the product gap concept is considered important [Research Office Lexicon, 2014].

The Polish MF displays total analytical inability. It does not publish analytic reports, makes access to data difficult and appears to obscure the financial reality in Poland. At the end of 2013, an analysis was published presenting data of selected local Polish Tax Offices [Więckowski, Jędrzejek, 2014]. In some regions during 2012, VAT tax collection receipts were negative. This reinforced the suspicion that enormous VAT recovery values that increase each year are a manifestation of very large scale VAT fraud. The Polish MF did not previously publish annual VAT recovery values. On February 10, 2014, such data was published for the first time [Dziennik Gazeta Prawna, 2014].

Since the most dramatic developments for Poland happened during 2012 and 2013, this paper is focused on an attempt to understand what happened throughout this period. Traditional approaches rely on calculating a VAT compliance measure – the VAT tax gap.

In order to obtain the full VAT collection picture, one should not only focus on VAT gaps resulting from the shadow economy in the EU accession states of May 1, 2004. Therefore, I also analyse other measures.

Measurable effects of VAT avoidance and evasion

Several indicators will be addressed in this work. The first is the VAT gap being the difference between theoretical tax liability according to tax law and the actual revenue collected [CASE, 2012, p. 29] on a timely basis (USA IRS).

There have been many top-down studies to measure the tax gap. Some such studies focus on the European Union as a whole yet, at the same time, present data specifically on Poland [Reckon, 2009, p. 41], [Case, 2013, pp. 37–38].

Many countries estimate VAT (or Tax on Goods and Services) tax gaps. For example, the UK has been assessing its VAT gap since 1992 and since 2009 has also estimated its direct tax gap. Such studies are highly politicised and subject to crtitcism as many economists believe that there are no reliable estimates of the overall tax gap [Gemmell, Hasseldine, 2013].

The IMF is currently preparing a new method to measure VAT gaps for roll-out to member countries in 2013 ("RA-GAP") and has applied it in Estonia [IMF Estonia, 2014] and Uganda. In particular, their method has been used to assess the British HMRC tax gap analysis program and has provided advice and guidance on further improving it [IMF UK, 2013].

The tax gap measure does not give direct indication of the level of tax fraud.

Top-down tax gap methodologies comprise the following steps:

1. Calculation of the portion of the total tax base attributable to consumption, broken down into products and services.
2. Calculation of theoretical VAT revenue through "taxation" of the theoretical VAT tax base at such rates relevant for particular goods and services.
3. Comparison of theoretical income calculated as above against the actual inflows derived from VAT proceeds for each year.

The tax base is calculated separately for the following consumption categories (sales/purchases) of goods and services:

- final consumption of households,
- final consumption of public entities and public benefit organisations,
- intermediate consumption and,
- investment.

In May 2013, PwC Poland issued a report in which an estimate of the minimum and maximum VAT gap was published [PwC, 2013, p. 14–15]. As for EU related cases, a final consumption value for households was obtained using the COICOP classification (Classification of individual consumption by purpose) for the period 2006 to 2011. This particular work used the EUROSTAT macroeconomic data. Tables of Usage showing flows between 47 sectors related to consumption of goods and services were employed. According to PwC, the VAT gap during the period 2011 to 2012 increased dramatically and could have ranged from 36.5 to 58.5 billion zloty (12.1 to 19.4 billion USD) in 2012.

The second group of indicators are *C-efficiency* methods. It has been observed that changes in VAT revenues have been driven much less by changes in the standard rate than by changes in C-efficiency [Keen, 2013]. C-efficiency is an indicator of the departure of the VAT from a perfectly enforced tax levied at a uniform rate on all consumption. Since the final consumption expenditure is a better tax base indicator than the GDP, this measure is appropriate to the Polish case as the largest contribution to Polish GDP came in the last 2 years from growth in exports.

C-efficiency = R(VAT)/ B *r, (1)

where R(VAT)/ are VAT revenues, r – standard VAT rate, and B the tax base.

Usually, a variant of the final consumption expenditure (FC) is taken as a tax base, sometimes called the tax base indicator, although there is a some difference between final consumption and the VAT base. National accounts contain data on final consumption expenditure but may not contain some otherwise useful data.

There are several variations of the C-efficiency method. In the simplest version

C-efficiency 2 = R(VAT)/ FC *r. (2)

This number would be 1 if VAT revenue collected was equal to the standard rate on all final consumption.

A more justifiable approach is to remove VAT revenues from FC as the theoretical basis for taxation should not include the tax itself. Then the equation (2) is transformed to the form:

C-efficiency 1 = R(VAT)/(FC-R(VAT av) *r, (3)

where R(VAT av) is theoretical VAT to be raised.

Finally, a VAT Revenue Ratio (VRR), is used that reads:

VRR = R(VAT)/(FC-R(VAT) *r, (4)

which is defined as the ratio between the actual VAT revenue collected and the revenue that would have been collected if VAT was applied at the standard rate to all final consumption.

The **Central Statistical Office of Poland** (GUS) does not calculate R(VAT av). This is done by the Polish Ministry of Finance that calculated the average VAT rate between 2004 and 2011. In 2011, this value was 16.5% and I adopted the same numbers for 2012 and 2013.

VAT avoidance and evasion indicators. Results for Poland

My calculations were based on Polish national account data from GUS [GUS, 2014].

Figure 1: Gross VAT revenues, net VAT revenues and VAT recovery values (VAT tax returned when reclaimed) between 2004 and 2013. Source: The Polish Ministry of Finance.

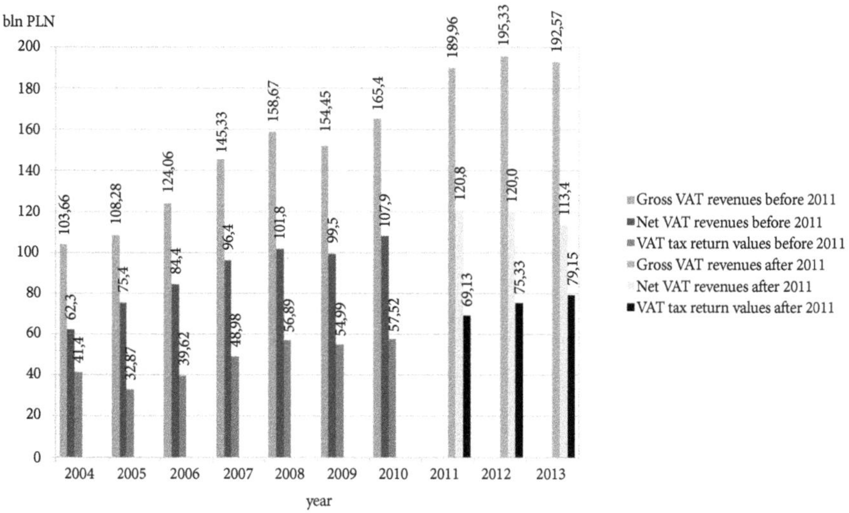

Note that since 2011, the standard VAT rate increased from 22% to 23%. In spite of this and the fact that final consumption expenditure growth for 2004 to 2013 was positive for all these years (although decreasing in 2012 and 2013), the decrease of VAT revenues is dramatic.

Fig 2. presents data suggesting VAT fraud reflected by decreasing VAT revenues.

Figure 2: The ratio of VAT recovery amounts to gross VAT revenues between 2004 to 2013 (left axis). Source: The Polish Ministry of Finance. VAT fraud (GUS) and PWC calculated tax gap (right axis).

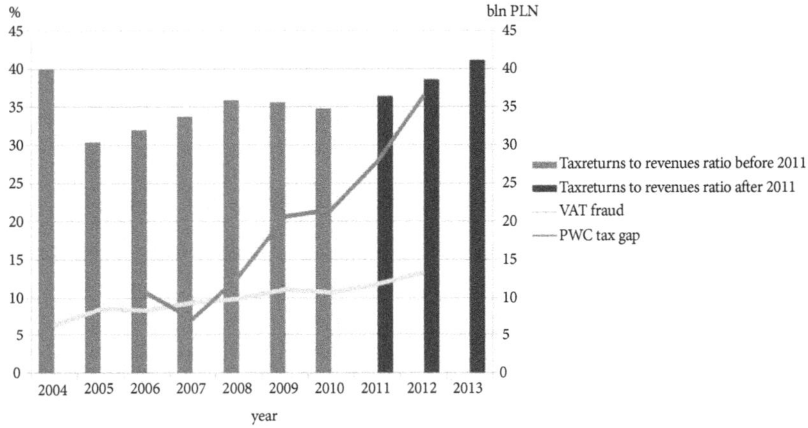

The PwC results can be compared to the previous results of Reckon and Case. For the 2006 tax gap, PwC estimates a minimum of 10.6 billion zloty compared to the 6.3 billion zloty estimate of Reckon, although the results should be the same as the minimum PwC calculations are based on the assumptions of Reckon. Similarly, the 2011 CASE result of 21.9 billion zloty is less than that of PwC being 27.8 billion zloty.

Fig. 3 shows a dramatic decrease of C-efficiency in Poland over recent years.

Figure 3: C-efficiency 1, C-efficiency 2, VRR measures together with const/ratio (proportional to the inverse ratio of VAT recovery values to gross VAT revenues.

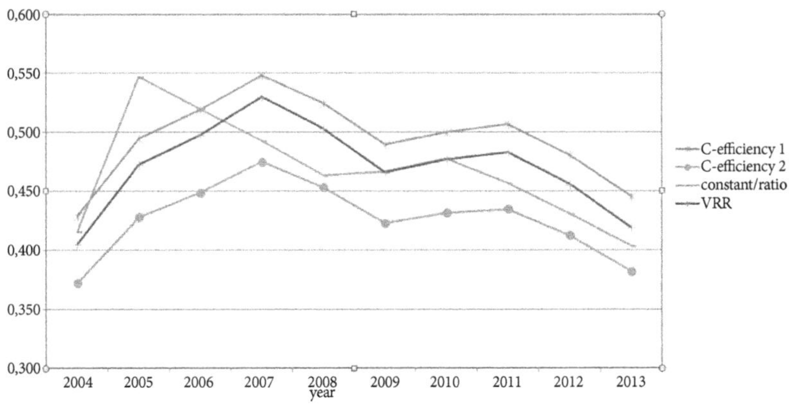

All C-efficiency indicators point to a dramatic drop of VAT collection efficiency, similar though not as steep to the one that happened in Latvia during the financial crisis in 2008. For up to 2010, my results for C-efficiency for Poland are basically in line with those of [Sopek, 2012. p. 292].

Selected regional Polish tax collection data

The first signal of a dramatic decrease of tax collection in 2012 originated from inspections of regional and local tax office data (Tab. 1). There is no common format for the data and tax offices often obscure the true situation. It is impossible for a person from outside of the Polish Ministry of Finance to aggregate all necessary data.

It is apparent that, for some local tax offices: Pierwszy Urząd Skarbowy Kraków and Podlaski Urząd Skarbowy Białystok, the VAT revenue collection is negative. This data points to significant organised criminal activity. Shadow economy models are clearly not suitable for describing tax collection in a country such as Poland (this view was also expressed in [Case, 2013]). The author is familiar with many investigations related to VAT fraud but the data is too scarce to build a bottom-up model.

Conclusions

This paper presents VAT avoidance and evasion indicators for Poland up to 2013 along with a critical comparison against previous results. The decrease in VAT collection efficiency between 2011 to 2013 is dramatic. The VAT recovery values increased by 10 billion zloty. This effect, to a large extent, is a result of fraud. I estimate the value of VAT fraud to be at least 15 billion zloty (since fraud was also occurring prior to 2011). This opinion is also expressed by *Instytut Studiów Podatkowych Modzelewski i Wspólnicy* [Dziennik Gazeta Prawna, 2014] although without deeper justification. This invalidates the claim of the Polish Ministry of Finance that VAT revenues are decreasing due to economic slowdown. These conclusions are corroborated by investigation of micro VAT statistics up to 2013.

- The relation of indirect tax revenues such as VAT or excise tax to GDP is a complex one. Poland is a crime plagued by financial crime with extremely inefficient and indolent prosecutor offices (the official statistical values of various crime categories are many fold smaller that estimates [Więckowski, Jędrzejek, 2014] and minimal analytical abilities unsupported by central databases.
- In 2013, GDP growth in the Czech Republic was negative but the VAT collection increased by 10% compared with 2012. This was achieved by

Table 1: Results of tax revenue collection in selected tax offices across the country in 2012 (in some cases compared against planned values)

Urząd Skarbowy (local Tax Office}	**Pierwszy Urząd Skarbowy Białystok**	**Drugi Urząd Skarbowy Białystok**	**Podlaski Urząd Skarbowy Białystok**	**II Urząd Skarbowy Warszawa-Śródmieście**	**Pierwszy Urząd Skarbowy Katowice**	**Drugi Urząd Skarbowy Katowice**	**Pierwszy Urząd Skarbowy Gdańsk**
Measure of performance	Plan/collection (mln zl.): CIT 16.0/13.1 PIT 462.6/514.0 VAT 197.5/134.6	tax revenues: 92%	tax revenues 5%	tax revenues 65.88% of the 2011 revenues	tax revenues and some non-tax revenues 89.44% of the plan	tax revenues and some non-tax revenues 81.25% of the plan	tax revenues: 152.9% of the plan

Sources of this data were provided by [Więckowski, Jędrzejek, pp. 456–457].

Table 2: Results of tax revenue collection in all tax offices in 2012 (compared against planned values) in the city of Cracow

Urząd Skarbowy (local Tax Office)	**Pierwszy Urząd Skarbowy Kraków**	**Drugi Urząd Skarbowy Kraków**	**Urząd Skarb. Kraków Krowo drza**	**Urząd Skarbowy Kraków-Nowa Huta**	**Urząd Skarbowy Kraków-Podgórze**	**Urząd Skarbowy Kraków-Prądnik**	**Urząd Skarbowy Kraków-Stare Miasto**	**Urząd Skarbowy Kraków-Śród-mieście**
Collection percentage of the plan	3.8 (the plan was ≥ 4%)	94.7	93.57	95	108.55	98.67	105.53	97

For 2013, not all data presented in Tables 1 and 2 were available.

Table 3: Results of tax revenue collection in all tax offices in 2012 (compared against planned values) in the city of Białystok (in some cases compared against planned values) in 2013

Urząd Skarbowy (local Tax Office}	Pierwszy Urząd Skarbowy Białystok	Drugi Urząd Skarbowy Białystok	Podlaski Urząd Skarbowy Białystok
Measure of performance	Plan/collection (in mln zl.): CIT 13.6/16.3 PIT 487.9/545.7 VAT 130.3/114.4	tax revenues: 87% of the plan	tax revenues: 32,12% of the plan

two measures. In the Czech Republic, vendors and buyers in the fuel industry have been jointly and severally liable for settling VAT bills since 2011. In 2013, the regulations were further tightened. As of October 2013, all companies trading in fuels must provide compulsory financial guarantees of 20 million koruna (approximately 3.5 million zloty) and must be entered in a relevant register. The registration is possible subject to fulfilment of certain criteria (e.g. no criminal record, no overdue tax liabilities) [PKN Orlen, 2014]. Secondly, tax investigations are operated with joint involvement of the police, prosecutor offices and tax offices; all parties having access to all relevant data, contrary to what is the case in Poland.

- The responsibility for the tremendous drop of potential VAT revenues in Poland in recent years lies partly in insufficient reaction of top officers of the Polish Ministry of Finance. Characteristicaly, the previous Deputy Finance Minister, Inspector General for the tax administration and the former Transport Minister Nowak were featured in one of tape recordings published by the Polish weekly, Wprost, in June 2014. The Deputy Finance Minister offered to tone down a tax investigation into Nowak's wife income statements. In the same recording he mentioned that "computers were thrown out of tax control offices" suggesting deliberate lack of using analytical tools for prioritising tax inspections.
- In the meantime, tax crime groups are corrupting everybody: politicians, lawyers, prosecutors, the media, university professors who write deficient laws, etc. Recommendations of the OECD Global Forum on VAT, 2014 seem surreal in this context. Using the example of the Czech Republic and Estonia [IMF Country Report No. 14/133, 2014], this report is one of the first claiming that tax fraud, not the gray zone, may be the main reason for tax gaps and that tax collection can be improved through thoughtful and diligent activities. Polish finances are now under increased EU and international scrutiny [IMF Poland, 2014], [Poland Convergence, 2014], which may provide the much needed stimulus.

Acknowledgements This work is supported by Polish PUT 04/45/DSPB/0105 grants.

Bibliography

CASE – Centre for Social and Economic Research (Project leader) and CPB Netherlands Bureau for Economic Policy Analysis (Consortium leader), *"Study to quantify and analyse the VAT Gap in the EU-27 Member States"* Final Report TAXUD/2012/DE/316.

Council Recommendation with a few to bringing an end to the situation of an excessive government deficit in Poland, COM (2013) 906 final, Brussels, 15.11.2013.

Dziennik Gazeta Prawna (2014), Chądzyński M., Przez eksport oddaliśmy więcej VAT, http://m.forsal.pl/makroekonomia/finanse-publiczne/przez-eksport-oddalismy-wiecej-vat.

European commission, (2014), Communication from the Commission - Assessment of action taken in response to the Council Recommendation of 10 December 2013 with a view to bringing an end to the situation of excessive government deficit.

Eurostat, (2014) news release 49/2014 - 27 March 2014, Labour costs in the EU28.

Gemmell N., Hasseldine J., Taxpayers' Behavioural Responses and Measures of Tax Compliance 'Gaps': A Critique, UK Tax Administration Research Centre, Discussion Paper: 002–13.

GUS (2014), CZĘŚĆ III Roczne wskaźniki makroekonomiczne http://stat.gov.pl/cps/rde/xbcr/gus/roczne_wskazniki_makroekonomiczne_cz_III_.xls.

H.M. Revenue & Customs (2013) *Preliminary Estimates of the VAT Gap for 2012–13*. London: HMRC. Available at: https://www.gov.uk/government/uploads/system/ uploads/ attachment_data/ file/263638/est-vat-gap-2013.pdf.

International Monetary Fund (2013), IMF Country Report No. 13/220, Republic of Poland: Selected Issues.

IMF Country report (2013), United Kingdom: Technical Assistance Report - Assessment of HMRC's Tax.

IMF Country Report No. 14/133, (2014) Republic Of Estonia Technical Assistance Report—Revenue Administration Gap Analysis Program—The Value-Added Tax Gap.

Keen M. (2013) IMF Working Paper WP/13/111, The Anatomy of the VAT.

Ministry of Finance, (2014), Szacunkowe dane o wykonaniu budżetu państwa w 2013 r., Warszawa.

Ministry of Finance (2013), Sprawozdanie z wykonania budżetu państwa w 2012 r. Tom I, Omówienie, www.mf.gov.pl/documents/ 764034/4311535/20130531 _tom_I_omowienie_2012.zip.zip, Rozdział 2 Dochody budżetu państwa, 07_ Cz I_2_RM_Dochody.pdf.

Najwyższa Izba Kontroli, NIK (2014), Wystąpienie pokontrolne, P/14/001Wykonanie budżetu państwa w 2013 r., część 77 - Podatki i inne wpłaty na rzecz budżetu państwa.

Namysłowski R. (2014), Liczby mówią same za siebie, Tygodnik Biznes i prawo PrawoPodatki i księgowość http://tbip.pl/podatki-i-9marca2014ksiegowosc/ liczby-mowia-same-za-siebie-882.html.

Poland Convergence Programme (2014), 2014 UPDATE.

PKN Orlen, (2014), An attack on the grey market, http://napedzamyprzyszlosc. pl/en/events/an-attack-on-the-grey-market.

PwC Report (2013), *Straty Skarbu Państwa w VAT – luka podatkowa, oszustwa, wyłudzenia oraz problematyka podatku od towarów i usług w Polsce*, Fundacja Naukowa – Instytut Badań Strukturalnych, Warszawa.

Reckon LLP, 2009, *Study to Quantify and Analyze the VAT Gap in the EU-25 Member States* (Reckon LLP, London).

Research Office Lexicon, (2014), Leksykon budżetowy, Luka produktowa, http:// www.sejm.gov.pl/sejm7.nsf/BASLeksykon.xsp?id=030C720783FB5A1CC125 7CEB003496B9&litera=L.

Schneider F., Raczkowski K. (2013), Size and development of the shadow economy and of tax evasion within Poland and of its neighbouring countries from 2003 to 2013: some new facts, [in:] K. Raczkowski, F. Schneider (ed.), The Economic Security of Business Transactions. Management in Business, Chartridge Books Oxford, Oxford.

Sopek P. (2012). *Financial Theory and Practice*, Tax expenditures and the efficiency of Croatian value added tax. Vol. 36 (3).

Więckowski J., Jędrzejek C., (2014), *Skala finansowej przestępczości zorganizowanej w Polsce i dlaczego jej zwalczanie jest tak nieefektywne*, [in:] K. Raczkowski (ed.), *Bezpieczeństwo ekonomiczne, obrotu gospodarczego. Ekonomia. Prawo. Zarządzanie*, Wolters Kluwer, Warszawa.

Jacek Bil[1]

Legislation and case law to combat crime associated with the settlement of indirect taxes in Poland

Introduction

The sector of indirect taxes is a significant element of the state budget supplying. As observed by K. Poznanski and M. Suchowolec tax revenues in Poland (especially in 2005–2007) grew at a very fast pace, which was a result of rapid economic development. Based on information provided by the Ministry of Finance in 2005–2012 the lowest growth rate of taxation was the case of income tax from legal persons. Another statement of the Ministry of Finance to reflect the tax revenue to the state budget in 2012, shows that the claims arising from the tax on goods and services accounted for 41.9% of total tax revenue. It is not without significance of proceeds of funds from excise duty 21.1% [Poznański, Suchowolec, 2014, p. 292]. The importance of indirect taxes provides even an estimate on the state budget for the period January-May 2014 according to which the income from indirect taxes is 77 501.7 million PLN (25 472.2 million USD). During the same period, revenues from income tax from legal persons amounted to 11 057, 3 million PLN (3 634.2 million USD), And income tax from individuals 16 765, 9 million PLN (5 510.4 million USD) [Ministry of Finance, 2014].

The mechanism of settlement of indirect taxes allows you to make tax deception (fraud), as a result the state budget does not affect claims of significant value. For example, in 2012 the state budget lost at least 36 billion PLN because of tax offenses. Poland is not the only country exposed to losses from fraud, such practices are reflected also in other European countries. Recognizing the problem resulting from value added tax frauds the need to combat tax evasion was indicated. One of the proposed solutions is the introduction of an inverted charge between counterparties. In Poland, in addition to the indicated solution joint and several liability for the obligations of the VAT supplier was

1 Captain Jacek Bil, PhD, Higher Police School in Szczytno, Department of Homeland Security, Institute for the Study of Crime and the Criminal Terrorism, e-mail: j.bil@wspol.edu.pl.

introduced. Offences relating to extortion value added tax in recent years continue to grow, which negatively affects the economic security of the state [Poznański, Suchowolec, 2014, p. 290].

The intention of this study is to identify some of the laws regulating the marketing of goods and services as well as products subject to excise duty and present relevant (from the point of view of the author) instruments which give the possibility for the authority of the activities aiming to combat the crime of tax fraud (VAT and excise duties).

International Monetary Fund, the Organisation for for Economic Cooperation and the European Commission carry out actions aimed at reducing the financial crisis, among others, by promoting trade in goods and services as well as products which are subject to excise duty. In the countries of the community average VAT rate tends growth, which is particularly evident in the case of France, Italy and also Cyprus (average VAT rate in the EU in 2008 amounted to 19.4% in 2014 it is 21.4%). The increase in indirect taxes affect economic downturn. Lowering tax rates or tax exemptions, which took place for example in Mexico, Paraguay, Kenya, Tanzania or South Korea resulted in increasing the impact of the budget. Studies conducted in OECD countries show that since 2009 only half of the planned income was implemented in respect of VAT. Inference of the reasons for the impact of the shortage of funds to the state budget from indirect taxes is not easy. On the one hand reducing the influence may be due to legislative changes, eg in terms of an increase in tax rates, on the other hand, can be caused by criminal activities [Ernst & Young, 2014, p. 8].

In 2013, Ernst & Young conducted a global study of indirect taxes, under which asked respondents to indicate the directions of the legislative changes relating to the marketing of VAT. Results of the study highlighted that the activity of legislative changes in respect of VAT is different. In some of the countries studied changes occur during the month, in other countries it is a period of three months or a year. The reason is to seek legislative changes to improve the state tax laws that will ensure increase in revenue to the state budget. The European Commission recognizing the need to reform the existing VAT rules has taken legislative initiatives aimed at introducing more modern trading system indicated tax. The proposed changes in the rules governing the marketing of VAT must be transparent to enterprises and should facilitate economic activity. It should be noted, however, that in many countries made changes bring the opposite effect, because the mechanisms governing the marketing of VAT fraud are used during their settlement [Ernst & Young, 2014, p. 8].

A similar situation applies to excise tax settlements. The main area of irregularities in the management of excise sector is tobacco, alcohol, and liquid fuels.

The economic growth is slow and uneven, even in the most developed economies of the world. In 2013 was noted global economic growth of 2.5%, and the World Trade Organization (WTO) predicts that this growth will be maintained until 2016 at 4.5%. It should be noted, however, that these are hypothetical predictions that can be shaken, among others by the introduction by the majority of members of the G-20 means that hinder trade. WTO has identified about 116 new restrictions, which include among others strict customs procedures and also an increase in tariffs [Ernst & Young, 2014, p. 12–13].

One of the means to prevent irregularities of the settelment of indirect taxes is the introduction of modern technology in the monitoring of trade in goods and services as well as products subject to excise duty. Authorities all over the world recognize the difficulty in conducting customs control. This highlights the need to use new technologies to access the actual data when conducting business control and customs controls. The use of technology leads to the prevention of irregularities in the settlement of indirect taxes [Ernst & Young, 2014, p. 14].

Taxes on goods and services

Tax on goods and services is an indirect tax, burdening expenses of consumption. The basis of its taxable marketing is understood as the value of materials supplied or services rendered. It (VAT) is charged at every stage of marketing. VAT is a tax on added value due to the fact that it charges only this part of the market, which is added by the taxpayer. It should be noted, however, that the tax base is the entire value of trading. Taxation of value added is created by the mechanism of deduction or refund of input tax in the preceding stage. To sum up, it should be noted that only the marketing made by the taxpayer is taxed, which is the difference between the purchase and the value of trading. Polish accession on the 1st of May 2004 to the European Union resulted in the need to adapt the rules (including tax rules) to the EU regulations. Common tax regulations in the European Union is nothing new, since already in the legislation claiming the European Economic Community adopted the harmonization of indirect taxes of the Member States of the Union. The first regulation that refers to the EU VAT harmonization was I of the EU Council Directive 67/227/EEC of 11 April 1967 on the harmonization of legislation of Member States concerning marketing taxes. The regulations adopted in cited document appealed primarily to the overall objectives and targets, to be achieved within the framework of the system of value added tax in force in the European Union. Another piece of legislation governing the harmonization of VAT in force until the end of 2007 in European Union countries was VI of the EU Council Directive 77/388/EEC of

17 May 1977 on the harmonization of the Member States relating to marketing taxes. This Directive, together with a number of the changes was interpreted by comprehensive regulation of the VAT system in force in the Member States of the European Union. At present, the current control system of value added tax in the European Union Council Directive 2006/112/EC of 28th November 2006 on the common system of value added tax. Cited EU regulations are very important both for the Polish VAT payers as well as for Polish the tax authorities [Bartosiewicz, 2013, p. 17–19] and law enforcement agencies.

Regulations cited above influenced the shape of Polish tax legislation, resulting in the Act of 11th March 2014 on tax on goods and service [Act, 2014]. The Act was introduced because of necessity of making changes in the Polish tax system (after the Polish accession to the European Union). The previous law regulating trade in goods and services of 8 January 1993 on tax on goods and services and excise tax [Act, 1993], required a thorough reconstruction, because it was illegible and incoherent. In the new version a division between VAT and excise tax was made. Although the said Act of 11 March 2004 on goods and services is essential for the settlement of VAT, it unquestionably should be noted that a number of important issues found in the provisions of the implementing acts [Bartosiewicz, 2013, p. 20–21], which include among others.: Regulation of the Minister of Finance April 4 2011 on the implementation of certain provisions of the Act on tax on goods and services [Regulation, 2011, April]. Regulation of the Minister of Finance of 28th March 2011 on the tax return for some taxpayers, invoicing, how to store them and the list of goods and services, which do not apply tax exemption [Regulation, 2011, March], Regulation of the Minister of Finance of 28 March 2011 on a tax representative [Regulation, 2011, March, tax representative], Regulation of the Minister of Finance dated 5 April 2004 on the forms of documents related to the registration of the taxpayer in respect of taxes on goods and services [Regulation, 2004, 5 April], Regulation of the Minister of Finance dated 7 April 2004 on confirmation of identify of a particular entity for the purposes of intra-Community transactions within the territory of a Member State other than the Republic of Poland [Regulation, 2004, 7 April], Regulation of the Minister of Finance of 29 June 2011 on the refund of goods and services tax to some entities [Regulation, 2011, June].

The Act on VAT is a document of a comprehensive character, as it relates (together with implementing regulations) to all aspects of taxation tax on goods and services, ie objective and tax scope of taxation:

a) time and place when the tax liability arose,
b) basis of taxation,

c) collection tax on imports,
d) rates and exemptions,
e) rules for deductions and tax returns,
f) reporting and registration obligations,
g) the principle of tax payments,
h) principles of tax documentation,
i) special rules for the taxation of certain entities and activities for certain goods and service [Bartosiewicz, 2013, p. 26].

Monitoring conducted criminal cases relating to phishing VAT indicates that special place to commit acts of that kind is Intra-Community marketing accompanied by the so-called carousel crime. The Act on tax on goods and services specifies the criteria for making such transactions.

Transactions are defined in the intra-EU law. In the preamble to Directive 2006/112 it was raised that intra-Community transactions carried out by taxable persons other than exempt taxable persons should be taxed in the Member State of destination, according to the rates and conditions imposed by the Member States. The concept of a Community trade is also held in the Polish legislation, as evidenced by the use of terminology indicated by the administrative courts and the Ministry of Finance. The transaction is therefore intra intra-Community supply of goods (WDT) and the intra-Community acquisition of goods (WNT), which take place between the Member States of the European Union [Selera, 2012, p. 21–22].

The Act of 11 March 2004 of the tax on goods and services in the art. 9 paragraph. 1 indicates that "the intra-Community acquisition of goods shall be understood as the acquisition of the right to dispose as owner of the goods, which are a result of the supplies are dispatched or transported to the territory of a Member State other than the Member State of dispatch or transport by making the delivery, the purchaser of the goods or in their favor" [Act, 2004]. In art. 13 paragraph. 1 of the Law specified intra-Community supply which is understood as "export of goods from the territory of the country on the territory of a Member State other than that of the country postage" [Act, 2004].

Another piece of legislation, which regulations are helpful for the prevention of crime associated with the settlement of VAT (including tax and excise duty) is the Act of 16 November 2000 on Anti-Money Laundering and Financing of Terrorism (hereinafter referred to as the Act) [Act, 2000]. Under this Act a national system of prevention of money laundering and terrorism financing is introduced. The central element of the system is the General Inspector of Financial Information (GIFI), who, as secretary of state in the Ministry of Finance is appointed and dismissed by the Prime Minister at the request of the minister competent for financial institutions. The tasks of GIFI stipulated by law are supported by the Department of Financial Information of the Ministry of Finance, which also acts as the Polish FIU (PFIU) [FIU is the central state agency responsible for receiving, analyzing, and reporting to the relevant authorities disclosures of financial information concerning suspected proceeds and potential financing of terrorism, as well as information required by national legislation and regulations]. The existing system in Poland of anti-money laundering and terrorist financing consists of: General Inspector of Financial Information The obligated institutions, which include among others.: credit and financial institutions, banks, cooperative savings and credit unions, investment funds, investment fund companies, insurance companies in respect of life insurance companies, factoring and leasing, payment institutions, the legal profession -notaries, lawyers and legal advisers, auditors and tax advisors, non-profit organizations - foundations, associations having legal personality and receiving payment in cash equal to or greater than the equivalent of 15 thousand. Euro intermediaries in trading of the assets - auction houses, exchange offices, pawn shops, secondhand shops, real estate agents, the Polish Post S.A [A complete list of obligated institutions was included in art. 2 item 1 of the Act of 16 November 2000. Anti-Money Laundering and Financing of Terrorism]. Cooperating units, which are government bodies and local self-government and other state entities, as well as the Polish National Bank, the Financial Supervision Commission and the Supreme Board of Control.

The Act of 16 November 2000 on the prevention of money laundering and financing of terrorism in accordance with art. 4 paragraph. 1 brings GIIF specific tasks that rely primarily on obtaining, collecting, processing and analyzing information in the manner prescribed in the Act, as well as taking action to counter the present investigation, and in particular the study of transactions for which it received GIIF reasonable suspicion, carrying out the procedure of transaction suspension or blocking the account to judgment, the dismissal of freezing the assets available and the request to provide information about transactions, transfer to competent authorities of documents justifying the suspicion of committing a crime, initiating and taking other activities to counter money laundering and the financing of terrorism, including conducting training employees obligated institutions in range of the tasks imposed on those institutions, control compliance with regulations on the prevention of discussed crime cooperation with foreign institutions and international organizations involved in anti-money laundering or the financing of terrorism and the imposition of fines provided for by the Act [Jasiński, 2014, p. 428].

Actions taken by GIIF in matters relating to defrauding the VAT refund and non-payment of the VAT concern many cases, which may be indicated by the data presented in the report of the General Inspector of Financial Information on the implementation of the Act of 16th November 2000 on the prevention of money laundering and financing of terrorism in 2013. It is this type of criminal activity causing the depletion of receivables of Treasury and contributed to the threat of legal business entities. Information provided by the obligated institutions and cooperating units the most often were affected by criminal activity in the field of fraud associated with the settlement of VAT. Activities in which abuse was made were associated primarily with precious metals, electronic equipment, components, biofuels and steel elements. As noted, indicated areas correspond to the information indicated in the reports of GIIF of previous years. Transactions described in these notifications are made by criminal groups using interconnected economic entities [Ministry of Finance, 2014, p. 17].

In order to prevent crime, tax legislator has introduced a number of criminal laws covering the behavior of the perpetrators of such acts for which criminal sanctions are laid down. These provisions were included among others in the Act of 10th September 1999 Penal Code [consolidated text. Coll. Laws of 1999. No. 83, item. 930, as amended. Amended] and the Act of 6th June 1997 Criminal Code [Act, 1997].

Criminal groups (acts of this kind are primarily committed by organized criminal groups) by making an offense connected with phishing VAT - both in the domestic and international marketing-related - Resort to procedures hindering law enforcement authorities conducting a detection process, including work on the basis of fictitious entities. State response to criminal activity is indicated, among others. legal regulation referred to in Article. 54–56 K. k. s, in which the legislator pointed out that crime is tax evasion (to operate under someone else's name), concealment of doing business on their own account or the actual size of the business as well as submission to the tax authorities of false declarations and statements. Another provisions referring to a tax offense related to the settlement of indirect taxes are art. 76, 77 and 78 K. k. s. under which indicates that a criminal act by the law is, among others. undue reimbursement of VAT, excise duties, expenses related to housing construction, as well as the untimely payment of tax, no tax or collection of tax at the lower of due amount.

Tax criminal activity was also penalized by the provisions of the Criminal Code. Described criminal activity is a scam, which according to Art. 286 §1 K. k is an act prohibited by law, which is to bring another person to the adverse regulation own or someone else's property in order to gain material benefits taking into account the object of the offense, which is certainly a value-added tax and excise duties. As mentioned previously addressed economic crime, among others. against the principles of the settlement of indirect taxes is committed by organized criminal groups. The legislature in art. 258 of the Penal Code defined the specificity of this type of criminal activity, within which indicated that criminal liability shall be the one who takes part in an organized group or association aimed at committing an offense or a tax offense. Qualified form of this offense proceedings relating to behavior consisting in the establishment of an organized criminal group or directing the group.

An important element of crime prevention are tax judgments to rule penalties for such offenses, based on the provisions of the Criminal Code. In jurisprudence there were voices of the impossibility of ruling the penalties provided for by the provisions of the Penal Code for committing a crime in the range of tax receivables (which was reserved only for the provisions contained in the Penal Fiscal Code). This image, however, has changed, according to this the Treasury perpetrators are also responsible for the crime penalized by law in the Penal Code. A positive (for the state) is the ruling of the Supreme Court order dated 10th July 2013 II KK 20/13. Under the present provisions the Supreme Court came to settle a dispute about whether the perpetrator of the crime associated with phishing VAT, acting by using fictitious business activities subject to criminal penalties as provided for by the provision of art. 286 §1 K. k. or penalty provided for in Art. 76 §1 K. k s Supreme Court in this decision argued that "a person who creates or co-creates an entity only for the use of procedures for refund of excess VAT and take action to achieve this objective by acquiring or counterfeiting documents related to this tax, then submitting them to the relevant tax office authority without conducting besides any business to be settled with the Treasury, may be widespread crime, as referred to in art. 286 §1 of the Penal Code, and not a tax offense defined in art. 76 §1 K. k. S [Supreme Court order dated 10 July 2013, KK II 20/13]. Indicated in the decision mechanisms of action of the perpetrator responsible mechanisms related offenses from phishing VAT by organized criminal groups, also in the course of intra-EU (criminal carousel).

Excise duty

Excise duty is an indirect tax levied on the consumption of certain products considered by the state as excise goods. This tax is a tax on single-phase, which is levied at one level of trade (unlike the tax on goods and services). Excise (commonly excise tax) is charged only at the stage of introduction of the goods on the market, further rotation of the commodity takes place without pre-emptive indicated tax. Just as the final entity VAT incur excise tax is the consumer. The specified type of tax a selective tax which means that it is applied to certain excise goods. A feature of the excise duty is the performance, flexibility, convenience and cheapness for paying subscription. Performance excise duty (like VAT) is visible at the financial impact to the state budget. Excise duty represents approximately 20% of the revenue to the state budget (tax VAT 40%). Flexibility excise duty is expressed by the fact that in a situation of recession and a decline in budget revenue yielding less pressure than other taxes on income. Another feature of excise duty - cheapness - manifests itself in a cheap consumption resulting from a single-phase issues (power at one level of trade). Convenience of duty stems from the fact that tax is paid by producers, buyers and importers of intra excise. Convenience is also due to the limited number of taxpayers (less), which also affects the easier process of investigation by the tax authorities [Parulski, 2010, p. 23–25].

Rules for the application of excise duties are laid down in the Act of 6th December 2008 on excise duty [Act, 2008]. It should be noted that the previous Act on Excise Duty, which was introduced after the Polish Accession to the European Union was imperfect and required a number of regulations, which made it unreadable both for the taxpayer and the tax authorities. The subject of Act entered in 2008 is to regulate the excise tax understood as: determination of excise duty payers, taxable representation, an indication of the tax base, tax rates and tax exemptions. The document regulates the rules relating to the production, processing and marketing of excise goods. The legislator indicates what conditions must comply with the entity you plan to be active in the production, processing, storage and reloading of excise goods in bonded warehouse. The Act also governs the rules for movements of excise goods both within the country and between the Member States of the European Union and in the case of international trade involving countries not members of the community [Parulski, 2010, p. 15].

The regulations adopted in this result among others the implementation of regulations in force in the European Union, which include, among others: Council Directive 2003/96/EC of 27 October 2003 restructuring the Community framework for the taxation of energy products and electricity [Directive, 2003] or Council Directive 92/12/EWG of 25th February 1992 on the general arrangements for excisable products and their holding, movement and monitoring [Directive, 1992].

As in the case of offenses relating to extortion VAT, so in the case of offenses related to incorrect billing of excise duty the State introduced a number of provisions relating to that type of crime. In addition to the common rules for VAT and excise tax (described above) according to the Article. 63 §1–3, art.64 §1, Art. 65 §1–3 k k. Pp. pointed out that a criminal act is a release, importation, production outside a tax warehouse, and sell and output from a tax warehouse of excise goods without prior marking with excise stamps. In addition indicated that the introduction of a fiscal offense from the tax warehouse of excise goods with excise stamps unmarked for the purpose of making their intra-Community supply or export of excise goods and receiving stolen goods [Directive, 1992].

Another provision in the field of management of excise duty is a disposition art. 66 §1, art. 68 §1 of the Fiscal Penal Code, under which an act prohibited by law is inadequate marking of products with excise stamps or trademarks inadequate labeling, as well as failure to determining the applicable excise with excise stamps. In art. 67 §1–2 kks legislator pointed out that it is a criminal act of counterfeiting or forging stamps or authorizations to receive banderole. Further regulations of the Act Fiscal Penal Code relating to excise duty underline that a fiscal offense is the production, import or marketing of excise goods without official verification, violation of condition of release from a tax stamp to mark the product, illicit trade in with excise stamps, as well as exposure on stamps risk of theft, destruction, damage or loss and untimely settlement of the state of wear of excise stamps, no records of excise stamps, failure to draw up a daily report or settlement of excise stamps with foreign trader.

Another piece of legislation relating to excise duty is the Act of 18th October 2006 for the manufacture of spirits, and the registration and protection of geographical indications of spirit drinks, where art. 41–44 specified that a criminal act is - the marketing of spirits from unlawful use of a geographical indication, production of spirits in accordance with the method of production and the technological conditions or quality parameters and production or bottling of spirits without the required entry in the register [Act, 2006] In accordance with the provisions of the Act of March 2, 2001 on the manufacture of ethyl alcohol and tobacco production is the production tax crime, pollution, purification and dehydration of ethyl alcohol or manufacture of tobacco products, including high-value, without the required entry in the register [Act, 2001] at the same legal act it is indicated that a criminal act by the law is the decontamination of contaminated ethyl alcohol or weakening contaminant and making a steady source of income from the commission of the offenses referred to in the rat. 12, 12a and 13 of the article spirits, and the registration and protection of geographical indications of spirit drinks.

Conclusions

The State reacting to irregularities related to the settlement of indirect taxes introduced into the legal system regulations, which on the one hand, define trading rules indicated taxes, on the other hand indicate criminal penalties for tax offenses. The implementation of EU legislation brought entrepreneurs facilitating the trade in goods and services within the European Union. Planned EU regulations transparency of tax rules should translate into a growth state, but this is not happening. Criminal groups using the "benefits" of Treasury regulations make a number of offenses, which translates decreased revenues to the state budget. Cited (selected) regulations according to the author are an effective tool in the fight against fiscal crime, but treatments are taken at the level of preparation of preparatory proceedings, which, however, are not favorable to the state finals in proceedings in the courts.

Bibliography

Act of 6 December 2008 on excise tax (consolidated text. Coll. Laws of 2009., No. 3, pos. 11).

Act of 16th November 2000 on Anti-Money Laundering and Financing of (consolidated text. Coll. Laws of 2010. No. 46, item. 276).

Act of 10 September 1999 Penal Code, (consolidated text. Coll. Laws of 1999. No. 83, item. 930, as amended. Amended.)

Act of 18th October 2006 for the manufacture of spirits, and the registration and protection of geographical indications of spirit drinks, (consolidated text. Coll. Laws of 2006, No. 13, item. 144).

Act of March 2, 2001 on the manufacture of ethyl alcohol and tobacco production is the production tax crime, pollution, purification and dehydration of ethyl alcohol or manufacture of tobacco products, including high-value, without the required entry in the register, (consolidated text. Coll. Laws of 2001., No. 31, item. 353).

Act of 6 June 1997, the Criminal Code (consolidated text. Coll. Laws of 1997. No. 88, item. 533, with later. Amended).

Act regulates trade in goods and services of 8 January 1993 on tax on goods and services and excise tax (consolidated text. Coll. Laws No. 11, item. 50, as amended. Amended).

Act of 11th March 2004 on tax on goods and service (consolidated text. Coll. Laws of 2011. No. 177, item. 1054, as amended).

Act of 11th March 2014 on tax on goods and service (consolidated text. Coll. Laws of 2011. No. 177, item. 1054, as amended).

Act of 23 January 2004 on excise tax (consolidated text. Coll. Laws of 2004., No. 29, item. 257, as amended. Amended).

Bartosiewicz A. (2013), VAT, 7 wydanie komentarza Adama Bartosiewicza i Ryszarda Kubackiego, Warszawa, Oficyna a Wolters Kluwer business.

Council Directive 2003/96/EC of 27th October 2003 restructuring the Community framework for the taxation of energy products and electricity (consolidated text. Acts. Gazette. EU L 283 of 31.10.2003).

Council Directive 92/12/EWG of 25th February 1992 on the general arrangements for excisable products and their holding, movement and monitoring (consolidated text. D. Office. L 76, 23.03.1992).

Estimates on the state budget for the period January-May 2014, the Ministry of Finance, 2014.

Ernst&Young, Indirect tax in 2014. A review of global indirect tax developments and issues, 2014.

Jasiński W. (2014), *Pranie pieniędzy. Zwalczanie i przeciwdziałanie*, [in:] W. Jasiński, W. Mądrzejowski, K. Wiciak, *Przestępczość zorganizowana. Fenomen. Współczesne zagrożenia. Zwalczanie. Ujęcie praktyczne*, Wyższa Szkoła Policji, Szczytno.

Poznański K., Suchowolec M. (2014), *Reforma systemu podatku VAT w Polsce*, [in:] K. Raczkowski, *Bezpieczeństwo ekonomiczne obrotu gospodarczego. Ekonomia. Prawo. Zarządzanie*, Oficyna a Wolters Kluwer business, Warszawa.

Parulski Sz. (2010), *Akcyza*, Komentarz 2 wydanie, Oficyna a Wolters Kluwer business, Warszawa.

Report of the General Inspector of Financial Information on the implementation of the Act of 16 November 2000. Anti-Money Laundering and Financing of Terrorism, Ministry of Finance, Warsaw 2014.

Regulation of the Minister of Finance April 4, 2011 on the implementation of certain provisions of the Act on tax on goods and services.

Regulation of the Minister of Finance of 28th March 2011 on the tax return for some taxpayers, invoicing, how to store them and the list of goods and services, which do not apply tax exemption.

Regulation of the Minister of Finance of 28 March 2011 on a tax representative (consolidated text. Coll. Laws No. 68, item 359).

Regulation of the Minister of Finance dated 5th April 2004 on the forms of documents related to the registration of the taxpayer in respect of taxes on goods and services (consolidated text. Coll. Laws No. 55, item. 539, as amended. Amended).

Regulation of the Minister of Finance dated 7 April 2004 on confirmation of identify of a particular entity for the purposes of intra-Community transactions within the territory of a Member State other than the Republic of Poland (consolidated text. Coll. Laws No. 58, item. 559, as amended. Amended).

Regulation of the Minister of Finance of 29th June 2011 on the refund of goods and services tax to some entities (consolidated text. Coll. Laws No. 136, item. 797).

Selera P. (2012), *Transakcje wewnątrzwspólnotowe w VAT. Analiza Praktyczna*, Warszawa, Oficyna a Wolters Kluwer business, Warszawa.

New Horizons in Management Sciences

Edited by Lukasz Sulkowski

www.peterlang.com

www.ingramcontent.com/pod-product-compliance
Ingram Content Group UK Ltd.
Pitfield, Milton Keynes, MK11 3LW, UK
UKHW020835290926
15470UKWH00004B/1364

9 783631 651902